Also by Peter Mansbridge

Extraordinary Canadians
One on One

Off the Record

Peter Mansbridge

Simon & Schuster

NEW YORK   LONDON   TORONTO
SYDNEY   NEW DELHI

SIMON &
SCHUSTER
CANADA

Simon & Schuster Canada
A Division of Simon & Schuster, Inc.
166 King Street East, Suite 300
Toronto, Ontario M5A 1J3

This Simon & Schuster Canada edition October 2021

SIMON & SCHUSTER CANADA and colophon are trademarks of Simon & Schuster, Inc.

For information about special discounts for bulk purchases, please contact Simon & Schuster Special Sales at 1-800-268-3216 or CustomerService@simonandschuster.ca.

Manufactured in the United States of America

10   9   8   7   6   5   4   3   2   1

Library and Archives Canada Cataloguing in Publication
Title: Off the record/Peter Mansbridge.
Names: Mansbridge, Peter, author.
Description: Simon & Schuster Canada edition.
Identifiers: Canadiana (print) 20210183144 | Canadiana (ebook) 20210183381 | ISBN 9781982169602 (hardcover) | ISBN 9781982169619 (ebook)
Subjects: LCSH: Mansbridge, Peter. | LCSH: Canadian Broadcasting Corporation—Officials and employees—Biography. | LCSH: Television news anchors—Canada—Biography. | LCSH: Television journalists—Canada—Biography. | LCGFT: Autobiographies.
Classification: LCC PN4913.M36 A3 2021 | DDC 070.92—dc23

ISBN 978-1-9821-6960-2
ISBN 978-1-9821-6961-9 (ebook)

For my grandchildren, Honor, Hope, and Ryder,
so they have some idea of what "Grampy" was doing
before they came along.

Contents

Off the Record

My First Prime Minister

Growing up in Ottawa in the 1950s, our family lived a *Father Knows Best* lifestyle. *Father Knows Best* was a TV show starring Robert Young and Jane Wyatt. It was the first family situation comedy on television, and it was a huge hit, portraying a family unit that navigated the postwar years by being close, always together. They ate breakfast together; father and the kids were always home for a mom-made lunch; and they gathered around the dining room table for dinner. It was all so perfect. That was us to a T. Or at least that's the way I like to remember it.

One day in the fall of 1958, after walking home along Fifth Avenue in Ottawa from my grade six class at Mutchmor Public School, I opened the door to our house to find my mother inside deep in conversation with two men in suits.

In the polite style of the '50s, I remained quiet until I was properly introduced.

"Peter," my mother said. "These men are producers working for the National Film Board, and they are planning a film on the Parliament Buildings." I listened while my mother carried on. "They've chosen Wendy to be in one of the lead roles in a story about two children visiting Parliament and touring the buildings. They still have to find a boy for the other role."

Wendy was my teenage sister. She was in high school at Glebe Collegiate Institute, and she was very popular. She was a cheerleader, a member of the Hi-Y, and had lots of As on her report card. You know the drill—the smarter, older sister. I loved her and she was my great protector as we grew up and still is to this day.

"I could play the boy. Why not me?" I said boldly, stepping some-what out of line with the *Father Knows Best* rules that seemed to govern things in our home.

"Oh, Peter," said my mother.

"Oh, yes," said the producers.

And that basically was it. They signed us up to star in *Michael and Mary Visit the Parliament Buildings*—two typically Canadian kids tour-ing the heart of Canadian democracy. There was an irony of course in that, seeing as Wendy and I had been born in Britain and immigrated to Canada just a few years earlier from what was then Malaya. We still had our English accents and our English passports, and I still wore British-boy-style shorts and pants. But that didn't seem to bother anyone at the NFB. The film was destined to be in every school in the country, and even now, I imagine that it's gathering dust on the bottom shelf of some basement storage room in a few schools.

The shoot was to take a week, which meant a week off school, which in turn meant both my parents and the schools had to sign off. They did.

The film was pretty simple in format. It wasn't moving pictures, but was instead still shots, slides. But at least it was in colour.

We set up and took location shots all over Parliament Hill. In the House of Commons, in the Senate, in the Hall of Honour, in the room dedicated to Canada's war dead, in the Peace Tower standing on the platform above one of the huge bells that toll out each hour across Ot-tawa. And the excitement built each day as we all knew the penultimate moment would come at the end of the week when we would meet and have a shoot with the prime minister, John Diefenbaker.

Diefenbaker had just won a huge majority in the 1958 general elec-tion earlier that year. At the time, it was the largest majority in Cana-dian history. The Saskatchewan lawyer-turned-politician was popular across the land, and his squeaker minority win in 1957 had upset more than twenty years of Liberal power in Ottawa. In the fall of 1958, there were great hopes that the Diefenbaker era would begin an exciting new period in Canada. The postelection honeymoon was still on as we moved our camera gear into the prime minister's office on the last day of our shoot.

These days, the PMO has space across Parliament Hill, its own building along Wellington Street overlooking the Hill, plus a spectacular wood-paneled office on the third floor of the Centre Block just outside the House of Commons. But back in 1958, John Diefenbaker kept his main office in a relatively small room in the East Block, and that's where we met. He was excited about the film and the scene it would include of "Michael and Mary" meeting the prime minister. We took lots of pictures and had lots of meaningful, at least for Wendy and me, small talk. Then someone said, "That's a wrap."

And with that, my first prime ministerial encounter had taken place. There would be many more with every prime minister from Diefenbaker to Justin Trudeau. In all, I have spent time with and interviewed eleven PMs, which is a pretty good figure considering there have only been twenty-three in total since Confederation in 1867. Okay, enough of that. I'm really starting to feel old now.

Back to John Diefenbaker.

When I was a reporter at CBC Winnipeg in the 1970s, there was a Friday afternoon ritual that would take place at the Winnipeg International Airport. Diefenbaker, by then an ordinary MP, or at least as ordinary as Dief could be, would always stop in Winnipeg to change planes on his way to his home riding in Prince Albert, Saskatchewan. And part of the stopover would include a news conference. He always had something to say, even if it rarely had anything to do with the questions reporters would ask him. Sitting there with his old cabinet colleague, Brandon's Walter Dinsdale, nodding beside him, "the Chief," as everyone called him, would ramble on about whatever misstep he felt Pierre Trudeau was making as prime minister. He wasn't that flattering about his own party leader either, his replacement, Robert Standfield. In other words, every Friday was all pure Diefenbaker. It rarely made national headlines, but there was always a full house of reporters anxious to get some clips for the weekend local news run.

One of those Fridays in 1974, I decided to finally bring with me a copy of the best picture taken of the then prime minister, my sister, and me in 1958. I waited until the news conference was over and went up to see the man.

"Mr. Diefenbaker, I'm sure you don't remember this photo shoot with the National Film Board, but it means a lot to me and to my sister, and I was wondering if you could sign it for me?"

He took the picture in his hands and studied it for a moment, showing it to Dinsdale beside him.

Part of the Diefenbaker myth was he never forgot anything or anyone. That he could walk into a rally and remember the names of people who were there to shake his hand. It was a great reputation to have, but most people thought it was perhaps a bit overblown. Nobody's memory could be that good. Or could it?

"I remember that day," the former prime minister said confidently. "Your mother was there, and she talked about how you'd come over from Britain as a family just a few years before."

I was dumbfounded. Speechless. I just stood there.

He gave up waiting for me to say something, pulled out a pen, and signed the photo: "To Peter and Wendy, with my best wishes now and always—17 years after. JG Diefenbaker."

POSTSCRIPT

John Diefenbaker never won another majority government after his overwhelming 1958 victory. He was a controversial figure throughout his political career, often fighting more with his own party than with the opposing Liberals. But he did accomplish changes that have lasted through history, perhaps the most important of which was the Canadian Bill of Rights. He also pushed into law in 1960 the ability for Indigenous Peoples in Canada to have the right to vote, which stunningly they had never had. And he included the first woman in a federal cabinet, Ellen Fairclough, as minister of citizenship and immigration. I'm proud to have my citizenship papers, officially earned in 1959, signed by Minister Fairclough.

Walter Dinsdale kept winning elections, eleven in all, and died in office in 1982.

John Diefenbaker died in 1979. He was eighty-three.

Wendy and I with PM John Diefenbaker in Ottawa in 1958.

–I–

A Penny on the Floor

MY SISTER IS THE CHRONICLER OF OUR FAMILY HISTORY. And that's a good thing, because while many Canadians have known me as a chronicler of our nation's history—and the world's too for that matter—I'd be lost on the little details about my early life if it wasn't for Wendy.

As much as she hates to admit it, Wendy is a couple of years older than me—I promised not to be exact—so she remembers when I came home from the hospital. And the fact that the next thing my father brought to our home in Bromley, Kent—yes, England—was a television set. Now, that's amazing because we were not well-off, and in 1948, having a television, still in its infancy as a medium, was an extravagance. But before you make the link between the television and what I ended up doing for most of my career, forget it. We were gone from that home in Kent before I was old enough to remember anything, and we left the television behind when we abandoned England for the colonies. Nope, not Canada, but Malaya on the other side of the world. At that time, my father was a bureaucrat working for the British Foreign Service and he was sent to Kuala Lumpur to help with the reorganization of the Malayan civil service, which led to the country's independence and eventual rebirth as Malaysia.

I was two years old when we left the port of Southampton on the P&O passenger ship RMS *Canton*. That voyage contains some of my first memories, including a great little story on which I have spent much time trying to determine its significance, if any, for the rest of my life.

This was a long trip. Twenty-one days in all. South along the coasts of France, Spain, and Portugal; through the Straits of Gibraltar and the Mediterranean; along the Suez Canal and the Red Sea. By the time we got to the Gulf of Aden, the ship's crew had organized a games day for the kids, and one of the games was a foot race for the youngest of us. I was dressed in my best British whites—shorts and shirt. And I had my lucky penny with me, one of those big, brown English pennies of the day. I don't remember exactly where I got it, but I assume it must have been from either my mother or my father. I do remember it was in the shirt pocket next to my heart.

There were about half a dozen kids roughly my age ready for the race, and the ship's steward lined us up and called out, "On your marks. Get set."

No one was really "set"—we were two- and three-year-olds after all; just keeping us in some form of a starting line was enough of a challenge.

"Go!"

And off I went. Now, I've never been a runner, but I guess those other kids really weren't either. Because, to my shock, I was in the lead. Waddling along at my full speed, which was more than theirs. Until the waddle caused a problem.

That beautiful, big, brown British penny popped out of my pocket.

I heard it hit the wooden deck. I looked down and saw it slowly rolling toward the edge of the boat and the ocean below. I couldn't let that happen. I stopped, reached down on my hands and knees, and rescued my fortune.

Proud of myself, I looked up, just in time to see everyone else cross the finish line.

With Wendy on board the RMS *Canton*
en route to Malaya in 1951.

So, what do we make of that little anecdote? Was it a harbinger of things to come? Would I pick money over progress in the future? Or would I focus on the finish line and leave the cash on the ground? When you're two years old, not all events will indicate what decisions you'll make in the years ahead. Genes, though, just may do that, and I had some pretty good genes.

My father, Stanley, was born in a Canadian military hospital in Folkestone, a small port town alongside the English Channel, in 1918. His father, my grandfather, was with the Princess Pats—the Princess Patricia's Canadian Light Infantry—and had been wounded on Vimy Ridge in that famous battle of April 1917, a place I would broadcast from many times during my career. Harry Mansbridge was evacuated to the

Canadian camp at Folkestone to recover from his wounds, where, in a story quite familiar to many other wounded and hospitalized soldiers, he fell in love with his nurse, a British girl by the name of Alice. One thing led to another, and my father was born.

After the war, the young family came to Canada, but my grandmother was homesick for Britain, and they moved back in the mid-1920s. Growing up, my father's dream was to become a lawyer, but a number of things got in the way. Like money. It was tight, and while he tried to supplement what my grandparents could put together by working at a bakery, he spent too much time eating "jambusters" and not enough saving, as he used to tell me. For the rest of his life after he left the bakery, he could not even look at another jambuster, let alone eat one. But mainly what stopped him from law school was the war.

By 1938, Stanley had joined the Royal Air Force, convinced that war was coming and wanting, like his father had done before him, to do his part. Harry had made his son promise not to join the army, where he himself had been a part of the trench hell that was the First World War, so my father chose the RAF. But air warfare didn't offer respite from a different kind of hell: tens of thousands of his Bomber and Fighter Command colleagues were lost over the skies of Europe, and for the rest of his life my father suffered in quiet remembrance of those friends who never came home.

Years later, when my parents were visiting me in Toronto, I told my father about a particularly good movie I'd watched about the air war called *Memphis Belle*. Now, it was about an American bomber crew but still, my father decided he wanted to watch it, so I rented it and set things up for him in a quiet area of my apartment. I had calls to make so I left him alone. When I returned a few hours later, the closing credits were running on the screen and there were tears trickling down my father's cheeks. The memories that haunt never leave.

He was a hero of the war; many of his missions, first in Hampdens, then in Lancasters, were described later as game changers in the conflict. He flew more than fifty missions on his two tours. By then, the odds against surviving were overwhelming. He was decorated with many awards, including the Distinguished Flying Cross personally pinned on him by King George VI at Buckingham Palace. His other medals were mailed to him after the war had ended. He looked at them then, but I don't recall him ever opening them after I was born. I have them now, still in their little faded cardboard boxes. And I do open them on occasion, hold them in my hands, my way of remembering my hero.

My mother, Brenda, was a knockout. She'd been turning heads since she was a child in Lincoln, north of London. She was the product of a broken family but had the benefits of a wealthy aunt who ensured that a single mother would still see her two school-age daughters attend a private institution. She graduated the same year the war broke out. Sixteen and gorgeous, she was focused on her job as a teller at a local bank, but also, and especially, young men. And there was a stable full of young men just down the road at the many air bases stationed in and around Lincoln. Parties, dances, picnics, and pub nights became commonplace for Brenda and the young women of Lincoln. Romances were common, but so too were the stories of romances cut short by flights that never returned.

I remember, after my father passed in 2005, my mother reached inside a case of personal belongings and brought out a carefully preserved set of RAF wings that she wanted me to have. I knew they weren't my father's as he was a navigator and these wings had belonged to a pilot. She leaned toward me and almost whispered, "He was such a dear boy. One night he never came home."

In 1942, at one of those Lincoln officers' mess dance parties, Brenda met Stanley. A year later, they married. A month after that, he was on a mission over La Spezia, the Italian naval port, when his aircraft got shot up pretty bad, and the decision was made to fly to North Africa instead of trying to make it back over the Alps to England. They headed for a remote air base in the desert near Blida in Algeria, landed successfully, but were unable to message home to let everyone know they were okay. For days, Brenda thought her new husband had been lost. But once the

Lancaster's engines were fixed, he returned home bearing gifts: bananas from Blida and silk stockings from a refueling stop in Gibraltar, two offerings worth their weight in gold in a Britain suffering from shortages and rationing. All was forgiven.

My mother and father were an interesting mix. She was always curious about the world around her, loved history and music, had an elegance of style and a spontaneous personality. He was more cerebral, constantly analyzing, planning, and recording all his decisions. After his death, my sister and I found a perfectly organized notebook in his possessions that logged the price of every single tank of gas he ever bought. Every. Single. Tank.

After the war, my father was offered a permanent commission as a senior ranked officer with the RAF, but he and my mother wanted to move on from the years of conflict and try to find a new home and a new way of life for their young and growing family. And that's why, after a stint working in one of Lloyds Bank's London branches, my father wound up back in the public service and we ended up on the *Canton*, my first of many voyages to the Far East.

Because of my father's position in Kuala Lumpur, we walked into a life none of us had ever seen before or since. He was thirty-four, my mother was twenty-nine, and we'd just left a semidetached home in Bromley and now found ourselves roaming around a huge home fit for

Mother and Father on a picnic in the summer of 1944, a month after Wendy's birth. The war was still on and my father was still flying.

royalty in one of the most prestigious addresses in the city of Kuala Lumpur: 6 Eaton Road. It had dozens of rooms, which we shared with the Ah Fooks, a Chinese family who lived with us as permanent house staff.

My mother loved this life. No cooking. No house cleaning. No nothing. And the three Ah kids—Ah Ho, Ah Ying, and Ah Chai—became Wendy's and my new best friends. They even taught us broken Chinese and Malay.

My father worked hard, but he played hard too. Countless days and nights were spent at the Selangor Cricket Club where he was a star bowler. My mother dressed up and helped run fashion shows. Holidays were spent on the coast along the straits of Malacca in Port Dickson. It was a beautiful area, but it wasn't without its perils. Wendy, barely nine years old, was attacked in the ocean by a Portuguese man-of-war, a jellyfish with lethal abilities. Another young child was attacked that same week in the same spot and didn't survive. Wendy did, thanks to the heroics of a number of people, including my father who pulled her out of the water, but it was close. All these years later, she still has the scars. Amazingly, she, and me for that matter, have never lost our love of swimming and especially of being at the sea.

There were other dangers too. During those years, a war of sorts was going on in Malaya as Communist insurgents tried to overthrow British rule. As a result, those working for the British government were targets. There were assassinations, one in particular of British High Commissioner Sir Henry Gurney, who was shot and killed by terrorists on a highway leading to a popular resort area called Fraser's Hill. A few months later, our family was driving along that same roadway when our car broke down. Wrong place wrong time for sure. We were stuck alone on the side of the road until an old truck came by filled in the back with vegetables. The driver offered to put my mother and Wendy with the veggies and take them to the nearest safe location and send someone back to rescue my father and me. I was only four and I had been sheltered from what had happened to Sir Henry and what had been going on in the jungles around us, but I happened to have a toy gun in my hands, and my father always told me afterwards that that was what had saved the day. He was joking of course, just trying to make his little son feel important, but he used to regale guests with the claim. We waited for help to arrive and it did, and that's the end of the story. Not quite capturing Osama bin Laden, but I'm afraid it will have to do for my part in battling terrorists in Southeast Asia.

Eventually, life in Malaya got to be too much for our family. My parents couldn't seem to shake war from their lives and find some calm to raise their children. Wendy was just finishing grade school and, if

Malaya, 1952. Practicing the anchorman
hand-on-chin pose in the family portrait.

we stayed in Malaya, she would have to go to Australia or England to achieve the next level of her education, and none of us wanted the family broken up for that.

That's when Canada beckoned. There were other options. England, of course, but it was still struggling with serious postwar economic depression, and Australia, which lost out when my mother weighed in. It was, for her, an issue of real substance. Put simply, she preferred the Canadian accent to the Australian.

"We can't have the children growing up sounding like that!" was her declaration.

We all laughed because she couldn't be serious. Could she? Probably not, but Wendy and I knew a closing argument when we heard one, so we started researching hockey, snow, and Mounties.

In April of 1954, this time on board the *Samaria*, we crossed the North Atlantic in search of peace, quiet, opportunity, and a new life. There were no foot races this time, but I do remember getting in trouble for dropping a few of my dinky toys from our deck into the frigid waters below. I was fascinated by the splash. My father was fascinated, and not in a good way, by the waste.

We landed in Quebec City, boarded a train, and headed for Ottawa, where my father was destined for a starting job in the lower ranks of the Canadian Civil Service. Within twenty years, he would work his way up the public service ladder to become assistant deputy minister of health in the Pierre Trudeau government of the early 1970s, and then be poached by Peter Lougheed to be chief deputy minister of the same department in Alberta. In all, it was a remarkable lifetime career of which I am still in awe.

While she was glad to be away from the conflict of Malaya, my mother missed the fancy home on Eaton Road with its high-society luxuries, 24/7 assistance, and its access to nightlife. While she adapted, Ottawa was not Kuala Lumpur. Not by a long shot. For the first while, we rented a small home in row housing, then moved to semidetached rentals.

Wendy and I went to Ottawa schools and we adapted too, although Wendy was told she would have to change her handwriting because it was too British and she spent hours—and not too pleasant ones—working on her penmanship. I've never quite understood what that was all about. Refining a British accent I get. But British handwriting? Seriously?

Regardless, we immersed ourselves in becoming Canadian. In Wendy's diary, she wrote about that in a series of short declarative phrases: "We learned the words to 'O Canada' before starting school. We cooked hot dogs in the Gatineau Hills, swam in the Chateau Laurier pool, studied the Group of Seven paintings, and marveled at the Rideau Canal system. We went to summer camp and learned how to eat corn on the cob."

In 1959, our family of four became a family of five when my brother, Paul, came along. That same year, we bought our first house in the middle-class district of the Glebe and a justice of the peace came to our home and we all pledged allegiance and became Canadian citizens.

By then, our daily dinner table conversations of the current news had become routine. We discussed the various news of the day, which was usually gathered from listening to and watching the CBC. We debated topical issues and were constantly challenged by our father to try to see, if not eventually accept, the "other side" of an argument. He had been a member of the debate team at his school and was a master at that art. He'd make an argument successfully, and then a minute later he'd argue the other side just as convincingly. Unbeknownst to me, those Mansbridge dinner table debates helped form the foundation of what would become my career a decade later.

The conversations I remember best happened in 1963. That year produced some of the most consequential news stories of my childhood, and together they crossed the spectrum of interests and possibilities. Where to start?

How about John Profumo, the dashing British minister of war? In today's parlance, we would call his story a "talker," and it sure was then too. Profumo had had an affair with a nineteen-year-old model, Christine Keeler, nothing new really for the British. But Keeler was also, at the same time, having an affair with a Russian envoy. This being at the height of the Cold War, it couldn't get juicier than that. A sexy, saucy, scandal of spies. Everyone hung on every tidbit of news that could be squeezed out of a sex scandal for the ages.

Or, still in Britain, the Great Train Robbery. Ronnie Biggs and his pals pulled off the biggest burglary of its time, with only the slightest of injuries to the innocent, and the boys almost got away with it. Overnight they became folk heroes, and it seemed no one was happy when they eventually talked too much and got caught.

In the heyday of the tabloids, these two were classic headline makers that had us talking up a storm at dinnertime. There was nothing boring in these stories and no one was in a hurry to get up from the table.

But then the issues got more complicated and far more important.

The situation in Vietnam began to look serious with our neighbours south of the border, and when the US suggested Canada should come into the war with them, our focus shifted to our newly elected government of Lester Pearson, who resisted the Americans and kept us out. In those early days of the US misadventure in Southeast Asia, that was a controversial decision. Should Canada be part of trying to stop the spread of Communism, which some in Washington described as a domino effect, where one country in Asia being toppled could lead to a cascade of others? The Mansbridges had seen that move attempted firsthand in Malaya, so there was no shortage of opinions on that one. The table discussion was a little more intense than usual.

Then Martin Luther King grabbed our attention. After the March on Washington, his "I Have a Dream" speech and his belief that "injustice anywhere is a threat to justice everywhere" planted the seed of new understanding. While we tended to look at America's civil rights problem as their problem, I was soon to realize it was our problem too.

As we got deeper into the fall of 1963, something else was happening that excited Wendy and me, even our mother a little, but my father just didn't seem to get it. It was about modern music, which was not my father's strong suit. He loved opera, and each summer when we embarked on the long drive to the Maine oceanside, he would serenade us with "Toreador" from *Carmen* while Wendy and I clasped our hands over our ears in the back seat! To us, this guy was trapped in another era, still upset that Frank Sinatra had squeezed out Bing Crosby, and he wasn't even ready to talk about that fellow Elvis Presley yet.

So, when four long-haired kids from Liverpool started making the charts, he was happy to dismiss them as "flashes in the pan." As you might imagine, Beatlemania was more of a four-way discussion than an all-family-fiver.

And then, on November 22, everything changed when President John F. Kennedy was assassinated. It was days before we could talk about it and, even then, no one really knew what to say. Kennedy had been my parents' generation and for them he brought great hope, but he was also young enough for us kids to believe that that hope included us. Suddenly, on a bright fall afternoon, he was gone, and with him so many of our dreams.

In many ways, that event was one of the last big Mansbridge family discussion nights. Wendy was leaving home to study nursing in residence at Ottawa's Civic Hospital; she would eventually go on to get a diploma in public health nursing at Dalhousie University in Halifax. With Wendy, my great protector, gone, things weren't quite the same. Paul was still in single digits, and while I tried to play the role of protector for him the way Wendy had for me, the age gap and my wavering attention span didn't help. I started focusing more on sports, playing football and basketball for Glebe Collegiate, than on family responsibilities and working on Latin and trigonometry. I discovered girls and beer, a combination that collided with my grades. In fact, I was a lousy student, lazy and bored, and some teachers openly asked why I couldn't be more like Wendy.

Short story, I never made it to grade thirteen and senior matriculation. University, much to my parents' disappointment, was not in the cards. But I was really itching to get going somewhere, so on my eighteenth birthday I joined the Royal Canadian Navy.

Why the navy? I liked the deep-blue serge uniform, and in the navy I could be a pilot, which had been my dream in my final years of high school. But really the uniform was the deciding factor. Off I went, first to Esquimalt on Vancouver Island, then basic flying training in single-engine aircraft at Camp Borden near Barrie, Ontario, and then Portage La Prairie, Manitoba, for advanced flying training in multi-engine aircraft.

While I loved the flying, once again I spent a little too much time focused on the social life available to a young officer in training. I bought a shiny red motorcycle to try to impress some of the girls in Portage and down the highway in Winnipeg. I loved that bike, so much so that I used to bring it into my room in the barracks to polish it up at night, which was fine until the day an unscheduled room inspection was ordered and I was grounded from going outside the base for a few days.

It was in Portage, though, that the navy finally caught up with me and determined that I was a risk to allow in the skies, let alone anywhere near the only aircraft carrier we had, HMCS *Bonaventure*. Instead, I was given the choice of going to sea or an honourable discharge which I accepted, and then took the long, lonely train ride home to Ottawa for another awkward conversation with my parents.

Just nineteen, I worked for a while at a gas station not far from Parliament Hill, but quickly decided it was time to break the bonds of home and try to make a name and a living for myself elsewhere. Something that could erase that look of shame that often crowded the look of love on the faces of Brenda and Stanley.

So, in the spring of 1968, off I went, west again, and the great adventure really began.

Beginnings

As the story goes, Julia Turner was just sixteen years old when she crossed Sunset Boulevard in Hollywood to go for a Coke in a soda shop on the other side of the street. Inside she was spotted by a reporter, who introduced her to an agent, who changed her name to Lana, and the next thing you knew she was a big star, a leading lady in the movies.

Well, I wasn't sixteen, I was nineteen, and I wasn't in Hollywood, I was in Churchill, Manitoba.

But after that, there are, as strange as it seems, some similarities to our stories.

I was a high school dropout, fresh from a short, unsuccessful stint in the Canadian navy, who moved west in 1968 looking for a new start. I found work as a baggage handler slash ticket agent for a little regional airline called Transair. How I got the job is a story I'll tell later. As I said, I was looking for a "new start," and tossing bags was certainly that. Transair trained me in Winnipeg, then sent me first to Brandon, Manitoba, and then to Prince Albert, Saskatchewan. I'd only been in PA a month or so when they decided to close down the station. They told me I was going to Churchill to fill in for a guy who was on two weeks' holiday. I got there. He never came back. And I didn't leave.

Which leads me to the day I was asked to announce a flight departure on the little public-address system. The PA system was set up on a podium right in the middle of the waiting room, which was filled with anxious passengers ready to board the daily Transair DC-4 flight to Winnipeg.

I clicked down on the microphone button: "Transair Flight 106 for Thompson, The Pas, and Winnipeg is now ready for boarding at Gate

One." We only had one gate, but it sure sounded like something you'd hear the big airlines say. "Passengers travelling with children or those requiring boarding assistance, please see the agent at Gate One."

As passengers started moving toward the gate, one person came in the opposite direction. Toward me.

"You have a really good voice," the man said. "Have you ever thought of being in radio?"

His name was Gaston Charpentier and he introduced himself as the manager of the CBC Northern Service Radio Station, CHFC, just down the road in Fort Churchill.

And that's when opportunity knocked. My "Julia Turner" moment. No experience. No background in the business. Turner had the looks, I had the voice.

Charpentier explained how the station was looking for a late-night announcer who could host a two-hour music show between 11 p.m. and 1 a.m. and then sign the station off the air for the night. He said he couldn't find anyone in town who was interested and asked whether I was. No audition. No HR interview. Part-time job for the asking.

I grabbed it. It meant more money, as I was only making $225 a month at Transair. And it sounded a little more interesting than "baggage handler." Charpentier said I could start the next night.

After completing my regular day shift at Transair, I went over to CHFC to learn the ropes. One of the regulars, a fellow from Calgary by the name of Bill Gray, gave me the rundown. We started in the record library, which in those days was a set of long bookcases with hundreds and hundreds of 45s, and dozens and dozens of LPs. Bill showed me how the cataloguing system worked and then we moved into the studio for the real training session.

CHFC was basically a one-person operation. During the early morning and late-night slots, the only person there was the on-call "announcer," so that person had to do everything. Cueing up records wasn't that hard, though there was a knack to it that had to be mastered. Same with the microphone. But this wasn't rocket science and if I could calculate the weight balance of a fully loaded DC-4 ready for its run to Winnipeg, I was pretty sure I could cue up a record. By the time I left the station, I was feeling comfortable about the next night when I'd be on my own for my debut.

The graveyard shift, as it was, actually ran from roughly eight thirty in the evening until signoff just after one a.m. I said good night to the announcer going off duty at eight thirty and was the only person left in the station. CHFC aired the CBC Radio network feed from Winnipeg for most of the evening, so my duties were minimal until the record show "Nightbeat" would start at eleven p.m. My first on-air moment was a thirty-five-second station break at 8:59:25. At that time, I would click open the microphone and confidently say the station identification and give the local weather report.

"This is CHFC Fort Churchill where the current weather shows a temperature of (whatever) with the winds from the (whatever). The wind chill factor is (whatever). Next on our schedule is (whatever)."

Those words were all typed out on a piece of paper and I just had to fill in the blanks. Easy peasy, right? Nope. Not that night.

I practiced the script—with the blanks filled in—over and over. But at about 8:50, the network line from Winnipeg suddenly went dead in the middle of their programming. Nothing, not even a hum. I was in shock. No one had briefed me on what to do with a situation like that. So, I had to draw on my memory as a youngster in the 1950s listening to the CBC at home with my parents, where things like that happened somewhat frequently.

I reached for the microphone switch, leaned toward the mic. And then uttered the first words I would ever say on the CBC: "One moment, please."

And then I switched off the mic and wondered what I would do next. Five seconds went by, then ten. I was about to really panic when, just as quickly as the feed had disappeared, it came back on and everything returned to normal.

The rest of my debut evening went fairly well. I was nervous and probably said some dumb ad-lib music things between records on "Nightbeat," but no one complained. I'm not even sure if anyone was listening, but by the time I left the building I felt pretty good.

Over the next few months, however, I quickly realized that if I was going to make broadcasting a full-time career, it wasn't going to involve music. It just wasn't my thing. Even back in my high school music class, the teachers could tell that I didn't, and wasn't going to, "get it." They started me on the trumpet but I couldn't hit the high notes, or in fact, any notes. Then the trombone. Finally the tuba. Nothing worked.

At CHFC, each week new records would arrive from the record companies. We'd sit around and rate the chances for each record. I remember the day Simon & Garfunkel's song "Bridge Over Troubled Water" arrived. It was so long, I said. Boring. It'll never make the charts. Bill Gray just shook his head.

As I said, music just wasn't my thing. But I knew what was. News and current affairs.

Ever since I was a child, I had been fascinated by the news of the day, whatever that news was. Along with history, current affairs was, as a result, my favourite topic.

So, in 1969, shortly after being offered a full-time job at CHFC, I suggested moving off "Nightbeat" and starting a daily newscast, which at the time the station did not have. They agreed and "The News with Peter Mansbridge" was born.

In the beginning, it was only a few minutes long, each evening at 5:30. I'd talk to the RCMP, the town office, the Port of Churchill, and the National Research Council, which operated the Churchill Rocket Range. Between them, there was always something to discuss on air.

And then, of course, the polar bears. You couldn't miss with a story on the bears.

But I needed more than content to do a newscast. I needed to know how to write, to interview, to edit, to line up, and to do all the other things real newscasters and producers did. But there was no one to teach me. I was all alone. So, each night, I would listen to the CBC newscasts

The only known picture of me at the CBC in Fort Churchill,
Manitoba, circa 1969.
University of Toronto Archives

from Toronto and Winnipeg, and to shortwave radio—the BBC, the
Voice of America, and, when I could tune them in, the big radio networks in the United States like CBS, NBC, and ABC—eagerly devour-
ing how others did what they did. I didn't copy, I learned, and soon "The
News with Peter Mansbridge" expanded to thirty minutes and included
interviews often done on location on a big, heavy, Nagra tape recorder
that I lugged around town and then edited back in my office.

I even started an open-line radio show in the mornings, called
"Words with Peter Mansbridge." It was a big deal for a little town of less
than two thousand where most everyone knew everyone, so there was
no anonymity if you were suddenly "on the air."

That first day was interesting. I opened the program with some nice
theme music and welcomed the audience to the new age of broadcasting: we were going to be just like the big cities down south. I asked
them to call in and share their thoughts on the topic of the day and then
waited for the lines to light up.

Nothing.

The show was thirty minutes long and no one called. Not one. Not even a wrong number. I talked for thirty minutes nonstop. By the end, I was almost begging. By day two, the show was called "Words *and Music* with Peter Mansbridge."

Over time the callers started dialling in, and that program and the daily news picked up a good audience. I began making a name for myself in both Winnipeg and Toronto because I would offer cut-down versions of my stories for their newscasts. They were almost always human-interest stories dealing with living in the north, or they were about polar bears. A polar bear story was a ticket to network exposure.

And then in late 1970, Herb Nixon, one of the most powerful names in CBC News at the time, called me up and said, "Peter, we'd like you to apply for an opening we have here in the Winnipeg newsroom." But there were more Churchill adventures to come first.

Bear Trap

Some people have a mission in life. Brian Davies is one of those people. I could see it in his eyes the day he walked into the Transair offices in Churchill.

Born in a Welsh coal-mining town, Davies eventually moved to Canada and joined the Canadian army. One day he took an injured dog to a shelter for care, and it was at that moment he decided his mission in life would be to protect endangered animals. He quit the army and formed the International Fund for Animal Welfare. There had never been anything like it, and it was Davies's energy and direction that got it worldwide recognition.

One of the first major issues he focused on was the commercial east coast seal hunt on the St. Lawrence River. He had actually been asked by the Canadian government in the mid-1960s to determine whether the hunt was conducted in a humane fashion. He was shocked at what he saw, and he went rogue. He organized tours for the international media to visit the ice where the slaughter took place, and when they balked at the trip, he tempted them with a celebrity tour guide—at the time, *the* celebrity, Brigitte Bardot. That did it. The world's sexiest star cuddling the world's most vulnerable baby seal. The media followed like they had been led by the nose.

With success on seals, Davies took aim at Churchill, Manitoba, and polar bears.

Churchill was right slap dab in the middle of the bear's annual migratory path along Hudson Bay, which made the town a pit stop for them to refuel. Target one was the town dump, but when it got overcrowded with fellow bears, or when the menu available wasn't sufficient for their liking, the bears would head into town, break into homes, and raid kitchens. Sounds cute, but it was dangerous and people did get hurt, a few even killed. So local and provincial authorities stepped in—the problem bears were either shot or captured and shipped off to zoos around the world. Brian Davies didn't like that, and he stepped in.

I was still working at Transair for half the week and was there when Davies arrived one afternoon with a good selection of European and American television and newspaper crews in tow. I was on the tarmac watching them disembark from the daily flight from Winnipeg and was more than a little disappointed that there was no Bardot evident.

Davies quickly made a deal with the local authorities, who knew that even without Bardot, there was power in the camera lens suddenly pointing at them and their town. The next "problem bear" to be trapped wouldn't be shot or shipped to a zoo; it would be handed over into the custody of Davies and the IFAW. He would then fly the bear south along the coastline and set it free and on its way.

A key part of the plan involved chartering an aircraft, and that's where Transair came into the picture. We offered him a DC-3 at a reasonable rate. We would take out most of the seats to make room for the huge steel bear trap but still leave enough seating space for some of the reporters and their cameras. A contract was signed, and when we got the word that a bear had been acquired, things were set for the next morning.

It was an early start. The bear was tranquillized to make things easier for everyone, and the cage was loaded and strapped down. The reporters, groggy from a long Churchill night, came on next.

The flight wasn't long, about an hour, but it was bumpy. Halfway to the destination, the bear woke up. I won't go into detail, but let's just say neither the sights nor the smells made for a comfortable ride. The fresh air from the tundra near the remote airstrip about 150 kilometres from Churchill where the plane landed was welcome. Once the trap was unloaded and the bear released, the reporters got their pictures of the bear disappearing over the horizon, Davies made a few comments, and things were declared a success.

Back in Churchill, the visitors left on the daily flight back to Winnipeg and sent their stories off to New York and Paris and Berlin and London and points around the world. And once again Brian Davies was declared the victor for delivering on his promise to "save the bears."

There was only one problem.

Bears travel. They travel fast.

And this bear, clearly marked for easy identification, had his own mission. He wanted back in Churchill at his favourite dump, and within a few days that's exactly where he was.

He was tagged, trapped, and sent off to a zoo in the United States.

POSTSCRIPT

There were two lessons from this. As a soon-to-be reporter, I learned it's never good to leave a story too quickly. Follow-ups are important.

And Brian Davies, he was no fool. He heard about the returning bear, and by the next year he had updated his program and flew the bears twice as far along Hudson Bay, where they found new excitement to keep them occupied and away from Churchill.

A Wake-Up Call

My clock read 6:21. In the morning. On a Saturday deep in the heart of the Churchill, Manitoba, winter of 1968–69. "Deep" in Churchill meant not just snow, but how far down the mercury in the thermometer was. So it was probably about minus 25 degrees Celsius—just another Churchill day.

I had woken up because my phone was ringing. I cracked open one eye and stared at my bleak surroundings. I lived in a hotel because I'd won a big hand in an after-hours poker game with the hotel owner in the bar downstairs and my winnings included access to the room for a few months. The room was elementary: a bed, a side table, a couple of hangers on the wall, an old black-and-white TV, a telephone I'd had installed. No bathroom—there was a shared one down the hall. The room was on the second floor and sat immediately above the bar, in fact immediately above the area where the local band played in the bar. They only knew a few songs, all country and western, and I distinctly remember the one they played most often: "On the Wings of a Snow White Dove."

Groggily, I picked up the phone.

"Hello?"

"Peter, it's George at Transair," said the voice at the other end of the line. "Aren't you supposed to be at the radio station?"

George was the caretaker, night watchman, and janitor; you name it, he did it all at the old Transair hangar out at the airport a few miles away. He was pretty old, probably in his late seventies, but he was a treasure. Everyone loved him. And for George, when the only thing to keep you company through the long nights was the expectation that the only radio station within hundreds of miles would sign on at 6 a.m., you tend to notice when it doesn't.

"Oh, shit," I said. "I forgot to set my alarm."

I jumped out of bed, threw on some clothes, and raced downstairs. Pushing the front door open, the cold, bitter Arctic air hit me. My major concern was, would my truck start? Transair had given me this behemoth of a five-ton truck to drive back and forth around the community as I was still working the day shift at the airline. Some nights and most weekends I worked part-time for the CBC and its northern service station, CHFC.

I unplugged the block heater, turned the key, and the truck's engine fired up. I gave it a minute or two and then backed it out onto Churchill's main road. The tires felt like rubber squares as I slowly guided the vehicle to the station. It was still dark, would be till almost ten in the morning in this northern land of winter darkness. But finally the station came into view.

I raced inside and, seeing as this station was a one-person operation during late nights and early mornings, my first duty was to turn the station "on." That didn't involve much, just the flick of a switch on the master control panel. Normally I would spend a few minutes picking some music selections from the library of 45s, cue up "God Save the Queen" to open the day's programming, and then join the main CBC network from Winnipeg or Toronto to first air the 6 a.m. news.

But by now, the clock read 6:45. That was not a time to play "The Queen." So what was I to do? Open the microphone and apologize? That's probably what I should have done, but that's not what I did.

Instead, I grabbed one of the first records I could find. I'm pretty sure it was "(Sittin' On) The Dock of the Bay" by Otis Redding. I cued it up, turned it on with no volume, waited about twenty seconds, and slowly faded the knob controlling the volume up, so everyone was in effect joining the song in progress. Then I tried to decide what I would say when Otis finished.

The song ended and I leaned into the mic.

"Otis Redding's classic on this cold Churchill morning here on the edge of our bay, Hudson Bay," I said, and moved right on to a weather update, and then into the next music selection.

I never said anything about my late arrival. I did enter the late start into the station's logbook. When the other staff started trickling in later that morning, there was no indication any of them had even been up in the 6–7 hour. No one ever said anything. The next time I saw George, I gave him a bottle of his favourite Scotch. Eventually, sometime much later, I did tell the station manager what had happened. He didn't blink.

But I had blinked. The whole episode scared me to the core. For fifty years at the CBC, I never turned up late again. Maybe for a few meetings, but certainly not to be on air. But that didn't stop me from having nightmares about that morning, fearing it could happen again.

Throughout the many years I anchored *The National*, I often had a version of the same dream. It would be only a minute or so before the broadcast began and I would somehow have lost track of time. I'd race to my dressing room, scrambling to find a tie, knowing the second hand of the clock was ticking down to airtime. I'd run toward the studio while trying to tie the knot. The floor director would be yelling for me to hurry up. I'd hear the intro music and see the opening visuals playing out on a monitor as I crossed the studio floor. But I knew I wasn't going to make it in time. I'd see the camera cut to an empty space—the space I was supposed to be occupying. I'd embarrassed everyone, but most of all myself.

And then I'd wake up. It was as if George had phoned me once again. This time to get me out of a nightmare.

The Prince and the Papers

I could see the helicopter approaching from the south, and I knew what it meant. My biggest broadcasting moment in what had been a very brief career so far was about to happen. How I would do might very well determine whether this would be a stepping-stone to better things or whether I would be heading back to the baggage counter at Transair.

It was the summer of 1970 and I had been assigned to CBC Radio's coverage of the royal tour as the Queen and her family came to northern Manitoba as part of the province's one-hundredth birthday celebrations. I was proud of my first press credentials card, bright red and stamped with my picture. My job was to provide two or three minutes of commentary as Prince Charles choppered out to officially open a Boy Scout jamboree about ten kilometres from the Churchill airport. I'd prepared for days. This was my first major broadcast. I'd be heard across

My very first press card.

the country. I knew my mother would be sitting in her Ottawa living room, nervous, as her son was about to make his "live" network debut.

The main anchor for the broadcast was the top man at CBC Radio at the time, Lloyd Robertson. He was in the studio while I was perched on what looked like a lifeguard tower standing alone in a strip of tundra, but it would provide a great overview of where the prince's helicopter would touch down. He'd shake a few hands, make a few remarks, and then fly back the short distance to Churchill to join his mother.

With me on the tower, placed on my knee, I had copious notes to refer to during my commentary. Facts about Charles, facts about his mother, facts about Churchill, facts about the helicopter—in fact, facts about everything that could possibly come up. I also had an old-style microphone that I had been told to depress the "talk" button on as soon as I heard Lloyd—Mr. Robertson to me back then—introduce me, and to keep it depressed and to keep talking for the few minutes allotted to me, describe the scene with Charles on location, and then throw it back to Lloyd.

I was ready. The helicopter approached. But instead of touching down not far from me as planned, it flew directly above me by about fifty feet. The downdraft lifted my notes away into the wind. I watched them flutter to the ground. I was now stranded, alone on the tower, my research gone, as I heard Mr. Robertson say, "And now, here's Peter Mansbridge."

I depressed the button and started talking. And talking. And talking. I didn't stop for twelve minutes. Charles had decided to enjoy his welcome and, as a result, stayed much longer than planned, giving me airtime I'd never imagined.

And the notes? I learned a big lesson that day that I've never forgotten and still use. Prepare for everything. Write everything down. Underline the key parts. Read them over, and then over again.

If you've done your research well, those actions will be enough. You'll never need to look at your notes again. Helicopter or no helicopter.

POSTSCRIPT

Lloyd Robertson became the anchor of The National *a few years later, and we kept working together as I took on bigger CBC assignments first in Saskatchewan and then in Ottawa. In 1976, he left for CTV and, as it would go, I eventually became the anchor of* The National *myself.*

Lloyd and I have remained good friends to this day. He was born and raised and had his first broadcast job in Stratford, Ontario, the small Ontario city where I live now. When I walk through Lloyd Robertson Park, I often think of that first broadcast together.

Two of Canada's best anchors, Bernard Derhome (SRC) and
Lloyd Robertson (CTV), with a baggage handler from Churchill in 2008.
University of Toronto Archives

The Three-Year Mark

There was a popular saying in Churchill when I moved there in the late 1960s. And people would take you aside and almost whisper it in your ear.

"If you stay for more than three years, you'll never leave."

By the summer of 1970, I'd been in the northern Manitoba port for two full years. And it had grown on me. I'd got married while I was in Churchill. My first child was born in Churchill. I'd started with the CBC in Churchill. There was a lot about the place I loved. In some ways, it had the benefits and excitement of being a rugged frontier town while still having the energy of progress. The town boasted about fifteen hundred people, but there were two Hudson Bay stores—which attempted to look modern though they were barely more than trading posts—government offices, two hotels, and a bustling deep seaport, despite that it was only open a couple of months a year because of long winter ice conditions. And then, of course, there was the National Research Council's Churchill Rocket Range—Canada's only venture into the space race.

Some of the finest scientists and researchers in the world would come to Churchill and bring the latest in space technology with them. I know because when I was working at Transair, I would book them on their flights back home to NASA in Cape Kennedy, in Houston, and in White Sands, New Mexico. They were fascinated by the mysteries of the northern lights, so visible from Churchill, and many of their experiments involved firing rockets into the aurora borealis.

But Churchill also had a dark side, one of racism and prejudice. There was a combustible mix of white, Métis, Cree, Chipewyan, and Inuit, although at the time most white people called the Inuit "Eskimo." When

I worked at Transair, I met many Inuit because they often flew back and forth between Churchill, where they went to school or received medical care, and their communities farther north in places like Arviat (then known as Eskimo Point), Rankin Inlet, Baker Lake, Chesterfield Inlet, Coral Harbour, and Resolute. When they did, to make it easier for white people like me, government departments booking their flights didn't have them travel under their names, but instead had them travel under an assigned *number*. I can remember actually standing at the PA system and calling out things like: "Would E-72549 come to the counter, please?" And you can guess what the "E" stood for. Today, I can't believe I did that.

So, in those days was Churchill, in many ways, racist in its practices and its actions? Yes. No question on that to me. Here's another example. In one of the community's two hotels, the Hudson Hotel, the drinking area had two levels: on the centre raised floor sat the white patrons in a large circle, while surrounding the circle was the lower area called the "racetrack." That's where Indigenous people were allowed. When I got to Churchill as a twenty-year-old, a product of white privilege who'd just left the tony upper-middle-class area of the Glebe in Ottawa, I assumed this was the way it was supposed to be and I didn't question it. No one, including me, stood up and called it what it was. It was just plain racist.

As I began working for the CBC and reporting on local events, I learned just how common deaths in the Indigenous community were, whether it was from murder, from fights, or from fires. I saw my first dead bodies while watching firefighters bring fatalities out of a burned-out building in the Chipewyan community of Dene Village on the outskirts of Churchill. I've seen many since, but you never forget the first one, especially when it's an infant. I can't remember what caused that fire, but many fires started in the village because residents, desperate for heat, began ripping their government-built houses apart to find wood to burn.

The whole Dene story was a disgrace. In 1956, the villagers had been forced, by Ottawa, to leave their homes on the Sayisi Dene First Nation at Little Duck Lake in northern Manitoba, where they'd lived a life of hunting, trapping, and trading, and move into Churchill and a more "modern" lifestyle. It was a disaster, and about fifteen years later, after terrible social unrest, the Dene succeeded in moving back to the wilderness and to living off the land.

In the early summer of 1970, I began spending some of my time working with young Indigenous kids, trying to involve them in activities that might make them feel more like members of the larger community. So, when the organizers of the upcoming Boy Scout jamboree asked me to design an obstacle course along a small lake near the campsite, I saw an opportunity. I'd met some young kids from Dene Village, who I felt would be great architects for a challenging course, so I asked them if they'd help me and they said yes. The course was a highlight of the jamboree and more than a little challenging for all the participants. It was a small gesture in the big scheme of things and most people in the community didn't even know anything about it, but for a few of the Dene kids, and for me, it felt like an accomplishment. I was lucky to get to know those kids, and some of us stayed friends in the initial years after I left Churchill. But to this day I wish I'd done more.

Eventually, I felt it was time to look for work in southern Canada. The CBC didn't have any openings that I was eligible for, so I started combing through the broadcast trade papers and magazines that came by mail to the station.

And then one day I saw it. A small ad that said something like: "Broadcast Position Available at CJBQ in Belleville, Ontario."

I figured this was right up my alley. Belleville was only a couple of hours from my old hometown of Ottawa, close to the shores of Lake Ontario, which was a beautiful spot in the summer. And it was home to one of my hockey heroes, Bobby Hull. Sounded perfect.

I spent a lot of time working on my application letter, trying to put my best broadcast experiences up front. (I'd only been in the business full time for less than a year!) I went into the recording studio and put together an audition tape with some of my best interviews, including my highest-profile interview at the time—Manitoba premier Ed Schreyer, who had been in Churchill for a working visit a few weeks earlier. Then I packaged everything up and walked over to the post office. I felt I was holding the future in my hands as I handed the parcel over to the postal clerk and sent it on its way.

And then the wait began.

In those days, mail wasn't exactly fast in remote areas like northern Canada. Perched on the edge of Hudson Bay, there were only three ways in and out. By water, which was primarily for the overseas shipment of prairie grain in August and September. By air, with the airline I had moved to Churchill with. And by rail. By road? Nope, no road. It stopped at Thompson a few hundred miles to the south.

Because of cost, almost everything was shipped by rail on the milk run from Winnipeg. And I mean "milk" run. Milk used to arrive in bags, and we'd buy enough for a week at a time. When it came, it was often twenty-four to forty-eight hours from turning sour, so the only way to make it work for a week was to freeze it and take one bag out at a time and let it thaw overnight. By the way, milk in a frozen block looks odd— it's yellow. But not to worry, it turns back to white by the morning.

Anyway, my application and my audition tape had gone out by rail for the journey to the desk of whoever was making the decision in Belleville. So I figured ten days to get to CJBQ, a couple of days for them to consider it, and another ten days for the reply to make it back. To be sure, I decided a month was a safe guess. Of course, I thought, if they're blown away by the audition they could just phone.

Six weeks later. No phone calls. No return mail. Nothing. I started thinking the package must have gotten lost. Seven weeks. Still nothing.

Then, at the two-month mark, a letter arrived. The envelope was thin.

I've long since misplaced the contents but I remember the letter's last line pretty much word for word. It was the kind of line that sears in the memory. It went something like this: "So thank you Peter for your interest, but at this time we don't see a future for you in broadcasting."

The CBC in Winnipeg felt differently. A few months later, Herb Nixon offered me a job in their radio and television newsroom in the Manitoba capital. I left Churchill in the early part of 1971—just before that three-year clock I'd heard so much about ran out.

POSTSCRIPT

Many years later when I was the chief correspondent of CBC News and anchor of The National, *I was in Belleville to give a dinner speech to a local group. I told the CJBQ story and it got a good laugh. After the event was over someone approached me at the head table. He was from CJBQ—a fairly recent hire in the management sector, I think he said—and with a nice smile he added, "Sorry." I laughed and we both agreed that, actually, things had worked out pretty well.*

Winnipeg Days

My Winnipeg days in the news business start with an admission: I really didn't know what I was doing.

I'd only been in the Winnipeg newsroom for a few hours when the assignment editor, Jake O'Donnell, an old newspaper veteran, yelled out my name: "Mansbridge, come here."

When O'Donnell called, you moved, and that much I did know. But when he told me he was sending me to cover the annual report of the Great West Life Insurance company, I wasn't shy. Don't forget, I was the guy who knew how to cover polar bears, not bottom lines.

"I have no idea what to ask for an annual report," I replied.

"Don't worry," said Jake. "I'm sending you with Dupasquier."

Dalton Dupasquier was the veteran CBC Winnipeg cameraman, a lanky, kind of goofy guy, who was going to be my guide on my first-ever television story. And thank God he was, and thank God Jake sent him to babysit me.

Dalton spent most of his day, not prepping his old film camera, but working the phones and the papers for stock tips. Dalton knew business, and he knew annual reports. At Great West Life, Dalton grabbed a copy of the annual report, ran over the numbers and the claims, and gave me three questions to ask. I did as I was told, and much to my relief, the story we got was the one deemed to be the most important out of the report.

In those days, most of local news wasn't as complicated. Fires, bank robberies, traffic accidents, school board meetings, city hall debates—the kind of stuff that almost "writes itself," as Jake used to say, and he was right.

Perhaps a little overdressed for a prairie farm report.
CBC

One day in 1972, Jake and the CBC Winnipeg managers had a new idea for me. There was a federal election called for late October, and they felt I was ready to take part in my first live special—no tape, no scripts, all ad-libbing commentary over breaking news. I was lucky, I was sitting beside a piece of Manitoba gold, veteran broadcaster Bill Guest. Bill Guest was a legend in Winnipeg. Extremely likeable and a man without airs. He hosted the morning CBC Radio broadcast, *Information Morning*, and the weekly television quiz show, *Reach for the Top*. He would anchor the broadcast and I would provide the colour commentary and analysis. The main broadcast would be done from Toronto, and we would provide short seven-minute segments every half hour with an update of the local results. But it was an exciting assignment and my first real opportunity to do what I was confident of—ad-libbing, not reading from a script, but reacting in real time to events as they unfolded.

The weekend before the election, Bill and I rehearsed how things would go with phony election results just to get in the rhythm. Bill was terrific and kept giving me useful pointers about how to use the monitors, how to make complicated graphics simple for the audience, and how to still have a good time while dealing with a very important subject.

Finally, it was approaching airtime. In our election-night studio, the floor director called out, "Sixty seconds."

My heart was pounding a bit, so I looked at Bill to help calm myself down. Instead, I was surprised. From the desk up, Bill appeared fine, but from my vantage point beside him, I could see his hands in his lap just below. They were shaking. A lot.

"Bill, you're not nervous, are you?" I asked.

His response was words I would live by. "Son, the day you're not nervous on a show like this is the day you've been in the business too long."

And with that, we were off.

"Good evening, Manitoba, and welcome to Election '72. I'm Bill Guest and with me is Peter Mansbridge."

POSTSCRIPT

It turned out to be one of the most exciting elections on record. Pierre Trudeau's Liberals won, but it was a two-seat squeaker that wasn't really finalized until the next day.

Bill Guest remained a friend and mentor until he was taken from us far too early, dying in 1985 of a heart attack at the age of fifty-seven.

Diversity in the Newsroom

It took a while for diversity to come to the CBC, and when it did, I would argue that it came first to the north. When I started working at the corporation's little radio station in Churchill, Manitoba, in 1968, there were no women on staff, but there was diversity.

James Arvaluk was one of the five announcers spinning records, and while all the rest of us were white and from the south, James was Inuit and from Pond Inlet on Baffin Island. Not long after I arrived, we were joined by Peter Irniq, further bolstering the number of Inuit on staff. And why not? The CBC Northern Service was established to reflect northern Canadians, not just white Canadians who had moved, often temporarily, to the north. Who better to tell the stories than the people who had lived them?

While I was honing my basic news skills, James and Peter were producing and hosting a weekly, thirty-minute Inuktitut broadcast that was heard across the north. They were rock stars in what was, at that time, the Northwest Territories and Yukon. Eventually, they used their early fame to establish careers as political figures in the north, and both had roles in the creation of the third territory, Nunavut. The CBC can and should take some credit for ensuring that there was a home for young Inuit in broadcasting then, which has led to a northern service with a significant presence of Indigenous women and men now.

So, diversity, to a degree, was something I noticed as soon as I started at the CBC.

But then, in the early 1970s, I was confronted by another reality when I arrived in Winnipeg. It was my first chance to observe the main network in operation. As I walked through the revolving doors on Portage

Avenue, the first person I saw was the switchboard operator. She was a woman. And it would be a while before I saw another one.

When I took the elevator to the fifth-floor newsroom, it was all men and it would remain that way for the first few years I was in the Manitoba capital. There were about twenty of us, acting like men often do. On my first day, I got roped into a game of 21 with the famed, and awfully nice, sportscaster Don Wittman. I left broke but "one of the boys." I can recall more than a few poker games going on in the late afternoon, right in the newsroom.

Then Bonnie Friedman arrived. She was hired as the newsroom receptionist, but she had other plans and it didn't take long for her to make them clear. One day when the "boys" were placing their orders with her for morning coffee, she'd had enough.

"Get your own goddamn coffee," she said in her New York accent. And they did.

Within a few months, Bonnie had moved upwards by demanding and earning consideration for promotion. Eventually, she became one of the best assignment editors I ever had.

She wasn't in the first wave of women in the news business at the CBC, but she was an early pioneer in a scene that began to shift quickly. With more and more women coming out of journalism schools, more and more women started to populate newsrooms and fill reporter, editor, and producer positions across the country. It was good for the CBC, good for journalism, and it was about time.

The foreign correspondent cohort, once the domain of the trench-coated Bogart types, began its transition too with Ann Medina, Anna Maria Tremonti, Adrienne Arsenault, Nahlah Ayed, Margaret Evans, Susan Ormiston, and many more making their marks with award-winning journalism in wars, earthquakes, and floods the world over. By the 1990s, there were more women than men in most ranks, eventually including management.

The problem—and it persists today—is that the overwhelming majority are white. The CBC, like many other organizations, is still playing catch-up in trying to reflect the diverse reality of Canada in its ranks. Our history, especially in southern Canada, includes Indigenous and Black people, who have mostly been ignored for key jobs. We also have a growing immigrant population of many people of colour. They, too, must be reflected at all levels of the nation's public broadcaster.

In general, the CBC is not doing too badly with on-air representation, but the commitment the corporation made was for more than that, and it has fallen short.

Here's the issue. The public needs more than just to *see* and *hear* diversity in the faces and voices of those on air; that diversity needs to be ingrained in the fabric of the company because it is in the fabric of the country. You cannot be a public broadcaster that serves only a slice of the public.

For all the talent in a company as massive as the CBC, it is not a democracy. The editorial decisions are necessarily made by a few key people. They seek input, but unless the decision makers at the big table bring in a multitude of perspectives, backgrounds, ethnicities, lived experiences, and diversity, the CBC will not adequately serve all Canadians.

In recent years, the people advocating those causes have given up waiting for change; instead, they are making it very clear that their treatment and their careers matter too.

POSTSCRIPT

James "Jimmy" Arvaluk wound up in the Nunavut cabinet and worked tirelessly to protect and promote Inuit culture. We saw each other occasionally, the last time in Pond Inlet in 2008. He died in 2016.

Peter Irniq was elected to the territorial legislature in 1987 but lost re-election to—wait for it—his old cohost, Jimmy Arvaluk. However, he landed on his feet, serving five years as commissioner of Nunavut, the government of Canada's representative in the territory. He was and still is passionate about all governments hiring more Inuit.

Another friend and colleague from the CBC Northern Service was Whit Fraser, who was based in Yellowknife, and the two of us exchanged stories about our communities on a weekly basis. At the time, a young Inuk woman by the name of Mary Simon was breaking barriers in another CBC northern station at Inuvik. Today, she and Whit are married, and Mary, in the summer of 2021, was named Canada's first Indigenous Governor General. Another barrier broken.

Bonnie Friedman was a continuing force at the CBC, eventually becoming The National's assignment editor based in Toronto. But just like the day she told us to get our own coffee, she suddenly told us goodbye in the early '80s. She went home to New York for a bit, and then really decided she'd had enough. The last I heard of her she was selling trinkets on a beach in Hawaii. I was jealous. She was the best.

The Wings on Her Lapel

Minor royals were still relatively major stories in the 1970s. Today, minor royals, even the Queen's youngest son, Prince Edward, travel in and out of Canada with little fanfare. Not so in 1971 when Princess Margaret, the Queen's younger sister and a rock star of sorts, flew into Winnipeg to officially open the new Winnipeg Art Gallery in the heart of the Manitoba capital.

Her plane was due to arrive during our suppertime newscast, and I was assigned to be at the airport to do the commentary for "live" coverage. It would be short, just a welcoming ceremony, and probably wouldn't last more than a few minutes. We'd only have one camera, but one was enough for a shot of the princess descending from the aircraft and being met by Manitoba officials. I'd be some distance away but equipped for the commentary.

I did my research. She was coming in on a regular Air Canada flight, and all officials including Air Canada agreed she would be the first one off the plane. The Manitoba delegation welcoming her would be led by the lieutenant governor, William McKeag.

The plane landed and began taxiing over toward the official welcoming area. I warned the control room we were just minutes away, and I heard the Winnipeg news anchor, Garth Dawley, begin his handover: "And now we are going to the Winnipeg International Airport where Peter Mansbridge is standing by for our live coverage of the arrival of Princess Margaret."

"Thanks, Garth, it's an historic day for Winnipeg," is the way I started things as the plane pulled up right on time and exactly in the spot where things had been designated.

As I talked briefly about the history of the moment, Princess Margaret's past trips to Canada, and the importance of the Winnipeg Art Gallery, the stairs were moved up to the aircraft and the door was opened. The big moment had arrived and I could see everything unfolding in front of me. A woman walked out of the door and stood at the top of the stairs.

"And there she is," I said. "Princess Margaret!"

But something wasn't right. She didn't have the normal fancy royal hat like her sister. And there seemed to be little decorative wings pinned to her chest.

In my ear, I heard someone yelling, "That's the stewardess!"

It *was* the stewardess.

A disaster for me.

And when I got back to the office later that evening, someone had put two pictures on my desk. One of Princess Margaret and one of an Air Canada flight attendant. It was suggested, only half-jokingly, that I do a report on the difference between the two for the late-night news.

Ahem. Note the tie tucked into the pants.
CBC

Russell Means

Russell Means will be remembered for a lot of things. Activist, actor, ladies' man. He was dynamic and likeable, and as a result always seemed to have a sizeable following anxious and ready to be at his side. And nowhere was that more apparent than at Wounded Knee.

Wounded Knee, South Dakota, on the Pine Ridge Indian Reservation, is sacred ground for members of the American Indian Movement (AIM), a Native American advocacy group, for two reasons.

In 1890, the United States Army massacred hundreds of the Lakota people who lived on the reservation at Wounded Knee. At least half of those who died were unarmed women and children. Washington saw it as a triumph and gave the country's highest military award for valour, the Medal of Honor, to twenty of its soldiers.

Then, in 1973, Indigenous activists chose Wounded Knee and its historic symbolism to make their case that treaties were not being fulfilled, not just on the Pine Ridge Indian Reservation but across the United States. They occupied the small town, commanding worldwide attention. As the site was surrounded by US marshals and members of the FBI, hundreds of journalists from dozens of television networks, including the CBC, travelled to South Dakota to cover the story. Followers and supporters, many of them young women, joined the protest. They listened to the movement's charismatic leaders and slept wherever they could find dry land. Aside from a few serious skirmishes, which included at least two deaths, the "incident," as it was called, ended peacefully after seventy-one days. The protest achieved what it had wanted—it put Indigenous issues on the front page.

One of the leaders of the occupation was Russell Means, who himself had been born not far from Wounded Knee. He was later indicted over the occupation, but the charges were dismissed for prosecutorial misconduct. That only increased Means's profile, and while he remained true to the original cause—he would go on to speak forcefully at the United Nations—he enjoyed his moment. So much so that he accepted Hollywood's beckoning to join the acting ranks and he appeared in several big-budget movies, including *The Last of the Mohicans*.

All this is to say that in 1976 I travelled back to Wounded Knee to talk with Russell Means about a number of issues, including whether anything had really been accomplished by the 1973 occupation. He argued that change takes time but that it would eventually come.

After we had finished our interview, Means and I walked the grounds where he had held court with his followers during the seventy-one days the world had watched. It was a casual conversation, the cameras weren't rolling, and he seemed quite relaxed.

At one point I asked him what it had really been like, what would be his lasting memory of the whole episode.

He looked at me, grinned, and half-whispered, "The five paternity suits I was hit with when it was all over!"

POSTSCRIPT

Russell Means kept up his activism and later his acting throughout the remainder of his life. He died at seventy-two in 2012. He is survived by his fifth wife and ten children.

Hair Raising in China

Anne Blakeney was visibly excited when I saw her at breakfast that morning. It was May 1976 and we were in China on a ten-day official visit. After days of briefings in Beijing, we were in Shanghai and finally getting a chance to tour something that wasn't tied to Anne's husband's trade mission.

Allan Blakeney was premier of Saskatchewan and was one of only a very few Western leaders who had been invited to China in months. The country's head of government, Chou En-lai, had just died in January. Mao Zedong, the chairman of the ruling Communist Party, was still alive but hadn't been seen in some time, and the assumption was he was ill. His wife, Jiang Qing, was leading the so-called Gang of Four in the shadows, trying to organize what would happen after Mao's death. She'd already spearheaded the "reeducation" and disappearance of the man many had assumed would be Mao's successor, Deng Xiaoping. But it was clear that Beijing (or, as we called it then, Peking) wanted to give the impression that it was still at least a little open to the world, as it had shown with Richard Nixon's visit in 1972 and Pierre Trudeau's visit the following year. So perhaps that was why Blakeney had been invited at what seemed like the last minute to come to China on a mission to extol the virtues of Saskatchewan potash to the Chinese. The premier's NDP government had just nationalized half the potash industry in the province, so he, as the only elected socialist in North America, was probably someone the Chinese felt they could comfortably sit down with and talk business.

I still smile when I hear the word "potash." I had to do quite a few stories on potash for *The National* when I was promoted to the CBC program as its correspondent in Saskatchewan in 1975, but that didn't mean the editors in Toronto had any idea what potash actually was. Almost every call I made to the "desk" in Toronto started with that question: "Mansbridge, tell me again what potash is?" Explaining that it was basically a fertilizer to make crops grow better often drew either a laugh or a yawn. In those days, it was never easy selling stories from the prairies unless there was a grain elevator in the background and someone talking with a straw hanging out of their mouth. "That's what the prairies is supposed to look like," a Toronto-centric editor told me once. I ignored the advice.

The problem for Allan Blakeney when we got to China was that there was—not known to us at the time—a serious backroom leadership struggle unfolding in Beijing hindering any meaningful trade talks, so the Chinese suddenly changed the itinerary and instead offered up what was basically a grand tour of some key landmarks in China: Beijing, the model rural commune Da Chai, Shanghai, and Guangzhou (then

A 1976 selfie on the Great Wall of China.

known as Canton). Most of the trip was by an old steam train and it was a fantastic experience—I felt like an extra in a 1930s adventure movie.

All that led up to this moment for Anne Blakeney. She had always had a fascination with herbal medicine, and she'd heard that one of the top places for such practice in China was in a research centre in Shanghai. She asked whether it would be possible, when we reached Shanghai, to visit and be given a tour. The Chinese responded positively and everything was quickly set for one of our mornings in the city.

I remember waiting for our transport vehicles to arrive outside our hotel with a few of the others who were going to take the tour. We had our "minder" with us from the Chinese authorities to make sure we didn't wander too far. But still, a crowd gathered, as so many younger ones had never seen Westerners before. At six feet tall and with a mop of blond hair—yes, I had some then—I was attracting particular interest from the two hundred or so people who seemed to appear out of nowhere. It was all very friendly as they laughed and pointed at this strange person who didn't look at all like them.

The vehicles arrived to take us to the herbal medicine clinic, and the visit lasted nearly two hours. As it ended, the clinic leaders offered up a question-and-answer session that all of us could take part in, but we knew this was Anne Blakeney's moment so we just listened. Sitting at what was a long table with about fifteen people in attendance, I heard the premier's wife ask detailed questions about possible remedies for some of the main medical issues of the day, from cancer to heart disease. I had no intention of asking any questions because it wasn't a news conference, but I'll admit there was one thing I really did want to ask but it would take some courage. My chance was moments away.

When Mrs. Blakeney wrapped up her questions, she turned her gaze away from the herbal doctors, looked down to the other end of the table, and said, "Does anyone else have a question?" Pause. "Peter, you always have questions, go ahead."

Yikes, I thought. Should I?

A few weeks before this trip, one of the women in the Regina newsroom, a wonderful journalist by the name of Sandra Lewis, had come up behind me while I was sitting at my desk typing a story. She suddenly gasped, "Peter, you're going bald!" I was horrified. At first I assumed she was joking, but as others joined in the chorus, I figured there must be some truth to it. That night I got into a contorted position in front of my mirror to check it out for myself. "Oh my God," I said out loud. "Sandra was right."

So there I was a few weeks later in Shanghai, centre stage for my question. And I calmly let the words out: "I've recently realized that I'm starting to lose my hair, and seeing as you have so many herbal cures for things, do you have one for that?"

All this had to go through a translator and as it did you could see laughter rolling across the room on the part of our Chinese hosts. Anne seemed to have a smile on her face too. But I figured the humiliation was worth it if they had something that could stop the unfolding recession on my scalp. Eventually came the answer. They did.

"Yes, we have a pill for that problem," said one of the lead specialists.

I responded immediately by passing a piece of paper and a pen across the table. "Please write the name out and where I could buy some," I said.

That brought even more laughter.

After handshakes, we departed, and as we were driving back to the hotel, I asked the "minder" whether we could stop at the place they'd written down and buy some of the pills. He thought for a minute and nodded.

Soon we were outside one of the old British bank buildings on the world-famous waterfront, the Bund, in the centre of downtown Shanghai. The main floor was like a department store and one counter was set aside for herbal medicines. A crowd quickly gathered, pointing and gesturing just like the morning outside the hotel. I passed the paper with the name of the pill on it and the translator added his own commentary. Everyone, the crowd included, laughed a lot. But the salesperson nodded to indicate they had the pill.

"How many bottles do you have?" I asked.

His answer came back: "Two dozen."

"I'll take them all."

More laughs. But I got those pills. All 2,400 of them.

I guarded the pills with my life for the long journey home. Even declared them at Customs in Vancouver. No problem.

When I got back to my apartment in Regina, I went over the story and checked out the dosage with my roommate, Ron Shorvoyce, who was the legislative reporter in Regina. I told him that I had to take fifteen pills a day for seven days and then take a week off before repeating.

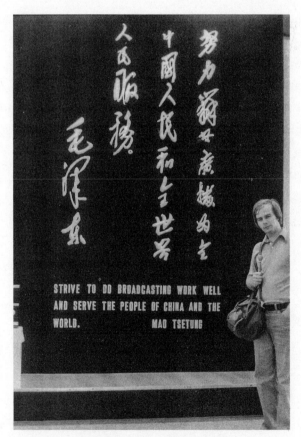

A poster on the street not far
from Tiananmen Square in Beijing.
University of Toronto Archives

Ron looked a little concerned. "What's in those pills?" he asked.

"I don't really know. They're herbal pills. Maybe it's a magic formula like Coke or KFC," I joked.

Ron didn't laugh. "You better get them checked out."

I booked an appointment with my Regina doctor, who had come to Canada from China with his family during the 1949 revolution. I told him the story. He said he would look at the pills, so I gave him a bottle.

About a week later, he called me back.

"Peter," he said. "These pills will do nothing for your hair."

"What?" I blurted back. "I brought all these bottles back for nothing?"

"Oh, they'll do something," the doctor replied. "I remember these pills from when I was in China."

"Well, what are they for?"

"They are," he paused. "Aphrodisiac!"

At that moment, I suddenly realized what everyone in China had been laughing about. I was upset, but the doctor wasn't. He still had one more thing to say.

"Peter, do you think I could keep this one bottle?"

Heroes in Broadcasting

For journalists of my generation, especially broadcast journalists, one name has always stood out among the rest. Someone to be inspired by, someone you could wish to emulate. CBS's Walter Cronkite.

He'd done it all: been there in Normandy not long after the Allied troops hit the beaches on D-Day; sat in the studio to break the news that John F. Kennedy had been assassinated; stood in Vietnam reporting back to America that their war could not be won; watched in awe and admiration with us as Neil Armstrong walked on the moon; and calmed the nation as he and it witnessed the first time a president, Richard Nixon, was forced to resign from office.

I recall coming home from school in Ottawa in November of 1963 to see my mother weeping at the television screen as Cronkite told the story of the Kennedy shooting in Dallas. He was emotional, and so was everyone else. He didn't hide those feelings. I watched his Vietnam reporting and understood why President Lyndon Johnson would always say that it was Cronkite's Vietnam journalism that cost Johnson his job.

So was Cronkite a hero of mine? You betcha.

Which brings me to January of 1978 and a favourite passion of Cronkite's: space stories. Kosmos 954 was a Soviet satellite that had been orbiting the Earth for only a few months when it was clear there was a malfunction, and the Soviets warned it would reenter the Earth's atmosphere and eventually crash somewhere on the planet. But no one could predict where. This had never happened before, and people around the world were understandably on edge. Well, as luck would have it, the satellite crashed in an extremely remote area of the Northwest

Territories. No one was hurt and, while there was some radioactive fall-out, it was considered minor. But it was still a huge story.

CBS was unable to get one of its reporters to Canada in time to do an item that evening for Cronkite's *CBS Evening News*, so they asked if the CBC could loan them a reporter and crew. After a year in Regina, I'd been promoted again to Ottawa and the CBC's Parliamentary Bureau, and as things turned out, the CBS assignment fell to me. I was pumped, to say the least. Talk about an opportunity. In those days it was rare that a Canadian appeared on one of the big-three American network newscasts.

There was no time to get to the crash site—in fact, it would be days before anyone made it to the remote area—so I had to do the story from Ottawa. I wrote a script, watched the edit, and fed the item to New York in time for Cronkite's 6:30 p.m. broadcast. Then I found a spot in the bureau's TV room and waited.

As the CBS opening graphics rolled out, the most famous television journalist in the world began his introduction with the same two words everyone in the business always used, but in the voice no one else had: "Good evening."

And then began his "roll-up" to the lead story, which concluded with the three words I never assumed I'd ever hear come from his mouth: "Peter Mansbridge reports."

The item wasn't that long, about a minute forty, but it had all the details that were known at the time. It ended with me on camera on the roof of our bureau with Parliament Hill in the background saying, "Peter Mansbridge for CBS News in Ottawa."

The screen cut back to Cronkite, who stared at his monitor for a second longer. One of my colleagues immediately reacted. "He looks impressed. They'll probably offer you a job."

The next day they did. A foreign correspondent's position in Johannesburg. I was more than flattered but eventually turned it down because I felt I owed the CBC my continuing loyalty as they had positioned me to cover the next federal election and it was expected to be called at any time. That moment, though, began a long relationship with both CBS and NBC where jobs were offered and negotiations were held. But more on that later.

After Cronkite retired in the early 1980s, I shifted my attention to NBC's Tom Brokaw. I'd always respected his journalism and his route to the top. He'd been a local reporter in southern California, a network reporter at the White House throughout Watergate, an anchor on the *Today* Show, and then in the '80s he became NBC's anchor of their *Nightly News*. In many ways, his rise to the top was similar to the trajectory I would eventually take.

Over the years, we bumped into each other a few times at international events, but I didn't really have a chance to talk to him at any length until the summer of 2014 during the seventieth anniversary of D-Day, an event of which both of us were in awe. Brokaw had written a book about the Second World War, one that was incredibly successful,

With NBC's Tom Brokaw in the American Cemetery in Normandy in 2014.
Stephanie Jenzer

selling hundreds of thousands of copies around the world. The title became part of the vocabulary—*The Greatest Generation*—describing those men and women who volunteered their service to fight Germany, Italy, and Japan in the 1940s.

Brokaw told me that he got pushback from some historians who quibbled with the word "greatest" and argued that there were other generations, like the Founding Fathers, who were more deserving of that title. He didn't agree and offered this defence, one he made with a smile on his face: "That's my story and I'm sticking to it!"

This conversation occurred as we stood together at the American Cemetery at Omaha Beach where US troops had landed early on that morning of June 6, 1944. Thousands were cut down by German gunfire even before they could reach the sand. In some ways, it was a slaughter, but in the end these boys, as Brokaw called them, persevered. For ten thousand, though, Omaha Beach is their final resting place.

It's easy to get emotional walking between the endless crosses, perched atop the bluffs overlooking the beach where so many took their last breath. So I asked the man who had chronicled so many of their stories what being there meant to him.

He paused. And then, gently and unashamedly, broke down.

After a moment, staring out at the sea of white markers across the cemetery grounds, he collected his thoughts.

"These boys . . . they came from the great plains, from the big cities, from small towns . . . and when they landed on this beach, they were nineteen or twenty years old. That morning the chances they were going to die were really good, but they didn't think that. They all supported each other.

"What I always take back from that is . . . the Depression formed them—they learned about deprivation, about working together, and about sacrifice. And when they made the ultimate sacrifice on this beach, you didn't hear anyone from their families whining that they had a hero in their family who died on D-Day, or died on Iwo Jima, or died on Okinawa, or died in Italy. They didn't say it was unfair. They knew the stakes were so big. And that's the lesson I take away from here."

Along the beaches of Normandy, you could use those same words where the Canadians fell, and the British fell, in those same hours on that same day.

We both stood there. Silent. The winds brushing through the leaves on the trees above us.

I'd always wanted that moment with Tom Brokaw.

POSTSCRIPT

Walter Cronkite retired from the CBS Evening News *in 1981. He lived a long life, writing and enjoying his favourite nonjournalistic pastime, sailing. He died in 2009 at the age of ninety-two.*

Tom Brokaw retired from the NBC Nightly News *in 2004. He still does frequent commentaries on NBC News and the occasional documentary. And of course, he's still writing, mostly with a look back at the military moments of recent American history.*

The Mystery Building

During the Vietnam War, the CBC had a bureau in Hong Kong. It was one of the premiere postings, and over the years, correspondents from Bill Cunningham to Joe Schlesinger to Colin Hoath would fly in and out of Saigon from Hong Kong to cover the conflict. But by the mid-1970s, with the war over, the CBC decided to close up shop, save money, and bring their last Hong Kong correspondent home.

In 1979, I was in Hong Kong as part of a small documentary crew covering the exodus of the "boat people" from Vietnam. It was a gripping story that had worldwide implications. Hundreds of thousands of Hoa people (Vietnamese with Han Chinese ancestry) were being persecuted by the Communist government, and the only way out was to pay

Covering an arrival of Vietnamese people at the entrance
to Hong Kong harbour in 1979.
CBC/Arnold Amber

enormous amounts of money for space on overcrowded boats, but there was no guarantee of where they would end up or who would take them in.

We spent time out in the South China Sea with Hong Kong officials intercepting some of the boats, and more time in refugee camps like the one that housed thousands in Hong Kong. We talked to some of the refugees and to the lone Canadian immigration officer, a twenty-something recent university grad who was making the "yes" or "no" decisions about whether to allow immigrant status to those who desperately wanted it. Canada eventually took in close to one hundred thousand Vietnamese boat people.

When we'd finished filming, it was time to screen some of our footage and start writing. The team was small, me and producer Arnold Amber. Our cameraman was a freelancer based in Hong Kong, and seeing as we no longer had a bureau there, he suggested a private film production house we could use in Kowloon, on the island side of the Hong Kong harbour. So, off we went. We took the Star Ferry across Victoria Harbour and walked to the building. It was already nighttime and dark. The office tower looked very quiet as we entered.

We got in the elevator and pushed the button to head up to the production house floor, but before we reached the correct number, the elevator stopped unexpectedly at a lower floor.

The doors opened, revealing a deserted, glass-walled office full of desks, chairs, and typewriters. And clearly spelled out in classy capital letters across the glass was: THE CANADIAN BROADCASTING CORPORATION.

POSTSCRIPT

I was never able to find out the story behind the deserted CBC office. It wasn't the old bureau, at least so said the correspondents who used to work out of the city. Was it an old lease that couldn't be broken? Or was it an expired lease for which the owners couldn't find new tenants? Who knows? One of those old CBC mysteries that occasionally haunt the place.

Dead Air

Words matter. And the wrong words matter a lot.

I discovered that during the first planned and promoted CBC News Special that I hosted. It was September 28, 1981, and it was real history. The Supreme Court of Canada, for the first time, had allowed cameras in its courtroom for a decision that would have enormous implications on the nation. The Trudeau government was attempting to "patriate" the Constitution—in other words, bring it home from Westminster where it had been stored, protected, and patronized by the government of England. All this was a result of the 1980 Quebec referendum and Prime Minister Pierre Trudeau's promise that he would implement a new constitution and make all regions of the country happy. A variety of provincial and Indigenous groups disagreed and had fought Trudeau in court. After spending a year listening to the arguments, the court would determine if Ottawa had the right to unilaterally patriate.

With cameras in the courtroom, we would have a front-row seat on the decision. As the host in the studio, this was a major milestone for me because it signalled my officially taking over the reins of the CBC News Specials, the unit that covered, as it happened, all major news events and had the opportunity to break into the regular programming schedule. To say I was a bit nervous that this first major event was bound to be a decision woven in legalese by the highest court in the land would be a serious understatement. But I was lucky because sitting beside me was the esteemed constitutional law expert Professor Peter Russell of the University of Toronto. I could throw anything his way, or so I thought.

The time arrived. We cut inside the courtroom to the chief justice,

Bora Laskin, and the country saw the first television pictures of the court's proceedings in its history. Laskin turned on the microphone in front of him and began to talk. We certainly saw his lips move but that was it. The sound was just a mumble.

I looked at Professor Russell, desperately hoping that the audio problem I was having was just my earpiece. I was wrong. He looked totally perplexed. Through my earpiece I could hear that the control room was in chaos with people pushing buttons and knobs, anything that might solve the problem. The biggest decision in the country's attempt at self-determination and we had no idea what was being said. Fortunately, there was one person who moved quickly to save us and break the story for everyone: Mike Duffy.

Mike was one of our most energetic reporters on Parliament Hill, and while we were in the studio he was standing outside the court waiting to interview some of the players as soon as the decision was made public. He could tell there were problems with the feed going to all the broadcast outlets, so he pulled his earpiece out and climbed over some tables to position himself right beside one of the floor speakers in the lobby area. He put his ear to the speaker and listened.

It was a confusing and complicated decision, but Mike took it all down and within minutes was on our air breaking it down in layman's language for the audience and for us. As Mike explained it, the court had decided that Ottawa did have the power to request the British Parliament to allow the Constitution to be brought "home," but at the same time it also ruled that Ottawa needed a consensus of the provinces to move ahead. It was a split decision with something for everyone.

Mike saved the day, in one of the most remarkable feats of peacetime journalism under intense pressure that I have ever witnessed. His exclusive launched us into hours of back and forth on what all this meant and how it would affect the constitutional debate, one that still lingers on to this day.

But on *that* day, the next thing everyone wanted to know was how

Pierre Trudeau would react. The problem was that the prime minister was in South Korea. We managed to set up a long-distance phone call (not always an easy feat in those days) with our chief political correspondent covering the trip, David Halton. The control room whispered in my ear that Halton was on the line and ready to talk.

"Well, everyone has been waiting to hear how Pierre Trudeau is taking this split decision from the court," I started, and then launched into the most memorable introduction of my career. "The prime minister is on the other side of the world in Seoul, South Korea, where it's thirteen hours ahead of us. Trudeau is in bed right now, but our David Halton is with him. David?"

There was dead air. I could feel the erudite Professor Peter Russell crashing almost headfirst into the desktop we were sitting at, convulsed in silent laughter. Eventually, David, pro that he is, picked up the story line and gave an appropriate answer.

Yes, words matter.

Relaxing after a broadcast with Mike Duffy in Ottawa in 1984.
(I quit smoking in 1994.)
CBC

POSTSCRIPT

Senator Mike Duffy has certainly had his issues since that day, but no one can take his reporter era away from him. He broke many a story over those years and has the awards to show for it.

Peter Russell is in his late eighties now and remains a professor emeritus at the University of Toronto.

David Halton was always the "class act" of our reportorial ranks and remains a close friend in our mutual retirements. His book about his equally famous father, Matthew Halton, Dispatches from the Front, *is a terrific read and should, in my view, be made into a movie.*

David has never let me forget that intro.

Diana

It was a day unlike any London had seen in decades, if ever. A royal wedding for the ages. A rather plodding, at times a bit odd, heir to the throne marrying a gorgeous, young teaching assistant while the world watched.

July 29, 1981. Charles and Diana.

The city, in fact most of the United Kingdom, was in a tizzy over the big event. Union Jacks were everywhere; so were pictures of the bride and groom. Selfridges and all the stores, big and small, were booming with the business of selling china sets of teacups and teapots, all mass-produced for the occasion. Matching Charles and Diana thimble sets were a special attraction. (Yes, I still have mine.)

Television networks from all over the world gathered in London to

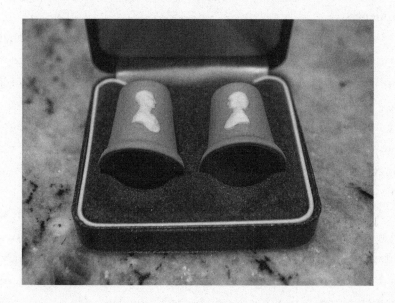

capture the nuptials for the hundreds of millions of people sitting in their homes, no matter the time zone, just anxious to see it all. As part of the global media contingent covering all the pomp and pageantry, the CBC was in attendance with Knowlton Nash and Barbara Frum anchoring from a London studio. I was positioned outside Buckingham Palace to give commentary whenever something of significance to the ceremony occurred at or near that spot, and not surprisingly there would be a lot. From the Queen's departure for St. Paul's Cathedral where the wedding would take place, to Diana's passing by on her way to the service, and of course when it was all over, the much-anticipated balcony scene with its "first kiss"—all would happen right in front of me.

The moment I remember most was when the carriage carrying Diana Spencer, soon to be Diana, Princess of Wales, accompanied by the Queen Mother, left St. James's Palace down the Mall and passed by me on its way to St. Paul's. The carriage was just a few dozen metres away and there were thousands of screaming Diana fans between it and me. Diana was waving, and then, I swear, and I swear to this day, she looked me straight in the eye. I was babbling away about some wedding trivia, but I froze at that moment. It only lasted a second or two, but it happened.

Was it an accident or did it mean more? Of course, I chose that it meant more. I decided that Diana was clearly smitten and ready to throw it all away for the baggage handler from Churchill turned TV reporter. Okay, so I have a vivid imagination, but that's the way I remember it, and as Tom Brokaw would say, I'm sticking to my story. Sadly, Diana ignored her better instincts and went ahead with the plan, dragged the long train of her wedding dress up the stairs of St. Paul's, and said "I do" anyway.

After that, I covered Diana a few times during the '80s when she was on her various Canadian visits to St. John's and Halifax; Toronto and Ottawa; and lastly for me, Victoria. I met her at a couple of the organized media receptions, but I guess the magic was gone. There were no eye-contact moments like that one on her wedding day.

All smiles after covering Diana in Victoria in 1986.
University of Toronto Archives

But seriously, the bigger picture post-wedding was a sad one for both the prince and the princess. Their problems, played out in front of the world, were eagerly pecked away at on the front pages and the television screens of the international media. Some of the problems were real— they clearly happened—but others were just palace gossip made real in the tabloids. None of it was pretty, and much of it can be condemned by journalism purists, but such has been the way of royal coverage for decades, if not centuries, and both Charles and Diana and all those who have come since were and are naive to think it would never apply to them. That's not to excuse bad, purely-for-profit journalism, it's just being realistic to the world of Fleet Street.

A lot of marriages don't work out, and this became one of them. Many couples identified with the way theirs crashed apart but never had to put up with the public shaming these two did. Sure, Charles and Diana were people of privilege, extreme privilege, but they were human too. The end was ugly. Details of their affairs were made public, even discussed by the principals themselves, and finally the divorce.

And, then, Paris.

It was a Saturday night at the end of August 1997. I was in a restaurant in Toronto after a round of golf with my friends, political analyst Allan Gregg and then *Maclean's* editor Bob Lewis. We were enjoying an after-dinner conversation when my pager went off.

"Get into the office. Diana. Car crash. Paris. It's bad."

Twenty minutes later, I was on the air. It *was* bad. It wasn't long before the official announcement: Diana was dead.

The next day I was on my way to London where we anchored *The National* for a week, exploring every possible angle of a heart-wrenching story. I hosted the coverage of the funeral along with my colleague Alison Smith. It was one of those broadcasts where we didn't really need to say much. The pictures were gripping, none more so than the two young princes, William and Harry, walking behind their mother's horse-drawn funeral cortege. Atop her coffin, in plain view of the cameras, was an envelope—Alison read out what it said, simply, "Mummy."

For everyone watching, in person or at home, it was a moment of high emotion.

As for me, so was our location in front of Buckingham Palace. It was, almost to the very spot, where I had stood sixteen years before, watching along with the world as she passed by on the way to her wedding. Now there I was, watching her casket pass by on the way to her funeral.

A Name in a Versailles Hat

Nearly four hundred years after France's Louis XIII picked Versailles as his favourite hunting ground, the leaders of the world's seven most powerful economies chose the same spot to have their annual summit. Of course, things had changed a bit since the seventeenth century. When Louis went looking for birds, Versailles was little more than a hunting lodge and hideaway for debauchery a mere twenty kilometres from the heart of Paris. By the time Louis the XIV gained the throne, Versailles had become one of the world's great palaces, and its famous Hall of Mirrors attracts tourists from across the world to this day.

And so it was that in June of 1982, France's president François Mitterand selected Versailles to host the eighth G7 summit. Much of the world was either in or sliding into recession, and the economic summit was to address the issues of sky-high interest rates, inflation, and unemployment. But that's not what happened.

In those days, the G7 summit was right up there on the international news agenda, ranking along with the annual major sessions of the United Nations and NATO and sporting events like the Olympics—dates not to be missed—and, as journalists, we got to travel to some of the most spectacular places in the world. Even though the economy wasn't exactly the most exciting subject to spend television time on, the CBC in its wisdom wanted a special half-hour show on what the summit had accomplished aside from regular news coverage. And that meant, as host of CBC News Specials, I had to be there. Hello Versailles.

Already, 1982 was shaping up as a banner year for news, and Versailles was looking to be a lot less about the economy than the summiteers had planned. In no particular order, here's what was happening.

Ronald Reagan was in the second year of his presidency and still a bit wobbly after an assassination attempt the year before. But there was a different kind of buzz that June for Reagan that had nothing to do with the summit. It was the fact that he was heading to Buckingham Palace as soon as the summit was over for a long-awaited, and much-heralded, meeting with the Queen. Two heads of state with two very different backgrounds, but it would be quite the moment. The cameras were ready.

Meanwhile, Margaret Thatcher was in an old-style war against Argentina of all countries. She had sent the military across the oceans to invade and recapture the British territory of the Falkland Islands, a place most people had never heard of until Argentina, just months before, had taken it by armed force and claimed it as theirs. But as odd as it seemed to many, the dispute had become a full-out war: destroyers and cruisers sunk on the high seas, dogfights in the air, and land battles on a series of remote, windswept islands in the South Atlantic.

Pierre Trudeau, for his part, wanted to talk about anything other than the economy, which had never been his passion, and was toying with the thought of doing a global peace mission. He was about to hit a few European countries to sound out the idea after things wrapped up in Versailles.

Host Mitterrand and West Germany's chancellor Helmut Schmidt knew that if one more thing of a noneconomic nature came up, it would likely mean the agenda would begin tilting away from the economy and in favour of international relations. And, of course, that one more thing happened. Right on the eve of the summit.

Israel amassed its troops along the Lebanese border, and hours later, with the G7 in session, they invaded. The possibility of a major Middle East conflict cast a shadow over the Versailles conference table, and with that, all the serious talk and the media questions swung to the noneconomic events of the day.

Now, to be fair, this was not a disappointment to the assembled media. The truth is economic stories are hard to tell and, unless you're working for the *Financial Times*, it's even harder to garner interest in them, let alone major play. War stories aren't easy to tell either, but they usually come with pictures that attract attention and with story lines that are much easier to follow. Armed with some of our best correspondents, we were ready to cover all the bases.

Those were the days when accountants didn't run the news services and the last thing anyone seemed to worry about was what the coverage was going to cost. And that certainly showed with the travel budget for the lineup of reporters, producers, and editors we had on location: our Paris correspondent David Bazay, our London correspondent Brian Stewart, our Washington correspondent Joe Schlesinger, our chief

One of Canada's greatest foreign correspondents
and one of my greatest friends, Brian Stewart,
on *The National* set in the early 1980s.
University of Toronto Archives

political correspondent David Halton, our Ottawa correspondent Mike Duffy, and me. Most of us were more excited about where we might be heading after the summit's final news conference than what any of the leaders had to say at it. And as soon as we put our half-hour news special to bed, we all gathered to decide who went where, the world seemingly on fire around us.

Executive producer Arnold Amber had secured a basement area in the palace for us to use as a workspace during the summit, and that's where we congregated. It reeked of history and a few other things—let's just agree that it was a pretty rough, unfinished area and it was unlikely any of the Louises had ever made it down there unless it was for a dalliance that lasted only a few minutes.

Amber was in charge of the CBC operation, and it was left to him to make the assignments for the various stories that loomed ahead. Most of us, no matter our normal duties, were angling for the Israel–Lebanon border—this was almost certainly going to be the lead story for the next few nights. The second best was Buenos Aires and the Falklands story. Amber was looking for a way to assign the stories without disappointing anyone. He decided it would be "choice by chance." He carefully wrote out topics on small pieces of paper:

Israel
London/Reagan
London/Falklands
Buenos Aires/Falklands
Washington
Trudeau

Then he folded them and placed them in a hat. Kind of a secret ballot in reverse. As we all sat patiently, yet expectantly, in the dank Versailles basement, Amber asked us one by one to walk up to the hat and pick our poison.

First up was Duffy, there in Versailles for his expertise on the economy. He pulled his piece of paper out of its spot at the bottom of the hat like he was picking a lottery ball out of a cage. He broke into a smile. We knew what that meant. Duffy's well-known luck had struck again.

"Israel," he beamed.

The groans fit the basement we were in.

It was all somewhat anticlimactic after that. Halton went with Trudeau, Bazay stayed in Paris, Schlesinger went to Buenos Aires, Stewart went to London to cover the war, and I went with him to cover Reagan and the Queen.

By the next night, most of us were in place in our new listening posts while Duffy was standing at the Israel–Lebanon border watching Israeli jets strafing Lebanese convoys. All because he'd picked a name out of a hat.

The Final Ballot

Running for the leadership of a party has changed a lot over the relatively short period I've covered political conventions. Today, thousands of party members—sometimes tens of thousands—vote remotely and electronically, and the results are known almost immediately. At least that's the way it's supposed to work. There are often technical glitches on timing, but the main idea is to be much more democratic and allow all party members to have a say in the decision of who should lead them.

It didn't always used to be that way, though, and some old-timers, like me, miss the old leadership convention days. While we concede the current method is fairer, the old days were much more exciting and made for great television. Between ballots, as lesser candidates dropped off and out, the arm twisting to try and attract their delegates was all out in the open. Deals were made, deals were broken, and the cameras witnessed it all, or most of it.

Like the 1968 Liberal leadership convention, when the then health minister Judy LaMarsh, desperate to stop a surging Pierre Trudeau, took to the convention floor between ballots and whispered in Paul Hellyer's ear, "Paul, don't let that bastard win, he isn't even a Liberal." She wanted Hellyer to withdraw his own bid for party leader and support someone else in an attempt to blunt Trudeau's momentum. Unfortunately for her, there was a microphone between her and Hellyer and everything was captured on air. But Hellyer couldn't make up his mind anyway, and the rest is history, including the fact that LaMarsh didn't make it into Trudeau's first cabinet.

Or the 1976 Progressive Conservative (PC) leadership convention, when the most unlikely of winners went from third place on the first ballot to first place on the final ballot, and someone most Canadians had never heard of became the leader of the party. The *Toronto Star* bannered the news of Joe Clark winning with this unforgettable headline: "Joe Who?"

The problem with those kinds of conventions, say the purists, is that the results are all cooked up by a small group of people, many controlled by the back rooms, all of whom are in attendance in whatever hockey rink the convention is being held. In other words, it may be wonderful to watch but it's not democratic.

Which brings us to 1983 and what many consider the most dramatic year in modern-day Canadian politics. The year started with Joe Clark as the leader of a very unhappy Conservative Party; their time in government in 1979 had lasted only nine months, and for many of them, Clark was the reason why. He'd tried to ram an austerity budget through a minority Parliament, and his government fell. In the election that followed, the dreaded Liberals—with Pierre Trudeau still at the helm—cruised back to power.

"Off with his head," said some, while others, like former Clark cabinet minister Elmer MacKay, just sniped from the background. Elmer, father of Peter MacKay, let it be known he thought Clark reminded him of dog food. If that wasn't bad enough, he added that it was the kind of dog food that stayed on the shelf because no one would buy it. (Something about chirping the party leader must run in the MacKay family, because in the dying days of the 2019 campaign, Peter had this to say about then leader Andrew Scheer: "Andrew is like the hockey player who has a breakaway on an empty net, and misses the net with his shot." Not quite dog food, but close.) Needless to say, by the time Clark got to Winnipeg on a frigid weekend in January of '83, the knives weren't hidden anymore; they were out in the open and his back was exposed.

Winnipeg was a review vote on Clark's leadership, and those who wanted Clark gone were working the hallways and the back rooms as soon as the delegates started arriving. Rumour had it that planeloads of newly signed-up members were being flown in from Quebec just to vote and then it was right back to the airport to fly home. They weren't there to support Clark; they were there to bring him down. Technically, Clark only needed 50 percent of the vote plus one to keep his job, but for some reason he'd set his own bar at 70 percent.

He didn't make it.

So, it was game on with a leadership race, one in which Clark would again run for the top job, but so would many of the members who had made no secret of the fact that they could do a better job if given the chance. Enter Brian Mulroney, who had finished a distant third to Clark on the final ballot in 1976. This time he'd got his ducks in a row and had a group of the party's biggest power players calling some of the shots behind him.

The vote was set for Ottawa on June 11, 1983, and it was going to be my first time anchoring such a major television news event. I was excited but I was also ready. I'd been covering politics, specifically PC politics, since the day I'd arrived on the Hill in 1976. I knew a lot of people in the party from across the country, and I had private conversations with

With David Halton in the anchor booth covering the
1983 Conservative Leadership Convention.
CBC

many of those who wanted the leadership in the lead-up to the vote, which gave me a chance to get some good "colour" for what was certain to be a long day on air. Of all the candidates, the one I wanted to talk with most and the one I left till last was Mulroney. Whatever happened when the voting ended, the odds were Mulroney would be involved in some fashion.

We agreed to meet the night before the vote in his hotel suite at the Chateau Laurier in Ottawa. When I got there, the door was open to the sitting room and there was a bit of a boisterous crowd inside. Mulroney was in the thick of it all, his wife Mila at his side. The others were members of his campaign team and they were busy trying to nail down what each had to do the next day when the action began on the convention floor.

I thought, "Well, so much for a private conversation; this is a zoo."

Mulroney must have sensed my concern because he immediately waved me to the other side of the room toward the bedroom. He followed me in and closed the door. He sat on the bed, I sat on a nearby chair.

"So what do you want to know?" he asked.

"I want to know how you see the day unfolding tomorrow."

Now, this was a guy who had been bitterly disappointed by what can happen in a convention when the floor dynamic takes over, as it did when he'd been considered a possible winner in 1976. But his speech the night before had been flat, and the next day he'd watched as the people he had counted on to support him when their own candidates dropped out walked right past his box to that of his unexpected competitor, Joe Clark.

"I'll never forget what Sinclair Stevens did to me in '76. I can still see him walking right past me, didn't even look up. I won't let that happen again," he told me now.

And then an amazing thing happened: He walked me through, ballot by ballot, the way he saw how the vote would unfold.

"I'll be second on the first ballot, second on the second, and probably still second on the third as all the also-rans drop off. Some will come to me, some won't. But while Joe will be first on all those ballots, he won't grow his vote. I will. I'll keep getting closer."

"So it goes four ballots?" I asked.

"Yes, and it will all come down to [John] Crosbie's vote when he drops out after three ballots. I have more of the Crosbie vote than Joe does, so I will win."

Now Brian Mulroney is often a man of bluster, and I'm sure that was a factor in that night's forecasting. But he also looked dead confident.

I asked him one more thing. "If you win, will you come to the CBC booth first so I can talk to you before anyone else?"

"Deal."

The next day, the voting lasted thirteen hours. It was far and away the longest I'd ever been in the chair. No commercials meant no pee breaks. Still not sure how I managed that.

With each ballot, the story unfolded—exactly the way Mulroney had predicted. The only possible threat to the prediction came after the second ballot when Crosbie's people tried to convince Clark's people that the only way to stop Mulroney was to have Clark abandon his first-place position and throw his support to the unilingual but growing Crosbie vote. Clark said no.

When the counting was all done, Brian Mulroney had the numbers, just like he had forecasted the night before sitting on his bed in the Chateau Laurier.

After a brief victory speech, he disappeared into the bowels of the Ottawa Civic Centre, and I wondered whether he'd forgotten his pledge the night before. No one seemed to know where he'd gone.

And then suddenly we heard footsteps coming up the staircase toward our booth hanging in the rafters overlooking the convention floor. The door opened, first for Mila Mulroney and then for an ashen-faced Brian Mulroney. He looked awful, pale, almost pure white.

We did the interview, but the whole time he looked like he was about to pass out.

An exhausted Brian Mulroney, with his wife, Mila, honoured his promise
to come to the anchor booth after his fourth ballot victory.
CBC

Someone took pictures of us, and a few weeks later one arrived in
my office mail. It was from the new leader of the opposition in his often
over-the-top tone:

"Peter: an outstanding journalist at an historic moment from an almost dead candidate! Brian."

POSTSCRIPT

*Brian Mulroney would win two majority governments, but after leaving office
in 1993, his party was decimated in an election which left them with only two
seats. As he slipped into private life, his public image took a major hit for his
role in the Airbus affair.*

*We still talk on occasion and have appeared at a number of events to-
gether, including in 2018 when I emceed a gathering in Winnipeg celebrating
the work Mulroney did in winning freedom for Nelson Mandela in 1990.
More than any other world leader, it was Mulroney's pressure that made that
happen. It remains one of his proudest moments, and Canada's.*

The Right Stuff

Like most people my age, I've been fascinated by space travel since I was a teenager. I lived through *The Right Stuff* years and grew up watching those first seven astronauts, all military pilots, jockey for a seat in the Mercury missions orbiting the Earth and some later in the Apollo missions to the Moon.

Many a morning in the '60s, I'd be up early to watch—and suffer from the endless delays—as Walter Cronkite anchored the CBS space coverage from the NASA facilities on Florida's Atlantic Coast. I was in awe of the astronauts and the courage they had to possess to be crammed into those tin cans and fired onto journeys that took them far away from the Earth. To me, these guys were heroes and therefore must live a hero's life. Wine, women, limos, the whole bit.

By the '80s, I was at the Kennedy Space Center in Florida covering the next phase of NASA's Space Shuttle program, both its successes and its tragedies. I witnessed the excitement of a few launches, felt the ground rumble even two miles away as the big rockets thundered their cargo into the sky. I was there to see Marc Garneau become the first Canadian in space and Roberta Bondar become the first Canadian woman to go into orbit. All the broadcasts cemented that image in my mind of the astronaut as special and worthy of the pampering they surely must get.

On one of my trips to the Kennedy Space Center, I was prepping for the next day's scheduled liftoff out at our portable studios across the Everglades from the launch pad when the decision was made to head back to Cocoa Beach where we were staying. I offered to drive and the three of us piled into the car and set out along the stretch of highway that's used only by those with the right accreditation for the Cape Canaveral area.

With Canada's first astronaut, Marc Garneau, watching Canada's
second astronaut, Roberta Bondar, launch into space.
University of Toronto Archives/Arnold Amber

So, when I saw a man hitchhiking, I said to my colleagues, "Let's pick
him up—he's obviously accredited."

No one argued and that's what we did.

The fellow jumped in the back seat with a smile and a thank you, and
then asked, "Where are you guys from?"

"We're journalists from Canada," we said.

"I'm from Canada too," he replied.

I could see him in the rearview mirror. "Oh, great, what do you do
in Canada?" I asked.

"I'm an astronaut."

Dream shattered. I couldn't hold back my astonishment. "An astronaut hitchhiking?"

He just laughed.

It turned out our astronauts weren't exactly paid that much and there
were limited expenses for them, certainly no cars to move them back
and forth. So they had to cut corners, including hitchhiking when they
had the chance. This was not what I had imagined all those years ago
sitting on the couch as a young teenager watching those early-morning
launches and imagining the "right stuff."

As I said, dream shattered.

A Call from CBS

In October 1987, I was standing in the checkout line at the front desk of the Essex House hotel in New York City. It wasn't a long line, but it was long and slow enough that I was starting to worry that it might cause me to be late for a meeting I had scheduled a few blocks away at the West 57th Street headquarters of CBS News.

As I waited, I stared at the floor and noticed a penny lying there seemingly unwanted. I thought for a moment. Should I pick it up? Would it bring good luck?

I stopped and picked it up. Just like I did all those years ago on the RMS *Canton* on its way to Malaya.

The penny gave me a surge of confidence. As I walked the few blocks to my meeting, I decided I had nothing to lose. I'd been to meetings at CBS before, in the late 1970s, and had been a bit nervous. At that time I was a young parliamentary correspondent in Ottawa, surprised that CBS was interested in me as a foreign correspondent in their South Africa bureau. This time there was no reason to be nervous. I had a great job at the CBC; at thirty-nine I was anchor of the Sunday night news and the lead anchor for all CBC News Specials like elections, conventions, and breaking news. Not to mention backup to the chief correspondent and anchor of the Monday to Friday *National*, Knowlton Nash.

CBS wanted to talk to me about their network morning show, the soon-to-be rechristened *CBS This Morning*. The network had a disastrous record in the mornings. Even when the legendary newsman Walter Cronkite had anchored the show in the 1950s. They had revamped the broadcast many times, including just nine months prior to my visit, but nothing had worked. They'd tried journalists, actresses, comedians, you name it, in the anchor chair, but they all, no matter how famous, couldn't pull the show out of morning television's last-place dumpster.

For some reason, they thought I could.

And where had they heard about me?

Howard Stringer was the new president of CBS News. Well loved by staff, Stringer had come up through the ranks and was determined to remake CBS into the global television leader it used to be when Cronkite was known the world over as the definition of journalistic credibility. When he surveyed the landscape of available "talent" for the morning, he settled on Kathleen Sullivan from ABC News as his female host, but drew blanks on a male. He ordered his search team to start screening tape from agencies that had walls full of video they'd pulled off satellites beaming newscasts from all over the world. Someone, without my knowledge, had recorded me and placed the tape along with a dozen others on Stringer's desk. There was something about what he saw that he liked, and the next thing I knew I was sitting across from him in his office.

Also in the room was David Corvo, who had been named the executive producer of this latest attempt by CBS to make mornings work.

After the expected small talk, Stringer went for substance. "What's wrong with our show?" he asked in his Welsh accent.

"It's simply not in the game," I replied. "NBC's *Today* Show and ABC's *Good Morning America* are hot off the top of their shows at seven a.m. with their best correspondents reporting from the White House or London or wherever, while you are fielding a bunch of unknowns, second-stringers at best. If you want to compete with Andrea Mitchell at NBC you have to give me *your* Andrea Mitchell and stop protecting her or him for Rather's six thirty p.m. show."

(Dan Rather had been named Cronkite's replacement on the main evening news earlier in the eighties and was trying hard to live up to the legacy.)

Corvo looked shocked. Stringer looked impressed. I kind of knew from that moment he was going to eventually offer me the job, but the dance continued on for about an hour. Picking up the penny had given me the self-assurance to speak my mind, not as a contestant for the job but as a broadcaster from a recognized network who felt like an equal and nothing less.

Then Corvo was instructed to take me out for lunch and book me to come down again the next week to do a studio test with Sullivan, the kind of test where they look for "chemistry."

What they didn't know about Sullivan and me is that we already knew each other. We'd met in London in July of 1981 at none other than the royal wedding of Prince Charles and Diana, the Princess of Wales. Back then, Kathleen was with a new network called CNN. We shared a platform outside Buckingham Palace and took turns doing "hits" into our respective network's special coverage. In between the hits we got acquainted. Bottom line, chemistry was not going to be an issue. And it wasn't.

A few days after that studio test, Howard called me at home in Toronto. He offered me the job, including a three-year contract totaling in the millions of dollars. Given that the Canadian dollar was worth about 70 cents to the US dollar at the time, Stringer's offer equaled a sum that stunned me. Keep in mind that at the time I was making about one hundred and fifty thousand a year at the CBC. It seemed, on the face, a no-brainer.

But it wasn't. Like many other Canadians facing a decision about leaving their existing job, country, friends, and family, it's a tough call. I had pretty much decided I was going to give it a go, but I told Stringer it was a tough call and I needed time.

Then some friends at the CBC ran a basic intervention. One of my best friends, correspondent Brian Stewart, joined by executive producers John Owen, Tony Burman, and the legendary Mark Starowicz, suddenly arrived at my condo late one night to argue that the CBC was in my blood and that public broadcasting would always offer more than what I could find at a commercially driven morning show.

As Starowicz said at one point, "Do you really want to interview cooks and actors and circus performers?"

Now, I like cooks, I would later marry an actress, and I wish I could juggle, but I got his point. He wasn't insulting anyone—he was appealing to my strongest journalistic senses. Senses I'd been grooming since those earliest days in Churchill. I was a hard-news guy, and Stewart, Burman, Owen, and Starowicz argued I'd regret any decision that went against that.

My friends were good but, in the end, it was Knowlton who tipped the scales. The following night, he and his wife, Lorraine Thompson, invited me to their apartment, and over hot chocolate (really), Knowlton said he was anxious to focus more on his book writing and was prepared to hand over the anchor job to me.

It was an emotional moment. He was sitting in his favourite living room chair; I was across the room perched on the edge of his couch. Lorraine was literally buzzing back and forth from the kitchen.

"I don't want you to go," said Knowlton, with a smile on his face and conviction in his voice.

It was an incredible gesture, one that I have wondered many times whether I could ever have done myself if confronted with the same situation.

On my way home I decided I was going to stay at the CBC. I'd spent my whole career, almost since that day at the Transair counter, secretly aspiring to the job of chief correspondent. Now it was there right in front

The person who put me in the anchor chair,
the great Knowlton Nash.
CBC

of me. Some things, I thought, are more important than money. Wait, let me say that again. Just to make sure I still believe it. Some things are more important than money.

At my place, I checked my voice mail. There was a message from Howard Stringer.

"Peter, it's Howard," he said. "I'm standing by the East River trying to decide whether to throw myself in the water. Come on, make up your mind."

I phoned Howard the next morning and told him. He immediately said he would fly up the next morning to try and see if we could make things work. He also said he would get Dan Rather to phone me. He would later ask Wayne Kabak, my agent at International Creative Management in New York, whether it was a "girl" issue, and said that if I didn't want to leave Canada because of my girlfriend, then CBS would do their best to find her a job too. Seriously. That was so 1980s. But that was never an issue.

It was simple, actually. I really loved the CBC. They had taken me from nowhere and been very good to me, and now the job of my dreams was sitting on the table, and I imagined all the great stories and experiences I would have in that job. I really liked Canada, and I really liked my friends, and I especially liked my family. I wasn't ready to leave any of them. While the salaries (even with a nice raise the CBC gave me) would never compare, I wasn't exactly selling pencils at the corner.

I kept that penny in my pocket throughout the two or three weeks of back and forth with CBS. It really was good luck. Not sure where it is now, but ever since that day in the Essex House in New York, whenever I see a coin on the ground with no owner in sight, I pick it up and believe good luck is just around the corner. And you know what? It usually is.

POSTSCRIPT

Knowlton passed away in 2014, Lorraine in 2020. Both were remarkable people. Knowlton had written the books post-retirement that he wanted to, and many were bestsellers.

Howard Stringer would go on to become the chairman and CEO of the Sony Corporation, the first non-Japanese CEO in the company's history. He is now a special advisor to the BBC.

Kathleen Sullivan remained at CBS for three years before moving on to other challenges in the broadcasting industry.

Dan Rather? He never called.

CBS This Morning is still in third place after many more attempts to reimagine its program.

In my final year in the anchor job at the CBC, 2017, I finally reached roughly the same salary that I had turned down thirty years before at CBS. But then again, it was never about the money.

Who knew? From Churchill, Manitoba,
to the cover of *TV Guide*.

Airport Connections

In 1988, I was off to cover my first Olympics in Seoul, South Korea. I'd just succeeded Knowlton Nash as anchor of *The National* the year before, so this assignment was a big deal.

Travel time to Asia is lengthy, of course, and in those days nonstop flights were few and far between. My flight had me routed through San Francisco with a change of terminals. Once I landed, I disembarked and began the long walk along the above-ground corridor connecting the two terminals.

I was travelling alone that trip and remember the walk clearly. At one point, I could see a lone traveler coming toward me from the other direction. The closer he got, the more familiar he looked. Suddenly I realized it was Yosuf Karsh.

Karsh was the most famous photographer of his time. Not just the most famous Canadian photographer. *The* most famous photographer. Period.

I knew all about him. How he lived in Ottawa and had his studios in the Chateau Laurier. How he'd taken portraits of every famous person in the world, including the classic Churchill shot where he'd pulled the British prime minister's cigar from his hand the second before pushing the shutter. It produced the famous Churchill scowl.

So, as the man approached, I wanted to say something, but . . . I chickened out. We crossed without a word.

Then to my shock, I heard, "Is that you, Peter Mansbridge?"

It was Karsh saying my name. It turned out that he was kind of a news junkie and knew the names of all the reporters who worked on Canadian television. He admitted that to me right there in the San

Francisco airport. It was a wonderful little chat and I felt so good as I walked toward my gate.

Then I suddenly thought of what I should have done. I turned and looked, but by then Yosuf Karsh was a fair distance away about to disappear into his terminal looking for his own gate.

"Damn," I thought. "I should have handed him my little travel camera and asked him to take a picture of me!"

POSTSCRIPT

Yosuf Karsh died in 2002 at the age of ninety-three.

The Chateau Laurier is one of my favourite hotels, and in the lobby between the front desk and one of the hotel bars is a room that is decorated with famous Karsh photos taken in his studio a few floors up. I always spend time looking at the photos. If you get the chance, I'd recommend you do too.

The Twenty-Four-Hour Suit

Most people remember the 1988 Seoul Olympics for the Ben Johnson fiasco. How Canadian emotions ran high, then came crashing down in forty-eight hours when the 100-metre dash, gold medal–winning, "fastest man in the world" was thrown out of the Games after testing positive for steroids. Canada was ashamed and embarrassed, and it showed in so many different ways. The worst was when some Canadian writers and broadcasters went from calling Johnson a "Canadian hero" to a "Jamaican-born runner" in an attempt to distance the shame.

The Johnson story was unquestionably *the* story of the Games, and it impacted sports, all sports, for decades to come. But those who thought it meant sports would be cleansed of drugs were wrong. It just meant that those who used drugs got better at cheating, as we still occasionally find out today.

So, yes, I was one of those who will always remember Seoul for the Johnson disaster. But I remember it for something else as well.

I was in the Korean capital to cohost the Opening Ceremony with the legendary sportscaster Brian Williams. Brian and I had been friends for years—we used to do the late-night local news and sports at CBC Toronto, and we'd always had a good time doing it. Then we both quickly moved up our respective ladders—he became the top broadcaster at CBC Network Sports and ditto for me at Network News. So, when in 1988 the corporation decided who it wanted face-first in the opening broadcast of the XXIVth Olympiad, they called on Brian and me. We were excited and focused—this was a big deal. We spent hours prepping for the broadcast which always features the Parade of Nations: Brian would talk about each of the 159 nations represented that year in terms of their athletes, while I'd focus on each nation's past or present history. And we'd ad-lib our way through the rest of the many hours we'd be on the air.

The Opening Ceremony was set for Friday, September 17th, but we had rehearsals and editorial meetings for the three days beforehand. After two days of cramming, Brian turned to me and said, "Let's go shopping. I know a place where we can get a suit made in twenty-four hours."

I wasn't impressed. "I know places like that, Brian. I once bought a twenty-four-hour suit in Hong Kong and it started falling apart after twenty-five hours."

"This is different," he insisted. "Famous people go there to shop."

So, I relented. After all, I was tired of reading up on countries that had never won an event and never would win an event. Time to see the sights.

Off we went to the Seoul tourist shopping heaven, Itaewon. Cosmopolitan dining, nightlife, and shopping are the hallmarks of the district and it was, as it usually is, packed when we got there. Brian led me to a pretty nondescript-looking shop marked with a Korean tailor's name. We went up a short flight of concrete steps and then we were inside. One of the tailors quickly latched on to us. Before I could say anything, Brian spoke.

"My friend is looking for a new suit, but it has to be ready in twenty-four hours."

No problem. We moved over to a huge pile of bolts of fabric, all different colours, and I picked out a safe navy blue.

I didn't see anyone famous.

Then the tailor moved me to a mirror and asked me to stand still while he took measurements. Then he took contact info. Then he took a deposit. The whole thing took at the most fifteen minutes.

I still didn't see anyone famous.

"You'll love it," bragged Brian. "You'll always thank me for this."

Twenty-four hours later, on the eve of the big show, we were back, ready for pickup. We had barely gotten in the store when, all of a sudden, sirens started blaring outside on the Itaewon street. We were all very aware of the constant threats that there could be an attack from North Korea to disrupt the Games, so that was the first thing that came to mind. I didn't know whether to hit the floor or dive behind a suit rack.

I did neither because, just as suddenly, the sirens stopped. Right outside the store. One of those black half-limo, half-SUV type vehicles had come to a halt at the foot of the steps and out jumped a couple of very serious-looking American plainclothes security men, carrying high-powered weapons and with little wires coming out of their ears. Behind them came a figure I was very familiar with seeing.

Lieutenant General Vernon Walters. This was a guy who had had—no other way of saying it—a hell of a career. He'd stood beside US presidents from Truman to Reagan. He'd covertly slipped Henry Kissinger into Paris in 1972 for the peace talks with North Vietnam. He'd secretly met with Pope John Paul II in the early 1980s to plot out the fall of the Polish Communists, which would eventually lead to the fall of Communism in Eastern Europe. Those are just a few of the things that were known about his accomplishments—let's not forget he was a deputy director of the CIA, so who knows what else he'd been up to.

And now there he was, walking up the steps of my Itaewon tailor shop.

Brian looked at me. He didn't say anything. He didn't need to say anything. The look of I-told-you-so was all over his face.

A few minutes later, there we were, General Vernon Walters—one of the most senior, most protected people in the world—and me, standing in our underwear together in a tiny Seoul dressing room, trying on our twenty-four-hour suits.

"Sir," I said. "All ready for the big day?"

"Always ready." It was the most I could get out of him.

He was gone as quickly as he'd arrived, and as the sound of the sirens slowly faded away, I stood there impressed. Vernon Walters and I share the same tailor, I thought. Funny how you meet some people, right?

The next night, I could see the general sitting in the United States
VIP box from our broadcast seats in the Olympic Stadium. As ambassador to the United Nations, he was representing President Reagan at the
Games and would stand when the American athletes entered the Parade
of Nations. Brian and I chuckled when we saw him—he sure looked
different than when I'd seen him in his boxers.

The broadcast went off well. Brian is amazing at those kinds of shows,
and my sidekick role was relatively easy. There was one moment near the
end, though, that wasn't easy.

Part of the tradition after the lighting of the Olympic torch is to release doves as a sign of peace and goodwill. It seemed especially important that year as we were just kilometres from the border with the South's
constant enemy, North Korea, with whom they were still at war.

With great fanfare, the doves were sent aloft. Brian said something
appropriately poetic about the moment, I watched, and we paused. Suddenly I was aghast.

I looked at Brian and whispered, "I saw them fly up and straight into
the flame. I didn't see them fly out."

Two very young looking guys in nice suits in Seoul, South Korea, 1988.
CBC

TV angles can be misleading. Sometimes you can't be sure. So, we said nothing else, nor, at the time, did anyone else. However, our eyes had not deceived us. Most of the doves had been burned alive, caught in the torch. They've used pigeons ever since.

POSTSCRIPT

The suit actually lasted a few years. I had to replace the stitching a month or so after getting back to Canada, which happens often in these quickly made outfits, but the material was top-notch. I'm not sure how long the general's lasted.

John Turner

My mother used to love telling the story of a day in the early 1960s when she was walking with a friend near Parliament Hill and an incredibly handsome man passed by and with a smile said, "Good day, ladies!" To which they both swooned.

It was John Turner.

If Canada ever had a perfect, Hollywood-style, political candidate, John Turner fit the bill. Smart, educated at UBC, the University of Paris, and Oxford as a Rhodes Scholar. A record-holding athlete as Canada's fastest man, sprinting 9.8 seconds in the 100-yard dash in 1947. A friend of the royal family, said to be close to Princess Margaret. A Member of Parliament at just thirty. And yes, my mother was right, he was incredibly handsome and was still turning heads in his nineties.

When I arrived on the Hill as a parliamentary correspondent in 1976, Turner had already left Ottawa. He'd quit his finance minister's portfolio in disagreement with Pierre Trudeau over wage and price controls. It was a matter of principle. He'd campaigned against them in 1974, and when Trudeau wanted to implement them shortly after, it was too much for Turner. He moved to Bay Street, kept quiet, and was seen as the "prince in waiting," ready to return when Trudeau was gone.

I realized that to cover Canadian politics effectively, this was someone I needed to know, so after connecting with a few mutual friends, we began a series of lunches in the early 1980s. We'd meet at Winston's on King Street West in Toronto, Turner's regular noon-hour haunt through those years. He had his own table for two near the front. He had his regular meal, sliced tomatoes and onions. And his regular drink, and let's just say it wasn't "soft."

The conversations were always interesting to me, often dealing with history and occasionally delving into present circumstances. But Turner was careful; he didn't violate any confidences. He was also very careful to suggest there were no serious differences between him and Trudeau. He often told me the story that Trudeau called him on Christmas Eve 1971 and asked if John and his wife, Geills, would take Margaret and him to a midnight mass, something the Turners always attended at Christmas. They agreed and drove there together. Turner said it was a wonderful evening of friendship and prayer. He never forgot it because of what else happened just a few hours later. Not long after they dropped the Trudeaus off at 24 Sussex, Margaret and Pierre headed to the hospital where Justin was born on Christmas Day.

By 1984, Trudeau had resigned, and Turner made his way back to Ottawa for what he hoped would be a triumphant return to political power. In the June convention that followed, he slipped past Jean Chrétien for the leadership, but things never really got better than that. Brian

With David Halton interviewing John Turner
during his brief moment in the prime minister's office in 1984.
CBC

Mulroney hammered Turner in an election that fall, winning the largest majority government in the country's history. Turner was left with just forty seats.

Some of Chrétien's supporters started sniping from the sidelines, and by the next election in 1988, things looked dire. Early polls in the campaign suggested they could get wiped out and lose half of what little they had in seats. Halfway through the campaign, I started hearing a rumble from some really good sources that a "coup" was being plotted, that a small group of party elders was considering going to Turner and asking him to step down mid-campaign in favour of Chrétien. If it was true, it was an unheard-of move. We went about trying to nail the tip down, but it was clear that if a "coup" was planned, it hadn't happened yet, and none of the major players were talking about it. So, we let it go. For the moment.

I'd only been in the top job, my dream job, for a few months at this point. I knew the stakes on this story. If I got it wrong, there would be tremendous pressure on the CBC to change course. But I was confident that the information I had been working with was solid. So was one of my best friends and closest advisors, our Ottawa bureau chief Elly Alboim, who was also working his sources, separate from mine, trying to get to the bottom of what was true and what wasn't. This was the biggest test of my career; it was not a time for self-doubt. It was a time I'd often reflect on in later years as the moment I really assumed the job.

Within days, the story charged back to full throttle. We heard that a couple of nights earlier, on a Saturday evening in Ottawa, one member of the group had visited Turner at Stornoway, the official residence of the leader of the opposition, and showed him a letter the others had signed. But Turner would have nothing to do with the idea. He tossed their written demands into the fireplace. Along with some of my colleagues, we locked down the various details of the story, confirming it with three sources including my main one, someone I have never revealed. Normally, two separate sources are needed, but knowing the impact this story would have, we wanted more. It took a while to get a third, and then a fourth source, and as we searched for it we had to pull the story from the air on the night it was first scheduled to run.

Finally, after days of working the phones, we had the sources and aired the story. It wasn't the lead that night, but instead ran third. There's no other way of describing the response other than the "shit hit the fan." Within minutes, Turner and his people issued a late-night, non-denial denial. In other words, they ignored the main claim and instead denied things I'd never said. The *Toronto Star*, at first, wrote their own confirmations in early editions of the next morning's paper, then dropped their original journalism and just covered the denials. Other news organizations turned on us, and on me. My journalism was questioned. My ethics were questioned.

Some papers had journalism professors write pieces which suggested that, even if the story was true, we should never have made it public, a logic I never understood. A major political party trying to dump its leader midway through a campaign and we should keep it a secret from those most affected—the voters? And this from those teaching young journalists the art of the trade? Stunning. Some journalists bought into the Liberal spin that Turner had been under the weather and that the party elders were just trying to prepare Chrétien if Turner had to drop out. They were wrong. I was appalled at some of the reactions from other journalists but I didn't let it bother me, nor did the CBC. We stood by the story and as veteran CBC reporter Don Newman, who had worked on the story as well, said at the time, "We know we're right. Screw them." Don sure had a way with words, and I've never forgotten them and the simple comfort they brought.

The controversy lasted a few days, and then it was suddenly replaced by Turner's comeback performance in the campaign debate. Accusing Mulroney of "selling Canada out with one signature of the pen" on the free-trade deal with the United States, Turner bounced back in the polls. Never enough to win, but enough to give Mulroney and the Tories a scare, and enough to save his job, at least for another year.

I've always been puzzled about how the other media and some professors dealt with the story we broke. To add insult to injury, when six months after the election, Turner's chief of staff, Peter Connally, told a postelection study group at Queen's University that everything in the story had been true, only the *Globe and Mail* reported it. The *Star* and many others ignored it.

One person who didn't let it get in the way of our friendship was John Turner. After he left active politics, we still saw each other for the occasional lunch, and he continued to tell me great stories.

He was passionate about democracy, always looking at me and reminding me that democracy doesn't happen automatically, that you have to participate, and that participation means public service. It's a line of his that I use and always credit to him when I talk to various groups, especially young people.

He was also passionate about the royal family, reminding me that he was the only Canadian invited to take part in the eulogies given at his friend Princess Margaret's funeral in 2002.

And he loved this quote attributed to Saint Augustine in 396 AD: "To him who God has given some talent, let him give some back." He lived by that.

POSTSCRIPT

John Napier Turner passed away on September 18, 2020. He was ninety-one. I will miss our lunches and his stories.

Rigging the Election

Television can be a complicated business, and for newspeople, the most complicated yet most rewarding night on the calendar is election night. For any news organization, election night is when you find out just how good you are. How ready you are. How responsible you are.

For starters, on television it's head-to-head competition on a scale you don't often see at any other time. You assemble your best journalists and your best guests. With computers tracking every one of the three hundred and thirty federal ridings in the country, you provide them with the best information so they can detect trends and make smart comments about what is happening.

Now, don't assume this all comes automatically on the night of the election, that somehow you sit down and immediately know how to follow the puck, if you will, as the results start tumbling in from one end of the country to the other. No, it means practice, and practice means rehearsals.

With elections often scheduled on Mondays, at the CBC we usually had everything ready in the main election-night studio for three full days beforehand. And we would take it very seriously with full-on "rehearsals" each day where all the election graphics would display votes "as they were being counted." Our computer specialists would have secretly loaded the computer with dummy results for every riding in the country, and our journalists would be tested on how they would react as the numbers came across the system. We'd spend hours each day doing this, and on the final day before the actual vote we would also link up with stations across the country so we could involve our roving reporters and guests as well.

Which brings me to the fall of 1988 and the election of that year. Mulroney versus Turner, Round Two. The Free-Trade Election. It had lots of names. Our rehearsal programs varied—in one, the Liberals won; in another, the Conservatives were the victors; and in one, it was a virtual tie, which really tested the on-air staff. But something else was happening that year too.

Huge satellite dishes had become a big deal, especially on the prairies where farmers, who had used rabbit ears since the dawn of TV—and, as a result, had very limited options—suddenly could receive dozens of signals from all over North America. They could also receive the internal signals from in-house network services that were only ever used to move material around between a network's stations. This rehearsal was an in-house movement of material, not intended for broadcast but easily watchable by those with the right satellites and the know-how to tune in the not-for-broadcast channels.

You starting to get the picture?

That's right. On that Sunday with our signal playing out across the country and being intercepted by satellite dishes in farmers' fields from Neepawa to Yorkton to Drumheller, all hell broke loose. The Canadian Radio-television and Telecommunications Commission got calls, the CBC president got calls; in fact, every official with anything to do with broadcasting got calls.

"The CBC is rigging the election!" "The CBC already knows the results!" "It doesn't matter how we vote, Mansbridge already has the outcome!"

While sitting at the anchor desk, I got a call from executive producer Arnold Amber, who was in the control room. I thought he was joking, but he wasn't. He told me I had to stop the show and start explaining what was happening to dish owners across the country.

And that's exactly what I did. It seemed odd, even laughable, to those of us on the studio floor, but it was also a sign of how easy it can be to lose trust, especially in what was becoming a rapidly changing landscape of television services. That was just the start. There would be huge tests ahead with, first, the 500-channel universe, then the Internet, and even today with streaming services altering how we watch. All of them have put the pressure on journalists to be more challenging, more accurate, and more transparent about the decisions we make.

When I had started back in those Churchill days, it really was primitive. Television was still a newborn venture. Black-and-white TV. Film that you physically cut and taped together. Very little competition. Those days were gone. Long gone. And while changes had been happening, the extent of them didn't really hit me until that day in 1988 when voices, who may not have realized it at the time but were at the leading edge of technological change, shouted from the prairies, "Hey, wait a minute!"

The election night team, 1988.
Left to right: (front) Barbara Frum, myself, David Halton,
and Wendy Mesley; (back) Don Newman
and Eric Malling.
CBC

The Wall

On the night the Berlin Wall started to come down, I was in Ottawa covering a constitutional conference. I know what you're thinking. That sounds like being in the wrong place at the wrong time for the wrong reason. Saying that the conference was part of the debate surrounding the Meech Lake Accord doesn't make it sound any better, does it?

Meech Lake was an important part of the never-ending Canadian debate about identity, but the Berlin Wall had consequences far larger. The world was changing in front of our eyes. All of Eastern Europe was about to crumble, and the very symbol that had underlined the divide between East and West was being dismantled, concrete bit by concrete bit. And yet I was in Ottawa watching first ministers haggle over how to rewrite the Constitution.

In the moments after the conference wrapped up on that historic night of November 10, 1989, the CBC phone lines were humming between those of us in our remote location in Ottawa and the editorial brain trust in Toronto, and it didn't take us long to pivot and redeploy our troops. It was decided I should be in Berlin and so off I went.

My knowledge of Berlin during the Cold War consisted of three things: the Wall where East Berliners had been shot and killed trying to climb their way to freedom; Checkpoint Charlie where legitimate crossings were allowed between East and West; and the Glienicke Bridge or, as it became known, "the bridge of spies," where East and West traded captured spies. Flying across the Atlantic through the night had me imagining all three places and wondering what the end of the Wall would mean not just to the big picture of international relations but to their place in history.

When we arrived, we went straight down to the Brandenburg Gate to scout out locations along the Wall that cut through the historic city. It was the perfect spot where we could anchor that night's broadcast. The "we" was producer Mark Bulgutch and me, so we were travelling light. The heavy lifting was being done by correspondents Claude Adams, Patrick Brown, and Brian Stewart, who had been there for the past few nights and were off trying to capture the news of the day. That news was that people from both East and West were pulling down the Wall. And specifically, on the eastern side, Berliners were trying to come to grips with the fact that they were soon to be free of the straitjacket of Communism they'd been living in since the end of the Second World War. For some, it meant celebration; for others, it meant retribution—breaking into the offices of the Stasi, the notorious intelligence agency that had funnelled information to their Soviet masters. East Berliners knew that some of their neighbours had been spying for the Stasi and they wanted to find out which neighbours. Payback was on their minds.

Mark worked out a deal with our colleagues at NBC that allowed us to use the platform they had erected for Tom Brokaw to anchor his *NBC Nightly News*. It was a great location, showcasing the background of the Wall, the people climbing over it, and those using everything from pickaxes to their bare hands to pull it apart. Given Brokaw's earlier time slot on the nightly schedule (6:30 p.m. Eastern, 12:30 a.m. Berlin time), his facilities would be available to us in advance of our first broadcast of *The National* at 9:00 p.m. Eastern, or 3:00 a.m. in Berlin.

When I stood in position, I looked in either direction, to my left and to my right, along the Wall. There were other anchor spots both ways. Some in use, but not all, because the reporters were from countries far and wide and they all had different time slots to hit their broadcasts on the other side of the world. It was still quite the scene and it made me think of one of the phrases Canadian philosopher Marshall McLuhan had made famous: "the global village." That night we were all standing in the same place, in a moment of history, telling the same story to

At the Wall, 1989.
CBC

people all over the planet. Technology and the story made the world a smaller place that night; it made it a global village.

As a journalist, you can only hope that during your time in the business you get the opportunity to tell a story from the very place and in the very moment when the world is changing. I've had a few, but that one was certainly the biggest.

Mind you, at that moment none of us knew with any real certainty where this story was leading. The Wall was coming down and that at least was certain. It had split the city for nearly three decades and had been the cause of much tension, much disappointment, and much heartache for the families who had watched their sons and daughters shot by East German guards as they tried to run and climb across the border. It was near the same spot where former US president John Kennedy had said in 1963, "Ich ben ein Berliner" to thousands of adoring West Germans. "I am a Berliner" became a rallying cry. But it was another US president, Ronald Reagan, who may have signaled the decisive blow to the Wall when, in 1987, also in Berlin, he called out to his Soviet counterpart, "Mr. Gorbachev, tear down this wall." Within two years it was coming down, and there's no doubt it would not have happened unless Gorbachev had given his approval.

But did the Wall coming down simply mean a new Berlin or was it more? Could it mean a reunited Germany for the first time since Hitler committed suicide in a Berlin bunker just a few blocks from the Brandenburg Gate in April 1945? Or could the demolition of the Wall signify the beginning of the end of Soviet Communism? Those were weighty, worldly questions, and I remember sitting on a bench in the early-morning hours with the Wall only metres away, contemplating how I would phrase them in the broadcast that was just about to begin.

In the end, we ended up somewhere in that worn-out old news phrase: "Who knows, who really knows." But there was no doubt the coverage of that night and those days signaled that tumultuous times were ahead and the map we had grown used to was going to be redrawn in a number of ways. And it was.

The next day, Mark and I drove into East Berlin through the famous Checkpoint Charlie, which had been the major crossing point in the divided city. Just days before, that route would have been a long, drawn-

With my colleague, coauthor (*Extraordinary Canadians*),
and friend Mark Bulgutch in Berlin in 1989.
CBC

out process requiring passports, permission, and a full going-over of the car and its contents. Not now. It was almost routine. Not much different than passing through Canada–U.S. Customs in your car. Within time, Checkpoint Charlie would become a tourist spot for those who remembered what it used to be.

Over the next few nights, we kept doing *The National* from the NBC location, and most nights there was a good crowd around the Wall, capturing their moment in history. Like everyone else, I grabbed a piece of the Wall. It's now in the fireplace we built in our home in Stratford, along with a few other similar mementos I've collected along the way: stones from the Great Wall of China, Juno Beach, Vimy Ridge, the tunnels beneath the Vatican.

But those nights, there was someone standing not far away from me, just on the other side of the Wall, someone who, unbeknownst to me, I would come to cover and to admire. She was a thirty-five-year-old research scientist with a degree in quantum chemistry. She was a passionate supporter of the movement toward freedom and was so moved by seeing the Wall come down that she soon ran for the first democratically elected government in the East. She won. And she kept winning. Until, at her retirement, she was acknowledged as the leader of the free world. A global village, if you will.

She was Angela Merkel.

The Soldier at the Door

The knock at the door was crisp and firm. If it had been in the middle of the night, I would have been worried, but it was early evening. Still, it was Moscow in 1989 and the Soviet Union wasn't always the friendliest of countries, so there was reason to be, at the very least, slightly concerned.

I had been in my room at the Metropol Hotel only for an hour or so. Built in 1899, it was the perfect location, overlooking Red Square, the Kremlin, and Saint Basil's Cathedral, though the accommodations had deteriorated since then. My room was tiny, with a small single bed, a cramped bathroom, and one towel the size of a facecloth. Maybe the knock at the door signaled a hotel housekeeping attendant with extra towels?

Unfortunately, it wasn't. When I opened the door, a soldier, or at least it was a man in a Soviet army uniform, stood before me.

I was worried until he took off his official Soviet army fur hat and, in broken English, said, "Twenty dollars US."

Now this was something you don't see every day. A Russian soldier trying to sell bits and pieces of his uniform. For cash. American cash. The moment had all the markings of a failed state.

And that's exactly what I felt I was witnessing. The first days of the once-great Soviet Union beginning its fall from grace. I had just flown into Moscow from Berlin, where I'd witnessed the Wall coming down, setting off tumultuous change in the Germanys. It would be a couple of years before the Soviet Union would fully crumble and Communism would disappear, but this soldier standing in front of me at my hotel room door was the start.

I bought his cap. And his army watch. And a few medals.

I later learned from my CBC colleagues that there were other soldiers on other floors doing the same thing that night and every night we were there. It was like being at the Dollar Store. A bargain on every floor, in every aisle.

It reminded me of stories my father used to tell me about when, as a wing commander in the Royal Air Force, he'd flown into Berlin in the summer of 1945 and they'd found piles of old Nazi medals in the streets of defeated Germany. He grabbed one, and for years I used to stare at it wondering and imagining about its personal history—who owned it, what was his story? At least I would always know where this Soviet stuff came from.

Later that evening, we decided to check out our bureau in Moscow and that meant a walk through the Metropol's lobby, which had lost some, if not a lot, of its former glory. I remember a small group of young Soviet women standing inside the hotel's front doors. Like the soldiers working the hallways upstairs, they too seemed very interested in ac-

Crumbling Communism. I'd tell you who that was with me, but I don't remember. (Must have been the vodka.)
Mark Bulgutch

quiring US dollars. Let's just say they weren't looking for help getting to the opera.

But onward to work. My producer, Mark Bulgutch, who'd been with me in Berlin, decided he'd head alone to the bureau just to ensure everything was in order for that night's broadcast of *The National* out of Toronto. He assumed he'd take a cab. But that's not the way things worked in Moscow during those days. Instead, you had to try and flag down a passing car, then basically beg for a ride by offering—you guessed it— US dollars. By the fourth car, Mark, who didn't speak Russian, managed to convince a driver to head toward the address he'd scribbled down on a piece of paper. Through the darkened Moscow streets he wondered and worried whether he was on a drive to oblivion. But his faith was restored when the car stopped in front of a tall apartment building and the driver nodded as if to say, "This is it." And it was.

The next morning things seemed to settle down, perhaps helped for me by a walk through nearby Red Square. The historic centrepiece of central Moscow, Red Square is a huge rectangular space that covers about eight hundred thousand square feet. It may well be the most familiar spot in all of the old Soviet Union because it was where the annual May Day parade had been held for decades. May Day was a chance for the country's leaders to show off their military might with a procession of tanks, trucks, missiles, and aircraft. For those around the world trying to forecast the direction of Soviet intentions, this was an important opportunity to assess the lineup of government leaders as they stood on the podium above Lenin's tomb. The most powerful leader was never hard to notice: he was always the one standing in the top spot—from Vladimir Lenin, to Joseph Stalin, to Georgy Malenkov, to Nikita Khrushchev to Leonid Brezhnev, to Yuri Andropov, and now to Mikhail Gorbachev, there was never any doubt who was in charge. What observers from Washington to London to Beijing always wanted to know was who was closest to the leader in the lineup because that could signal who had influence and who didn't—and of course who could be next at the pinnacle of Soviet power.

Walking beneath the podium area, I looked up, remembering that I'd witnessed this spot for as long as I'd watched television. Those old, grainy, black-and-white TV pictures were coming to life in real time, along with memories of my parents trying to read in those lineups what it all meant during some of the darkest days of the Cold War.

As I walked across Red Square on this cool November day in the Soviet capital, I couldn't stop thinking of the soldier from the night before and how the fact he had been selling off his uniform could be a metaphor for a coming collapse of the Soviet system. And then I looked at the stones that made up the parade ground. Maybe they held the key to what should have been our first sense of what was to come. And it hadn't happened that week or even that year. It had happened two years before.

Does the name Mathias Rust ring a bell? He may have been the person who showed the world that the Soviet Union wasn't what we thought it was, at least not anymore. Just nineteen years old and living in Hamburg, West Germany, Rust had a private pilot's licence. One day in 1987, he told his parents he was going on a flying adventure to build up his flying time, which back then was a meagre fifty hours. He rented a Cessna and flew to the Shetland Islands, then to Iceland, then to Norway and Finland. In Helsinki, he rested for a few days before climbing back into his plane and announcing to air traffic control that he was heading to Sweden.

But after a half hour, he switched course and headed straight for Moscow.

At the time, everyone believed that the Soviet Union was a superpower on a level with the United States. It had, among other assets, the largest air-defence system in the world. Well, not on May 28, 1987. Just after Rust crossed the border, a Russian MiG fighter scrambled to intercept Rust but mistook the Cessna for a domestic flight and disappeared. Rust never saw another plane, and no one ever tried to contact him.

The next thing he knew, he was thirty feet above Lenin's tomb and buzzing over those walking through Red Square. Rust decided to land, and to avoid hitting anyone he picked a nearby spot by a bridge that had been cleared for maintenance. After two hours of being hailed a hero by tourists and even some Soviet security officials, Rust was arrested for violating flight rules, found guilty, and sentenced to four years in jail, of which he served one.

But the real damage was to the Soviet Union. It was humiliated, the minister of defence was forced to resign, and the head of air defence was sacked. If they couldn't stop a Cessna, how could they stop a missile?

Now, I'm sure it's a stretch for me to draw a line from Mathias Rust in 1987 to the soldier at my door in 1989 and the eventual collapse of the Soviet Union in 1991, but there is something about the symmetry there.

Our visit to Moscow lasted only a few days. There were the usual high-level meetings between then Prime Minister Mulroney and President Gorbachev, a few news conferences and signing ceremonies, but what I remember most was the soldier selling his uniform and what it seemed to represent. The events in the years that followed seemed to underscore that truth.

The CBC went all out with banner ads in the daily newspapers
to advertise the fact we were broadcasting from Moscow.
CBC

High School Crush

There's a scene in the first of the Indiana Jones movies, *Raiders of the Lost Ark*, where one of the university students in Jones's archaeological class goes eye to eye with her professor. The prof, played by Harrison Ford, is in full flight describing in detail some dig he'd been on while the young woman student is clearly swooning. She closes her eyes, and stenciled on her eyelids are the words "I love you." Jones does a double take and tries to ignore it.

Ahh, teenage fantasies. Most of us had them at one time or another, and they were usually about one of our teachers. I was no different.

Like a lot of the boys in my Ottawa high school English class in the early 1960s, I had a thing for Miss Bruce. We used to talk about her in the halls in the way young boys do.

"She's gorgeous."

"If only I was older."

But then again we knew Miss Bruce was "taken," as the saying goes. She had a boyfriend. He used to come and wait for her outside class some afternoons. And we all knew who he was. We recognized him because we watched him every Saturday afternoon.

You've probably never heard of *Club Thirteen*, but in 1961 a new television station in Ottawa decided to copy the highly successful Saturday afternoon ABC television show *American Bandstand*, hosted by Dick Clark. CJOH, one of CTV's first stations, called their Saturday teenage dance show *Club Thirteen* after the station's channel number. And they picked Miss Bruce's boyfriend to be the host. His name was Peter Jennings.

Yes, that Peter Jennings. Soon to be a network news anchor in

Canada, then in the States, he would become one of the most recognized and respected television news journalists in the world.

But when I saw him standing outside Miss Bruce's class, I didn't think about his job, just how lucky he was to have our teacher as his girlfriend. A career in broadcasting was the furthest thing from my mind. Back then, my hopes were to be a pilot, a lawyer, or an underwater archaeologist. The closest I ever got to thinking about broadcasting was one summer when I wrote to Ernie Calcutt, a local radio sportscaster, asking for advice about getting into sports journalism. I was only half-serious and by the time he wrote a very kind letter back, inviting me to visit his station, CFRA, I'd already moved on to thinking of flying.

I've often looked back at my Peter Jennings connection and seen some

The Gathering of the Giants. From left to right: (front) Sidney Gruson, Allan Fortheringham, and Richard Gwyn; (middle) Barbara Amiel, Lloyd Robertson, Jeffrey Simpson, Morley Safer, Barbara Frum, and Robert MacNeil; (back) Henry Champ, myself, Peter Gzowski, and Peter Jennings.
University of Toronto Archives

similarities. We both came from successful families, we both grew up in Ottawa, we both dropped out of high school, neither of us graduated from university or college, and we both began our journalism careers in local broadcasting. And, obviously, we had similar taste in women.

Peter's father was a nationally known CBC journalist, Charles Jennings, a pioneer in Canadian broadcasting. One would think that would have made it easy for Peter to get a start. It didn't. In fact, Charles Jennings was outspoken in his feelings about nepotism. However, with Charles out of the country on assignment, the CBC hired Peter to host a children's radio program and he never looked back. By the time he was doing *Club Thirteen*, he was also hosting the evening news program. And then the Americans came calling and off he went to New York, first as an anchor and then a correspondent, before circling back to anchoring in 1983 and on.

It was a long time between the days I used to see Peter in the hallways outside Miss Bruce's English class and the next time I saw him in person, in November of 1990. The University of Western Ontario had organized a fundraising gala in Toronto called the Gathering of the Giants, a pretentious-sounding name for a dinner for a group of well-known Canadian-born journalists. From the States came ex-pats Jennings, Morley Safer, Robert MacNeil, and more. From Canada the list was long and impressive, including Barbara Frum, Lloyd Robertson, and Allan Fotheringham. The evening was fun and informative, filled with sketches and speeches. And it delivered on its main purpose of putting money into the university's journalism program, which was operated by a friend of most of us, Peter Desbarats. Peter Jennings and I sat next to each other and enjoyed a few laughs about our respective careers and the irony of our first meeting. However, he wasn't shy about gently giving me some shade for my decision a few years earlier to stay at the CBC and turn down a multi-million-dollar, three-year deal from CBS.

"It worked for me, it would have worked for you," was his message. We agreed to disagree.

We kept in touch occasionally. The next year, we were both in Madrid anchoring our respective broadcasts at a Middle East peace conference in the Spanish capital looking for that elusive deal between the Israelis and the Palestinians. I remember Peter had an eye infection that had left one eye seriously bloodshot. I asked him how he could possibly go on camera like that. And so he showed me a little anchorman tradecraft— how to cut down the angle on camera by tilting your head a certain way. And guess what? Not only did it work for him on this occasion, but it also worked for me when I had a similar problem a few years later.

Peter's time in the anchor chair for ABC was nothing but a class act. Countless wannabe anchors modelled their style after him, but what he had that most of them did not was his stellar journalism background. From those early days covering the Ottawa scene—yes, even on the dance floor—to his years covering war after war in the Middle East, he always had the experience and the contacts to draw upon. He also had what the American broadcast executives like to call "a mid-Atlantic accent," so he was never out of place no matter where he was. But he was truly one of a kind.

And what about Miss Bruce? Well, Phyllis Bruce became a rock star of her own. She kept wowing the boys at Glebe Collegiate Institute in Ottawa for a few more years before moving into the world of publishing. A senior player at some of Canada's top publishing houses, she is now the editor of Phyllis Bruce Editions, a wing of Simon & Schuster Canada. She has guided and edited some of Canada's most famous and most decorated writers, including Charlotte Gray, Helen Humphreys, Frances Itani, Ken McGoogan, James Raffan, and Richard B. Wright. She has also been named a Member of the Order of Canada.

Peter and Phyllis married other people, but they remained good friends throughout his life until, tragically, he passed away, losing a battle with lung cancer at the age of only sixty-seven in August of 2005.

And before you ask, the answer is no. Phyllis is not my editor or my publisher. She's not even my agent. I wouldn't be able to concentrate.

A Man, a Feather, and a Statue

One of the most striking images of the divisive national debate surrounding what was known as the Meech Lake Constitutional Accord involved a man by the name of Elijah Harper.

Harper was born in 1949 on the Red Sucker Lake reserve in northern Manitoba. He was educated first in the residential school system, then at the University of Manitoba. At twenty-nine, he was elected chief of the Red Sucker Lake First Nation, after which he entered provincial politics, joining the NDP and winning his riding of Rupertsland in 1981, the first Indigenous person to do so. His meteoric political career kept on surging when he was appointed to the provincial cabinet a few years later. And it was as a Manitoba cabinet minister that he became a national figure.

The Meech Lake Accord, negotiated in 1987 and designed to bring Quebec into the constitutional family, proposed amendments to the Constitution of Canada. By 1990, Prime Minister Mulroney and the ten premiers had signed the deal, but every legislative body needed to agree. It was a long, drawn-out process, and significant opposition to the Accord came from different parts of the country. Elijah Harper's concern was that Indigenous Peoples did not have the appropriate say in how the Accord came together. Sitting in the Manitoba legislature seat holding an eagle feather, he was the lone government member—there was only one needed—to crush the deal. He did it despite conflicting advice from those closest to him; some said it could ruin his political career, others talked of the bravery of being the lone voice.

Most people who know about Meech Lake know about Elijah Harper and his feather. What they don't likely know is this part of the backstory.

Some of the Manitoba opposition to Meech Lake came from a former provincial Liberal leader by the name of Izzy Asper. Asper had been out of active politics for more than ten years but was still a major player behind the scenes both provincially and federally. The federal Liberals weren't fans of Meech Lake, and their former leader Pierre Trudeau made no secret of the fact that he was against it. Asper was the same, so he raised money for a campaign, which he then helped organize, especially in Winnipeg.

I had known Asper since the early 1970s when he was the leader of the tiny Manitoba Liberal Party. And after he left office to, among other things, start Global Television, we became good friends. We'd often have dinner when I was in Winnipeg and when he was in Toronto. He was bold and brash and loved to tell stories; some I could use, and some he'd make conditional upon confidentiality. This one kind of fell in between the margins.

The night before the final attempt to pass the Accord in the Manitoba legislature, things looked uncertain. There was a lot of pressure on the Manitoba government of Conservative Gary Filmon to keep its promise to support Meech Lake, and while Elijah Harper had hinted his unease, it looked like he might finally go along with the majority of the legislature.

That's when Asper made his move. At least this is the way he told me the story as we sat having a drink in the bar of the Winnipeg Inn at the corner of Portage and Main a few years later. After many conversations about Meech Lake, Asper knew Harper well, and he had scheduled yet another dinner for that night. The talk was good, but Asper felt Harper still needed an extra push.

After dinner, he walked with Harper down by the Assiniboine River just outside the Manitoba legislature, best known for its Golden Boy statue sitting high on top of the legislative dome. However, there is another statue down by the river that is more important: Louis Riel. The Métis leader who was hanged for treason in 1885, but is now regarded as a hero who fought for Indigenous rights.

Asper stopped by the statue, looked up at Riel, and said to Harper, "Elijah, if you do what's right tomorrow, there will one day be a statue of you right here next to Riel."

POSTSCRIPT

Israel "Izzy" Asper remained a force in backroom politics and in broadcasting and journalism until his death in 2003.

Elijah Harper went on to serve as an MP in Ottawa, then as the commissioner of the Indian Claims Commission; he won many humanitarian awards, received numerous honorary doctorates, and was named to the Order of Manitoba. He died of heart disease in 2013. His body lay in state in the Manitoba legislature. As of this writing, there is no statue to Elijah Harper next to that of Louis Riel.

Seat 1A

I was in a cab on my way to the Charlottetown airport. I'd flown in from Toronto on an early-morning flight to give a noon-hour speech in what is one of my favourite cities in one of my favourite provinces, and now I needed to make the early-afternoon flight out of Prince Edward Island to be back in Toronto in time to do my job anchoring *The National*. I asked the driver to hurry.

I'd already picked up my boarding pass that morning to save time, and I took my ticket out of my inside suit jacket pocket to double-check I still had it. Yes, there it was. Seat 1A. The flight back to Toronto, unlike the direct nonstop from Toronto in the morning, was to be a connecting flight, so it meant a switch in Halifax from the small, dozen-passenger propeller-driven flight to a bigger passenger jet to Toronto. Seat 1A would allow me to get on last and off first, further saving time if the connection was tight.

I got to the airport and went quickly through security. This was in the 1990s, pre-9/11, so security was fairly basic. I showed my boarding pass to the Air Canada agent at the gate and was directed across the tarmac to the waiting aircraft, which had already boarded the other passengers.

As I approached the stairs, the pilot slid his window back and called out, "It's great to have you with us today, Mr. Mansbridge."

"That's very kind of you," I replied and walked up the stairs.

As I got to the top, I turned to my right to slip into 1A. Too late, someone was already sitting in it. And he was big. Could have passed for an offensive lineman in the CFL.

I decided maybe discretion was best. I noticed that 2A was open and

I proceeded to sit there instead. There were only single seats on each side of the aircraft, so all was fine.

The door was closed, and the flight attendant began her routine of explaining how seat belts worked. When she finished, she went back to the door to the cockpit, opened it, and leaned in to talk with the pilots. Then she turned back and headed straight to the fellow in 1A.

"The pilots were wondering if you'd like to sit in the jump seat for the flight over to Halifax?" she told him.

"Absolutely," said the man, who likely never had been offered such a cockpit view on previous flights.

Now, did I say he was big? Well, he certainly was and the scene of him trying to make his way through the cockpit doors attracted the attention of all the other passengers on board. The flight attendant could see the concern being expressed and she was determined to deal with it by making another announcement: "Everything is okay," she said. "That was Peter Mansbridge."

The Iron Interview

Most called her "the Iron Lady"; some called her "Attila the Hen." Both may have been understatements. The British prime minister Margaret Thatcher was tough, very tough. She was convinced she had to be to achieve her goals and to command respect as the first woman to lead her country, and she made a habit of making punch lines of those who opposed her. Some, in the old-fashioned British way, would last for the ages.

"If you want something said, ask a man. If you want something done, ask a woman."

"Don't follow the crowd. Let the crowd follow you."

"It may be the cock that crows, but it's the hen that lays the eggs."

Aren't those great? But wait, there's more.

"Standing in the middle of the road is very dangerous. You get knocked down by the traffic on both sides."

"Being powerful is like being a lady. If you have to tell people you are, you aren't."

"The problem with socialism is that you eventually run out of other people's money."

Ah, yes. Thatcherism. Great quotes for sure, but none of them uttered in an interview with me. I got nothing out of Lady T except a parade of verbal slaps in the face.

In 1993, she was touring the Western world selling the book of her years in power before the Conservative Party finally revolted and, convinced she couldn't win the federal election again, kicked her out of the leadership and 10 Downing Street. The book was called *The Downing Street Years*, and not surprisingly, as political memoirs tend to do, it painted her in a pretty glowing light. I was happy, though, that she and her publishers had picked me to do the exclusive Canadian interview. When it was over, I wished she'd picked the competition.

We met at the King Edward, Toronto's oldest posh hotel. Lady Thatcher arrived with her entourage, but she seemed to be a bit put-off already before we even got started. She didn't smile through a greeting, sat down with a "let's get it over" look about her. That happens occasionally when an interview subject arrives out of sorts, but some casual chat usually gets you into a better space before the interview starts. Not so this time.

I'd interviewed Mrs. T years before when she was PM, but that was only for a few minutes, almost a scrum at an international conference. This would be different. One-on-one for half an hour. It would be a chance to get into some matters of substance. I wanted to ask her about her experiences in power to understand how power is wielded, how decisions are made, especially when those decisions affect lives. I assumed she'd lighten up her mood a bit. I was wrong.

I started by welcoming her to Canada, and then got into it with a question about dealing with the weight of leadership during war and used her description in the book of the decisions surrounding the Falklands War with Argentina in 1982.

"During the early days of the war, before the fighting started, with your fleet on its way across the Atlantic, were there ever moments when you thought, 'Am I absolutely sure about this?'"

"I really don't think you could've read the full book," she said, then she went on defending her actions while picking me apart as if I were an Argentine army platoon private.

Actually, I had read the book and I told her so, but that didn't seem to matter. Question after question was met by the same barrage, almost always including a variation of the "you obviously never read my book" line. At one point, I tried a different tack.

"Could Margaret Thatcher have served under a Margaret Thatcher?"

"That's a silly question to ask," she replied.

Now I knew what it was like to be a backbencher in her Conservative Party. Chopped liver. After a while, I knew the interview was lost. If someone had been marking it as a duel, it was no contest. The Iron Lady prevailed.

But there was still one more moment to come. After the interview was over, the lights turned off, and the camera stopped rolling, she smiled. "Peter," she said, as if I were her favourite nephew. "Would you like me to sign your book?"

I resisted telling her what she could do with the book, and instead meekly smiled back, and said, "Oh, yes, that would be wonderful."

I'll always regret never taking the interview beyond the argument of whether or not I had read the book. I should have countered with: "Did you write it?" Because, according to the British papers, it had been ghostwritten by three professionals. But I didn't go there. Should have but didn't.

POSTSCRIPT

Baroness Thatcher died in 2013 at the age of eighty-seven. The signed book still has a place of "honour" in my library.

Interviewing Margaret Thatcher.
Since this is *my* book, I decide who makes it into the picture!
CBC

Mothers and Monarchs

My mother was born in Liverpool, England, and while she didn't dislike the royal family, she didn't exactly praise them either. Whenever she did bring the topic up, it was usually about the Queen's choice in hats, dresses, and coats. My mother was fussy about clothes, and she was no fan of the styles and colours Queen Elizabeth was almost always, in public at least, dressed in. I'd explain that the distinctive colours were there for a reason—people in crowds wanted to see the Queen, and that was a lot easier if she was wearing colours that made her stand out from everyone else.

Over the years, my mother's arguments became more political. What exactly did the royal family offer for all the money it collected from the public purse? Why were there so many of them? And so on. She also was surprised that the CBC spent so much time covering the royals when they visited Canada. Of course she never complained that it meant her son would be on television more often.

In 1994, I got a call from the governor general, my friend Ray Hnatyshyn, who was organizing a guest list for the Queen's upcoming visit to Victoria, where my parents were living in retirement. The list included many dignitaries from the British Columbia capital mixed with many of those of the more "common" variety. And that's what the GG wanted to talk to me about.

"Do you think your parents would like to be invited?" he asked.

Perfect, I thought, finally my mother would get to see Her Majesty up close. My father had been awarded the Distinguished Flying Cross by the Queen's father, King George VI, in 1943 at Buckingham Palace for his service in the Royal Air Force during the Second World War. I

Mother and Father in Malaya, 1954.
Could they be better looking?

was confident that he would be subdued about the opportunity to see the Queen but would also enjoy the moment, which he did.

And so, the engraved invitation arrived, and my mother started to get quite excited. She would pick out an outfit that would capture the moment and make *her* stand out.

When the big day finally came, my parents filed into the reception room along with a few hundred others and waited with great anticipation. With all the associated fanfare, the Queen and the Duke of Edinburgh entered and began slowly circulating among the attendees.

My mother was standing with a small group in the middle of the room when suddenly she heard a voice beside her.

"What a wonderful event."

She turned her head and there, right beside her, was the Queen. Elizabeth II in all her royal glory. My mother froze, jaw dropped.

"Are you from Victoria?" asked the Queen, trying to encourage a short chat before moving on.

Nothing. My mother, never one for a loss of words in the past, could say not a word. She was awestruck. The woman she'd watched from childhood to adulthood, the woman whom she'd sung the anthem for over decades, whose image had adorned her currency, her stamps, the walls of almost every office she'd ever visited—all of that and more— was standing right beside her, looking straight at her, and talking directly to her.

Nothing. She told me later that her mouth never closed. It just stayed open. Frozen with no words coming out of it.

Finally, the Queen, amused I imagine, smiled, and moved on.

I never heard my mother criticize the Queen again.

Lead Foot

I love to drive on the open highway early in the morning and watch the sun come up. I especially like it when I'm on my way to my log cabin in the Gatineau Hills north of Ottawa. And that's exactly what I was doing one day in the 1990s.

By then I'd been anchoring *The National* for almost a decade, and as a result, I was fairly well-known. I'd already won half a dozen major awards for my journalism, and I was often recognized in airports, hotels, restaurants, and shopping malls. Some people would come up and start talking; others would simply give a nod of recognition. It was all very nice, and I never found it invasive.

Well, on that day, while I was enjoying the drive between Perth and Carleton Place, I got a little carried away. My foot was heavy, as they say. And the next thing I knew, there was a car with flashing lights right behind me.

The OPP. Ontario's Provincial Police. And the officer was signalling me to pull over.

I did, coming to a stop on the side of the road. As he walked up to the driver's-side window, I knew I was in trouble. I readied my licence, vehicle registration, and car insurance.

At the window, he was polite and to the point. "Can I have your papers, please?"

"Yes, sir," I said and handed the three documents over.

He looked at them, then at me, and said with surprise: "Peter Mansbridge!"

I'm sorry, but all I could think of was, "God, I love this job."

But he had other things on his mind. "We were in Sea Scouts together in 1962 in Ottawa!"

I *had* been in Sea Scouts in Ottawa in 1962, and while he didn't look familiar to me, I said, "Of course, yes, I remember."

And then followed a couple good minutes of recollecting friends, camping trips, and jamborees. We shared a few laughs but, as these conversations often go, we quickly ran out of things to say. An awkward pause ensued. Until he said, "So, Peter, what do you do now?"

And then he gave me a ticket.

The Highest Blessing

In an old frame church in Malpeque, Prince Edward Island, in 1998, Cynthia Dale and I got married in a very small ceremony. Aside from the minister, the only two other people in attendance were one of Cynthia's best friends, fellow actress Sheila McCarthy, and one of my best friends, Sheila's husband, the superb stage and screen actor Peter Donaldson. Pete and Sheila were working in PEI that year filming the TV series *Emily of New Moon*, and they helped arrange for us to slip in and out of PEI, thereby keeping our nuptials private.

In fact, we didn't even tell our families. It was an elopement. Both of us had been previously married and had been through divorces, and we just felt it would be easier all round if we kept things simple.

The wedding was wonderful. We had a sumptuous meal that evening in Summerside, and then early the next day we flew back to Toronto to connect to a flight to Rome, where we had planned a short honeymoon. The first few days in Rome were what anyone would expect being in Rome—magical—and we continued with our theme of keeping it all private. No one knew we were there, or at least that's what we thought.

Somehow the Canadian embassy to the Vatican got wind of our presence and someone there thought it would be a good idea to host a small luncheon in our honour. We were a bit embarrassed, but we didn't say no. The luncheon was very special, and we met some truly lovely people, one of whom became a friend: Archbishop John Patrick Foley, a member of the Vatican cabinet and a senior media advisor to Pope John Paul II. As it turned out, Archbishop Foley knew about the CBC, and I knew about him from his frequent appearances on American television.

At the end of the luncheon, Archbishop Foley leaned over to us and whispered, "Would you like to meet the Pope?"

I'm not Catholic, and although I'd briefly met the Pope before during his 1984 visit to Canada, this was different. Cynthia, who is Catholic, felt the same way and was excited about the possibility.

"We'd love to," we said.

"Can you come by the Vatican tomorrow morning?"

Tomorrow was a Wednesday, the day the Pope held his weekly general audience with thousands in attendance, but there are always a few who are taken aside and get to meet with the Pope privately after the general audience is over.

So, the next morning we met Archbishop Foley in an anteroom, and he prepped us for the soon-to-be papal encounter.

"Just try to be natural and speak clearly," he advised. "His Holiness speaks many languages, but it helps that you are clear."

The next thing we knew, we were being ushered into a special room with official Vatican photographers in every corner. And there he was, John Paul II, standing alone in the middle of the room waiting for us to walk in. The leader of the world's Catholic community with his arms half-outstretched in the pose that had become famous throughout his time as pope.

We approached, Cynthia wearing a broad smile as she accepted his greetings. I suddenly found myself bowing, holding his hand, and kissing the Ring of the Fisherman. Again, I'm not Catholic, and I don't recall anyone telling me to do that, but it just happened in the moment.

The four of us talked very briefly, with Archbishop Foley explaining how I'd anchored coverage of the Pope's visits to Canada in 1984 and again in 1987. John Paul II talked about how much he'd enjoyed Canada and that he hoped to return one day. With flashbulbs popping in the background, the Archbishop manoeuvred the conversation around to why we were in Rome, knowing full well what that would mean.

"Peter and Cynthia are here on their honeymoon, Your Holiness. They just got married on the weekend."

The Pope took the cue. Standing in front of us he said a few phrases in Latin, smiled, and placed his hand lightly on our heads.

The audience was over. As we left the room, I looked at Cynthia for guidance.

"What was that?" I asked.

"He just blessed the marriage."

Someone had once told me divorce meant it was awfully hard to get permission from the Church for remarriage. So much for that theory, I thought.

Outside the reception room, Archbishop Foley was all smiles. He proceeded to take us on an insider's tour of the Vatican, and we got to see some pretty special places that you don't get to see on the regular tour, from the Pope's personal chapel to a da Vinci that has never been photographed.

When we arrived back at our hotel later that day, there was a package waiting for us at the front desk. A stack of 8x10 photographs of Cynthia, myself, and John Paul II—one of which we handed to Cynthia's devout

How does that old joke go? Who are those
old guys with Cynthia Dale?
The Vatican

Catholic parents shortly after we got off the plane from Rome back in Toronto.

Any possible debate about the decision to elope seemed to end with the photographic evidence of a papal blessing.

POSTSCRIPT

John Paul II would visit Canada one more time for World Youth Day in 2002. After twenty-six years, his papacy ended upon his death in 2005.

John Patrick Foley was an American, born and raised in Pennsylvania. He was elevated to Cardinal in 2007. He remained a friend to both Cynthia and me until his death in 2011.

Sheila McCarthy is still acting and directing. Her husband, my friend Peter Donaldson, lost a battle to cancer in 2011. Sheila asked me to take some of his ashes to our favourite golf courses in Scotland. I did, and I still hear him laughing at some of my shots as I pass the spot where the winds took him away.

Thumbs Up, He's Dead

May 2, 2000, was a Tuesday. It wasn't a particularly busy day in the news business, and we weren't exactly excited about the broadcast we had lined up that night. The story slotted for the top spot was about a squabble during Question Period in the House of Commons. While the Ottawa bureau was all jazzed about it, the story wasn't moving anyone around the main desk in Toronto. But with little more than half an hour until the opening of *The National* rolled out of the control room of Studio 52, the odds were that yet another gong-show Ottawa political mashup was going to lead the broadcast.

Needless to say, it was one of those nights where comments from grizzled veterans of the news business can get a little dark.

"Maybe there's a plane flying out there somewhere in trouble," said one of those particular types who may have been me. In fact, it was me. There was an audible groan in the area, and we moved on.

As host and chief correspondent, I sat at the main desk for *The National* surrounded by half a dozen key players, but the real power at night was held by the show producer and the lineup editor. The show producer that night was Nigel Gibson and he had to worry about everything, from the look of the show to the content of the items, to the writing of reports, to the continuity that I would be presenting. Across the desk from him was Mark Harrison, the lineup editor, whose job was exactly what the title implies. He had to decide which items would make the broadcast that night, what length each one would be, and what order they would be in. While it was ultimately his call, the three of us would always discuss the decisions and almost always would come to an agreement. But not always. The others at the desk, the writers, would not be shy about chiming in as well. The best nights were nights of disagreement with everyone engaged in the debate before Mark would make the final call.

To me, a newsroom without debate isn't a good thing; you need a good discussion about options, preferably every night. But most nights, there are not a lot of options. And May 2, 2000, was one of those nights.

Stockwell Day versus Jean Chrétien blah blah blah looked like a lock.

But then Martin Power walked over to the desk.

Martin was the nighttime assignment editor, which meant he was responsible for ensuring that the items being sent in from reporters across the country and around the world made it successfully to the videotape playback room. He booked the transmission lines and the satellites to make that happen. He also monitored news developments to check that we didn't miss any late-breaking stories. And he answered the phones. He was a busy guy, a kind of a jack of all news trades.

As he walked toward our main desk, something he rarely did, he had our attention. It was clear he had something to tell us.

"I just had a tip," he said. "A caller said the Friendly Giant has died."

It was about 8:20, forty minutes to the first edition of *The National*.

The Friendly Giant was a national institution. In fact, for most if not all the people in the newsroom that night who had grown up in Canada, Friendly was THE national institution. His might have been the first Canadian kid's TV show they had watched, thrilled by being invited every day to go across the drawbridge with a giant named Friendly into his castle for stories with his friends, puppets Rusty and Jerome. After pointing to a circle of chairs, "one little chair for you, and a bigger chair for two more to curl up in, and for someone who likes to rock, a rocking chair in the middle," Friendly would tell everyone to "look up, wayyyy up." If you are a Canadian of a certain age, those words and phrases live with you forever. I know they did for me as one of Friendly's earliest viewers.

For a fraction of a second after Martin spoke, you could hear a pin drop, but only a fraction.

"Oh my God, that's a lead," one of us said, knowing it was a story that would touch millions.

But at that moment it was just a tip and not confirmed. It had to go through the normal story-vetting process and the clock was ticking. Martin would try to confirm the story. One of the writers and I would work on how we would open the show and tell the story. Mark scrambled to find an editor to begin pulling video stocks from the film library.

The Friendly Giant was Bob Homme, an American-born Canadian actor who had first developed the idea of a children's show based on a castle setting when he was at the University of Wisconsin, Madison, in the early 1950s. After graduating, he brought the idea to Canada, and the CBC grabbed it. When it debuted in 1958, the show influenced the lives of millions of Canadians, and not just kids. Mothers got their first break of the day when Friendly began his fifteen-minute spot every morning.

When I first started filling in for Knowlton Nash as the anchor of *The National* in 1981, I used to find it a little overwhelming at times, partly because the broadcast shared the old Studio 2 on Jarvis Street in Toronto with—wait for it—that icon of my childhood, the Friendly Giant. *The National* was on one side of the room, Friendly's castle on the other. I'd be looking into the camera delivering the news when just off camera I could see where Rusty and Jerome were there hanging on the castle wall!

Bob Homme had an amazing run, almost thirty years at the CBC, entertaining a number of generations. And then in 1985, the castle closed its drawbridge for the last time, and he headed off into retirement in rural Ontario.

Back to 2000. It was now 8:45. Fifteen minutes to air. The potential opening headlines were ready, the continuity for my read was in the prompter, and the video obit was still being edited but was going to be ready. Just one thing missing. The most critical thing. Confirmation.

Martin was frantically working the phones trying to get someone close to the Homme family to sign off on the news. His family was, understandably, not answering the phones at their home in Grafton, Ontario, just east of Cobourg. Obviously, if we couldn't get the confirmation, we couldn't run the story. Martin kept trying. We all chipped in on the effort, calling anyone who might be able to help.

Then it was time for me to head down to my dressing room and makeup. I put on a tie, got a quick powder, and touched base with the studio crew, then I headed back to the newsroom. I was notorious for not taking my position at *The National* desk until the last minute, and this was certainly going to be one of those nights.

I arrived back at my newsroom seat, sat down, and glanced over at Martin at his desk about thirty metres away. He wasn't looking at us. He was on the phone. It was almost five to nine.

I looked back and forth at Mark and Nigel. Mark was preparing to move the Chrétien-Day story back to the top. I started to get up out of my chair but took one last look over at Martin. He was just wrapping up a phone call, rising slowly out of his chair. He looked over at us, at first expressionless. A look that seemed to capture everything that had happened in the past near forty minutes: journalists desperately trying to do their job, under stressful deadline conditions, on a story that would matter to millions. But even then, what unfolded next is something you can only see in a newsroom.

Martin broke into what seemed like a half-smile. And then he held up his hand and gave the thumbs-up sign.

Nigel relaxed, Mark moved to his seat in the control room, and I slid into position in the studio with about thirty seconds to air.

The opening rolled and I began the broadcast. "Good evening. For a generation of Canadian kids, he was known simply as the Friendly Giant. A man who taught them to love books and music. In real life, his name was Bob Homme. Tonight, we begin *The National* with sad news. Bob Homme died this afternoon after a battle with cancer at his home in Grafton, Ontario."

When the newscast had ended and we gathered back in the newsroom to relive those last, action-packed moments before the show, I decided something right then and there. If I ever decided to write about my days in this, at times, crazy business, I had found a phrase that sometimes captures the atmosphere in a newsroom fighting the clock. "Thumbs Up, He's Dead."

Chrétien Style

Prime ministers, in fact most politicians, don't really like reporters. We kind of get in the way by asking questions and chasing our prey down hallways for answers. And politicians certainly don't like journalists if they think they make them look bad. And that's where Jean Chrétien and I had a problem.

I first met Jean Chrétien in 1978. In those days, he was the minister for industry, trade, and commerce.

As he walked into his office for our interview that day, it was clear he was a person comfortable in his own skin. The walls around his desk were decorated with some of the objects and artwork he'd acquired in what I think was always his favourite portfolio, the one he'd held from 1968 to 1974: Indian affairs and northern development. Indigenous art was all over the walls, and when I asked about it, he talked about his frequent travels out of Ottawa to visit with Indigenous leaders from coast to coast to coast and how he and his family would summer in the north almost every year. He bragged about the fact he'd held that cabinet position longer than most, that while his relations with Indigenous leaders often got heated, they knew who they were dealing with—he wasn't just passing through, as was the criticism of so many other ministers who had held the portfolio, and still is.

But Chrétien was pretty much a junior minister back then, never considered part of Prime Minister Pierre Trudeau's inner circle, and most observers thought he'd never reach beyond where he was. They were wrong. He kept climbing, and I was one of those who admired what I saw. In 1977, he was appointed finance minister, then justice minister in the early 1980s; he was also Ottawa's point person on the 1981 constitutional talks which led to the 1982 patriation of the Constitution. But still, a lot of the Liberal Party's top people, including some of its most astute political fixers—and most of the press gallery, including me I'll admit—didn't see him with the "royal jelly" needed to be prime minister.

While many made fun of his chances, his sights never wavered. He almost knocked off the so-called prince in waiting, John Turner, for Liberal leader when Pierre Trudeau stepped down in 1984, and after Turner couldn't win the PM's office in two elections (1984 and 1988), Chrétien finally achieved the party's top rung in 1990. To a lot of people's surprise, it was straight into the modern-day Canadian political history books.

As Liberal leader, Jean Chrétien won three majority governments in a row. A three-peat. Back to back to back majorities in 1993, 1997, and 2000. No one had done that since Sir Wilfred Laurier had won four in a row a century ago. And everyone else since Chrétien has been a piker compared to him, the guy who wasn't supposed to make it. In the past fifty years, Brian Mulroney has come closest by winning two in a row, but both Trudeaus, Diefenbaker, and Harper only managed one majority at a time; Pearson, Clark, and Martin only minorities; Turner and Campbell zip.

Okay, that's the background. Now, about our relationship.

He was a very popular prime minister at the beginning of his three majorities. He was funny, politically savvy, and he had a smart team around him. His time in office came during a period when *The National* was trying different ways to use television to make the PM accountable. We abandoned the year-end interview format as tired and predictable, replacing it instead with a town-hall format where I'd moderate the session but "ordinary" Canadians would ask the PM their own questions. Chrétien loved the first one in 1993. He was in his element, and the crowd clearly liked him. The second one the next year was much the same. But time moves on and so do people's moods. The Canadian mood was shifting with harsh government cuts to stem the deficit and a generally difficult overall economic situation. We had just done a lengthy series on *The National* called "Hard Times, Hard Choices," and so we weren't that popular around the government benches on Parliament Hill.

But Chrétien was keen to have a third town hall. And so were we. We prepared as we always did. We asked for viewers to write in with the question they would ask if given the chance, and we also talked to our stations across the country to see who they were aware of that was vocal in their regions. We put all those names together, then researched the people to make sure none were partisan in the sense that they worked or actively supported one of the parties. And we made sure our final list had a diverse view of the country and the issues confronting it.

Then we brought the people to Ottawa and readied them for their moment with the PM. This time I did add a new twist. In the general pep talk I gave the crowd before Jean Chrétien was to walk into the hall, I suggested something different. I'd noticed in past years that when someone would ask a question they would stand, but when they finished the question, they would immediately sit down. That left the PM speaking to the room at large or to the cameras. It wasn't personal, and better TV for a town hall would be personal. So I suggested they stay standing until they heard the answer, and even followed up if they felt they needed to. Staying on their feet would force the PM to look directly at them. It would be real dialogue. It would be personal.

The questions that year were tougher, given the challenges in the economy, and having the people stand totally changed the dynamic in the room. I'll never forget the woman from Saskatchewan who told her story of hard times, how the current economy meant she couldn't find a job in her hometown. Chrétien gave a bit of a message-track answer and she, still standing, said, "But what can I do to support my family?"

A not-so-happy Jean Chrétien at a
CBC town hall in the 1990s.
CBC

The prime minister's advice: "Maybe it's time to move."

It came across as insensitive, as did some of his other answers. It was not his finest hour, and he took a beating in the media for it.

The prime minister's office made it clear they were unhappy. They accused us of "setting him up," picking only certain questioners and even accused us of writing the questions. None of that was true but, needless to say, there were no more town halls, and year after year our requests for one-on-one interviews didn't meet with success either.

Until we got close to the 2000 election.

As if nothing had ever happened, our annual request was met with approval and we were given a date and a time for a one-on-one. It was set for 9 a.m. at Rideau Gate, the official government guesthouse across the street from 24 Sussex Drive, the prime minister's residence.

Chrétien was in a good mood and the interview went well, even if it failed to produce any real news. He sat as he often did with his arms crossed in front of him, playing defence in the way he'd learned from years in public life.

When it was over, he suggested I come across to 24 Sussex and join him for an informal, off-the-record chat. These sessions happen occasionally, and I'd had them with other prime ministers in the past and some since. They can be useful and often lead to stories. So, I thought, let's see what happens.

I joined the PM in the living room. He opened up the conversation by saying he had something for me, and an aide appeared with two glasses and what was obviously a bottle of liquor.

"One of my Caribbean fellow prime ministers gave me this," he said. "It's the best rum in the world."

He poured two glasses. And I mean poured.

"But, Prime Minister," I said. "It's ten a.m., not my normal drinking time. Plus, I have to get back to Toronto to do *The National* tonight."

He wasn't buying it. He wanted me to drink his rum.

So, I sipped. I'm sure it could have started a car, it was so strong.

He encouraged me to stop sipping and instead finish things off. I did.

I don't remember anything else after that. It might have taken a few years, but revenge had been had.

Before the rum, 2000.
CBC

POSTSCRIPT

I used that story to introduce the twentieth prime minister of Canada at a party organized for John Turner's ninetieth birthday in June of 2019. It got quite a few laughs from the audience of old pols who knew well the Chrétien style.

As I sat down at the table we were sharing, Jean Chrétien looked at me before he moved toward the podium for his speech. He smiled and said, "Gee, I don't remember that at all."

Growing up in Ottawa in 1957 with no home team,
you had to pick between Blue and Red. I picked Blue.

The Royal Canadian Navy, Victoria, 1966. I'm
in the top row, second from the left.

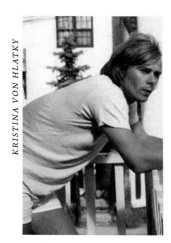

Winnipeg, 1975.
The hair days.

"Hurry hard!" I loved curling in my Manitoba
days. Left to right: Marv Terhoch, me,
Bob Culbert, and Bill Moreham.

My first network TV news special was the 1975 NDP leadership campaign
that elected Ed Broadbent. Clockwise from middle right: Larry Stout,
John Warren, Peter Daniel, Don McNeill, and the new kid on the block.

Ottawa, 1977. Still perfecting the soon to be anchorman pose.

With my friend and future Governor General, Ray Hnatyshyn, in Ottawa in 1978.

In Vancouver's Gastown with cameraman Dave Hall and editor Mark Carroll on a day off during the 1979 election campaign.

Wide awake with Mike Duffy on a plane of sleeping
reporters covering the Trudeau campaign in 1984.

1987: One of the early iterations of what would eventually
become "At Issue." Left to right: David Halton,
Brian Stewart, me, and Jeffrey Simpson.

Ottawa, 1986. Seriously now, do either of these
two guys look like they believe the other?

Getting the thoughtful anchorman pose down perfectly,
while Joe Clark nails the former prime minister look
in the House of Commons in the 1990s.

This photo is from around 1990 and it's full of a generation of news stars. Can you find them? Keith Boag, Ian Hanomansing, Paul Workman, Karen Webb, Denise Harrington, Wendy Mesley, Susan Ormiston, Gillian Finlay, Eve Savory, Der Hoi Yin, Dan Bjarnason, Tom Kennedy, Anna Maria Tremonti, Neil Macdonald, Brian Dubreil, Paul Adams, Saša Petricic, Kevin Newman.

Broadcasting along the Thames in London with cameraman Brian Kelly, circa 1995.

Catching some rays in Cape Dorset, Nunavut, with
Fred Parker and Sat Kumar in the late 1990s.

Resolute, Nunavut. Friends for life.

Travelling business class, armed forces style on a
Hercules from Kandahar to Kabul in 2006.

I travelled the world with these three. Left to right: Fred
Parker, Jonathan Whitten, Mark Harrison, and me.

MARK HARRISON

I love Vimy and am always honoured to be there, as was our team for the 90th anniversary in 2007. Left to right: Brian Kelly, Fred Parker, Adrienne Arsenault, me, Sheldon Beldick, Jon Whitten.

STEPHANIE JENZER

Inside a long forgotten tunnel at Vimy Ridge, amazed by the writings and carvings from young Canadians waiting underground for the battle in which some say Canada was born.

A personal fave: With my son Will at a
Toronto Raptors game in 2001. Even
Vince Carter couldn't keep him awake.

People are convinced this was photoshopped. It wasn't. The two
former presidents were in Toronto for a joint appearance circa
2010. They're laughing because I asked them where I should send
them a copy. Surprisingly, they didn't hound me for one.

Broadcasting with my friend and colleague Brian Stewart in 2015 from Apeldoorn in the Netherlands, where they always remember Canada.

Prepping for an "At Issue" panel with Chantal Hébert in 2016.

I did the "sync clap" ahead of all interviews. To "soften up" guests (especially prime ministers), the running joke was that it was my job due to budget cuts. Some laughed, most didn't.

With Governor General David Johnston in Trafalgar Square, London, in 2016.

A selfie aficionado, Mayor Naheed Nenshi in Calgary, circa 2016. It was freezing that night—minus 30 degrees—as we raised money for food banks with the CP Holiday Train.

I'm sure Mark Critch always wanted my job. He was devastated when they picked four others over him.

The two fingers that have always done my typing at work (and on this book) in my typically cluttered and disorganized desk at the CBC.

My last day in the studio, June 28, 2017, standing on the shoulders of an incredible team at *The National*.

With Fred Parker, my one and only director for thirty years on *The National*, on my last night doing the broadcast in Ottawa, June 30, 2017.

Seconds after my full-time career at the CBC came to an end on Canada Day, July 1, 2017, in Ottawa. The expression says it all.

PMO

Doing a Zoom call with Prime Minister Trudeau for my podcast, *The Bridge*, on Sirius XM Canada in March 2021.

WILL MANSBRIDGE

Each year on my birthday, I jump from this rock in the Gatineau Hills, as I did here in 2020 with the latest update, yelling, "I'm 72 and still jumping!"

In the War Zone

War correspondents are a breed of their own. Incredibly brave yet incredibly smart. They're not there to be heroes, they're there to cover a story.

Some of the foreign correspondents I've been lucky enough to work with have been through it all, seen death and destruction, been targeted themselves, yet been focused on telling the truth as best they can about what they see. The Schlesingers, Fungs, Arsenaults, Tremontis, Stewarts, Macdonalds, and many, many more. My own experience with conflict has been extremely limited, and what I've learned I've learned from many on the list above, in some cases from being in situations with them.

In 2000, during the second Palestinian uprising against Israel, the Al-Aqsa Intifada, our Jerusalem correspondent Neil Macdonald offered to take me to Bethlehem where much of the conflict at that time was taking place. We were anchoring *The National* in Israel for a few days, trying to tell the story of the uprising and what both sides were saying.

It was a bright, sunny day. We drove the short distance to Bethlehem, a city with so much biblical history, and Neil got us through various checkpoints by being Neil. We had all the right identification, but Neil refused to accept any delays from the guards and spoke calmly yet confidently as we were going through.

We had arranged to visit a local hospital and interview one of the main doctors. When we arrived, we learned that the power had been turned off after the latest gunfight, which meant surgeries and basic care were hindered. It also meant we couldn't set up lights for the interview, so instead we moved closer to one of the windows on the second floor of the hospital and began recording.

As the doctor spoke passionately about trying to save lives under difficult conditions, I suddenly felt a hand on my shoulder firmly pulling me back toward the darkened area of the room.

"Jeez, Peter, they're shooting at the hospital and you're sitting in the window," Neil said.

I had heard some distant *rat a tat tat* but innocently, or foolishly, hadn't connected that noise to gunfire. For Neil, it was just another day of being smart and careful in a conflict zone and making sure he didn't end up bringing a bloodied anchor back to the office.

It was a basic lesson for me, and even though I had taken courses in how to handle myself—like all of us who travel into questionable areas do—being in the real deal means staying sharp. I hadn't.

Many of those who have real-time experience explain that there is a price to pay for working in a war zone and that it takes time to decompress after being there. Some of what is witnessed is never forgotten and can come back to haunt. Many of the women and men I've worked with carry that with them always. They don't complain. They do their job, but they do it very carefully. I've been so lucky to call them colleagues.

This picture was taken at Base Camp Kandahar
in Afghanistan just after returning from a patrol
with Canadian soldiers outside the wire.
That face captures what relief looks like.
Mark Harrison

It Can Be Ugly Out There

When I was in Israel covering the latest Palestinian uprising, suicide bombings or attacks on Jewish shoppers were not uncommon. They seemed to be happening every few days. We covered the story as best we could, given the challenge Middle East stories always presented: no matter what we did, what we said, or what we showed, neither side of the Palestinian-Israeli divide was left convinced that we weren't biased against them. In all my years, I never received more mail charging me with bias than I did on this subject—not even from Liberals and Conservatives in Canada constantly whining about how hard done by they felt they were.

One day, I was working in our Jerusalem bureau when there was the clear sound of a huge explosion outside the office. To me, it seemed like the blast could have been right outside our building. The more experienced war correspondents said it was close but probably a couple of blocks away. My adrenaline was rushing; to them it was another day in the uprising.

My crew and I rushed out the bureau door, down the elevator, and into the street. There were sirens blaring and people running. There was a faint hint of smoke about three or four blocks away. We ran in that direction, each of us trying to take some of the equipment load from the cameraman who had come with us.

Within minutes we were there. And it was a scene of expected chaos. Jerusalem was used to suicide bombings, and this was another one. The bomber had been on a bus. The windows were all blown out. There were people standing, bleeding, and in shock. Others, still in their seats. And clearly some who would never know what had happened. There were first responders trying to help, others literally picking up the pieces. It was horrible but it was life for Israelis at that time, and by that night it would likely be the same life for some Palestinians caught in what had become a constant cycle of revenge.

We did what we needed to do. We shot the scene, talked to some survivors, and I did a short piece facing the camera that would help this segment fit into the documentary we were putting together.

Then my cell phone rang. It was Toronto, wanting me to go on the air for a "talkback" with one of the CBC News Network anchors about what was happening. I agreed. And moments later, I was on the air describing the scene.

And then the Toronto anchor asked me, "Peter, how many people are dead?"

Then I did what I shouldn't have done. I lost it. "I have no idea," I said angrily. "I just got here. This only happened minutes ago. It's a bloodbath. They are picking bits and pieces of body parts, strips of flesh, off the ground and the walls. I have no idea how many bodies that will total."

The line went silent. There were no more questions.

Later, the show producer and the anchor sent me notes to apologize. But they hadn't been wrong. In fact, it was me who learned a lesson that day. If the positions had been reversed, I almost certainly would have asked something similar. Too often, in the comfort of the anchor chair on the other side of the world, we lose touch with the reality of what it's really like out there. And we forget how real, sometimes ugly real, the situation is for the reporters who are just trying to do their best under horrific circumstances.

A Call in the Night

There are times when television can feel awfully distant from the out-side world. The images on that September morning in 2001 were incredibly powerful. Planes, full of passengers, smashing into the Twin Towers representing America's economic might. Within an hour or so, those buildings collapsed more than a hundred floors into poisonous dust. Thousands were dead. A similar horror simultaneously unfolded at the Pentagon in Washington.

Over the next few days, I spent hours that never seemed to end in the studio. People ask me what it was like to do a broadcast like that. I tell them that it was draining and emotional, yet in a way, I was constantly shielded from reality.

During the challenging hours on the first day when rumours were rampant about more planes and more targets, when "facts" kept changing, it was most vital to keep focused. Keeping focused meant trusting my eyes and my instincts, believing what I could see and feel. But that's where the issue of feeling "distant" can come in.

Looking at a monitor in a comfortable studio is not the same as being in the street watching people leap from a hundred floors up. Being in the studio can give you an artificial sense of reality. During those initial hours of broadcast, there were moments when I actually felt, perhaps just subconsciously, that I was watching a movie. I was saying all the right things, but deep inside I'm not sure I was fully comprehending the crushing impact this was having on people watching from across the country.

It was the middle of the night, around four a.m., about eighteen

On air for forty-four hours on 9/11 and 9/12.
CBC

hours after I'd first sat in the studio taking over from Mark Kelly, who had done a brilliant job anchoring in the initial hours of the story. I was exhausted, yet the adrenaline was still pumping. This break wouldn't be for a quick nap; instead, it would be a quick shower and suit change. All of that I could do in my dressing room just down the hall from the studio.

I walked in and right away saw the red message light blinking on my phone. It had to be family because the number was private. It *was* family.

"Dad, I'm watching. It's such an awful story. I want you to know that I love you."

It was my twenty-eight-year-old daughter, Pam, calling from Winnipeg. The message lasted barely ten seconds. I broke down.

When I pulled myself together, I realized that I had been missing a crucial part of the story. Because what Pam did was happening everywhere. Daughters were calling fathers, mothers were calling sons, brothers were calling sisters, friends were calling friends. Reaching out. Comforting. Connecting. Telling each other they loved them. What they'd seen had made them want to hug, hold close, and reach out to the people who mattered to them. Their world had been threatened in ways that were unimaginable, and they wanted to touch someone close to make sure they were okay. It was one of those "the world will never be the same" moments.

Pam may never understand the difference that call in the middle of the night meant to me. But I do. And I'll never forget it.

The Pilot

Some of the hardest-working people during a breaking news broadcast are "chase producers." They have to find guests who can give background and explain certain elements of a story, one that's suddenly been thrust, not just on the public, but also on the journalists covering it. Needless to say, I was always in awe of those who performed the chase function at the CBC.

Never had there been more pressure on all of us than on 9/11, when we all needed help understanding what had just happened. The chase people were desperately looking for experts in all fields from airlines to terrorism to foreign affairs to rescue operations. And they found a parade of never-ending "talkers" who could help us on all counts. On days like that, networks have people watching other networks, and if they see someone particularly good they'll try to poach them. That's just how it works.

Well, a couple of hours into our programming we were looking for another airline expert to go with the ones we already had. Our people got a call from one of our western stations; they suggested a retired American airline pilot living in their city who was said to be very good at explaining the basics of what a pilot would have been going through that day. The chase people reached out, pre-interviewed him, and booked him to come into our local studio so he could be hooked up with me.

He arrived and he was terrific. His descriptions put the viewer right inside the cockpit of a plane in trouble, giving us a pilot's-eye view of what might have happened. By the time he was off the air, other networks in Canada and the United States had seen him and were able to book him for their shows as well. Score another success for the chase people.

Two weeks later, after things had started to settle down, we found out something else about him. He wasn't a pilot, never had been. He was a fake. A con man. Nothing more than a flying enthusiast. We were horrified.

I talked to a couple of my Air Canada pilot friends who had been at home watching, and they were equally surprised. Mainly because they couldn't find fault with anything the guy had said. He may have been a fraud, but he knew his stuff.

Of course, that didn't and couldn't satisfy us. We eventually admitted what had happened and made sure our other network friends knew too. And you can be sure it's a story I tell when I'm asked to speak with those training to be our future chase producers. I tell them verification is key—make sure your guests are who they say they are. The lesson is simple: you never assume anything until you've done a full check, especially on a day like 9/11.

Buying Time

I've always had a thing for watches. It started when I was quite young. I used to hold my father's watch in my hand when he'd take it off after returning from work in the evenings. And every once in a while, my mother would let me hold her father's gold pocket watch, which she kept hidden away with her most precious things. He'd been a ship's officer for the White Star Line in the heyday of transatlantic passenger travel before the First World War. He'd never been on White Star's most famous liner, the *Titanic*, but my mother said he had been on a few of her sister ships, so I always had this image of him standing on the main deck holding this very pocket watch looking out at the North Atlantic. I'm not sure if he ever did, but I had that image anyway. I almost begged my parents for a timepiece I could call my own. I was about ten when I finally got my own watch. A Timex. I earned the money to buy it myself by doing that film about the Parliament Buildings for the National Film Board in 1958. I treasured the Timex and kept it close for years.

I think it was those three timepieces that began my fascination with watches, a fascination that continues today. I can't pass a watch counter or flip by a watch advertisement without having a closer look. I have dozens of watches. Dozens. I almost feel guilty admitting that because most of them I never wear, but the ones I cherish have special memories attached to them—mainly because of where I bought them, which was nearly always while on assignment in far-flung regions of the world.

In January of 2003, I found myself in Baghdad. The international situation was tense. It was pretty clear that a war in Iraq was imminent. The only way it could be averted it seemed, was if Saddam Hussein would allow inspectors into his country to go wherever they wanted to look for what the Americans and the British were convinced were there: weapons of mass destruction (WMD). Saddam teased them for months, but the answer always ended up being no.

Saddam wasn't talking, but Iraq's number two, foreign affairs minister Tariq Aziz, had decided he would. As a result, I managed to land what was a bit of a world exclusive by getting an agreement with him for an interview. I was in Jordan when the word came through that he would talk, so I managed to grab an evening flight from Amman to Baghdad, landing with ample time to prep for the early-evening interview the next day. I was helped in that by talking with our two correspondents who were covering the larger story, Nahlah Ayed and Don Murray. During lunch, we moved off the story at hand and I tried to bring them up to date on the latest CBC politics, always a popular theme. Somehow that turned into me telling Don about my watch fascination and he was quick with an idea.

"Why don't we go down to the *souk*? They've always got a selection."

The *souk* is an Arab street market, and they sell the whole gambit, from food to silks to jewelry and everything in between. So off we went and, sure enough, there were a few stalls with watches.

Now, let's be frank. When you are in a street market looking for watches, whether you're in Baghdad, London, New York, or Toronto—we aren't talking about the real thing here. They're fakes. But there are fakes and there are *fakes*. I used to grade them this way: for twenty-five bucks—US of course—you could get one where Rolex was spelled without the "e," but it would likely stop working by the time you got back to your hotel, and the vendor would be gone when you got back to ask for a refund. For fifty dollars, things improve. Somewhat. But the watch is not going to last. And then, finally, the third tier: 100–150 bucks. That's where it gets pretty hard to distinguish from the real deal. That was my market. And my new best friend in the Baghdad *souk* had a few examples to offer.

There was no doubt which one caught my eye almost immediately. It was a Rolex. Spelled correctly. Beautiful stainless-steel band, black watch face, date including the year, full stopwatch functions. I was impressed. Don, for his part, was already bored and tapping on the real watch he was wearing. Time to go.

The seller and I haggled over the price. He wanted two hundred, I offered one hundred. No surprise then that we settled on one fifty and everyone seemed happy.

Two hours later, I was sitting across from Tariq Aziz in his office with the watch on my left wrist. If you ever screen that interview you might just see it. And no, he didn't lean over at one point and say, "Hey, man, nice watch."

Five years on, I was in Beijing for the 2008 Olympics. It was a busy time as we were hosting *The National* from Beijing, and each day I was off doing some feature interview or mini-documentary about life in the Chinese capital that had transformed so much since my first visit in 1976. But every evening when I returned to the broadcasting centre, one of my colleagues, usually one of the team from CBC Sports, would say, "Mansbridge, they've got great watches at the main Beijing flea market."

My reputation had clearly preceded me. When an afternoon off loomed, I was on my way.

The flea market was actually a huge, multi-floored building, but the selection was pretty brutal. Mostly first-tier with the odd second-tier watch available. This was not going to work, I decided, and made my feelings well known. Finally, one of the sellers motioned me over. In broken English he talked about a different watch place, a few blocks away, that would make me happy.

So we trudged over, crossing streets, going down narrow alleyways, and finally we found it. From the outside, it was a very basic, unmarked door, but inside was like a miniature Birks. Clean space, glass showcases, and lots of watches. And most were the third-tier kind I liked. I was like a kid in a candy store. A fake candy store, mind you, but still. It didn't take me long to find a few I'd take home: a Panerai, a Cartier, a Breitling. There was a bit of haggling, but I did not feel taken advantage of—beyond the fact that I was clearly being taken advantage of; it wasn't a charity.

Before we left, the sales guy leaned over and whispered, "Do you want some handbags?"

The next thing we knew we were a few doors down the lane and in another spot not much bigger than a large walk-in closet. But there were thousands of handbags there. Top fakes. Gucci, Prada, Louis Vuitton. I couldn't help but wonder why they didn't try making fake BMWs, Mercedes, Audis.

I'll spare you the examples of street watch buying in Hong Kong, Rome, and Paris. None were as good as Beijing and Baghdad. However, what has always remained unclear to me is where exactly these "replica" watches are made, who makes them, and under what conditions they work. I have to assume that the labour is cheap and the conditions aren't good. And that's the bad side of this story, and my encouragement of the sale can legitimately be seen as a failure on my part.

Here's the surprising part. All those watches still look terrific. No metallic fading. And, even years later, they still work. Haven't done a thing with any of them since the day I bought them. Not even a battery. Go figure.

The Gathering Storm

There was something about Tariq Aziz that made Westerners feel comfortable. He spoke impeccable English, which helped. He dressed like a Westerner, which made him acceptable to Western TV audiences. And he always sounded like someone you could make a deal with, which, as it turned out, was part of his problem. Too many people claimed he was all about making deals for profit, either for himself or for his boss. Now I was about to meet him face-to-face at a critical moment in world history.

Tariq Aziz was Saddam Hussein's number two for years—first as Iraq's foreign affairs minister from 1983 to 1991, and then as deputy prime minister, as he was when I met him in Baghdad in 2003. But he was more than all those positions. He was the face of Iraq when you couldn't see the real face: Saddam himself.

After Iraq's invasion of Kuwait in 1990—the beginning of the Gulf War—Aziz spent days shuttling around the world with US secretary of state James Baker trying to avert a war with the United States and its coalition partners. Day after day, the two men would stand together in front of the world's media looking temptingly close to making a deal.

In the end, they didn't, and the US-led forces eventually blew the Iraqi army, literally, out of Kuwait in Operation Desert Storm, a weeks-long conflict in early 1991. As the Iraqi forces fled Kuwait City for home, they were chased by coalition fighter jets and the results were not only devastating but horrifying, especially in one area just a few kilometres from the border that became known as the "Highway of Death"—a six-lane highway leading to the Iraqi port of Basra. The hundreds, if not thousands, of Iraqi military vehicles trying to make their escape were sitting ducks. For years, the burned-out carcasses of Iraqi trucks, oil tankers, armoured personnel carriers, and jeeps littered both sides of the highway. More than a decade later, travelling by that same spot as a second US-Iraq war was about to take place, I was able to see some of that old destruction still left over from the first one.

Iraq was bloodied and beaten, but Saddam Hussein was still standing, and that meant Tariq Aziz was too. Once more he became Iraq's voice on the international stage as it rebuilt and flexed its muscles. The bully Saddam, with his strident swagger, caused Washington to ready its trigger finger for a second time, while Aziz, always with the face of a diplomat, tried to calm things down. But that only worked for so long, and by the end of January 2003, in a post-9/11 world, things were again on the verge.

As tensions rose, I flew into Baghdad for one reason—an interview with Aziz. At that point, Saddam Hussein wasn't giving any interviews, although he had my request sitting on his desk. Okay, so maybe it wasn't on his desk, maybe just on some flunky's desk down the hall. Whoever had it, no one got back to me. Except Tariq Aziz, and he was still a catch.

He hadn't given any interviews for a few weeks, and the situation with Iraq seemed to be reaching a breaking point. Another UN report on the issue of whether Iraq had weapons of mass destruction was due at any moment. So, as dusk fell over the historic city at the junction of the Tigris and Euphrates rivers, I drove toward what had been Aziz's office for years: Iraq's foreign affairs building. Along the way, at almost every turn, there was either a huge billboard showing Saddam or a statue of Saddam. Driving those streets felt eerie. I couldn't help but think that all of those features would be destroyed because the Americans were hell-bent on regime change, which meant throwing Saddam out of power. And Aziz too.

I arrived at the building and was ushered up to the top floor—I think it was the seventh floor. Given the evening hour, there were very few people around. We were directed to set up our cameras in the waiting room next to the deputy prime minister's office and were told Aziz was inside his office, working, but would come out in due course. Then his aides left us. Alone. Which I found a bit odd, but at least it meant we were free to set up as we wished.

It quickly became clear what Aziz was doing. We could hear it through the seemingly paper-thin walls. He was watching CNN and their "live" coverage of the UN announcement about its latest Iraq report. And that was interesting because CNN was banned in Iraq for everyone it seemed, except the guy who obviously found it the best way to get the latest developments.

If that wasn't enough of a surprise, it got better. When Aziz eventually opened the door to greet us, he was alone. No one else had been with him. A good part of the world was on the edge of war, and one guy without officials, briefers, or even an apparent phone call to his boss—we would have heard that through those walls—was about to give his country's reaction to the report which many felt could determine whether there would be a war or not. To me it had the feel of amateur hour in a very high stakes situation. But this was Tariq Aziz, no stranger to high stakes.

It was the diplomatic Aziz who walked into the waiting room with his hand outstretched. "How are things in Canada? I love Canada."

He actually did have a connection to Canada, as one of his relatives lived just outside of Toronto and he had visited in the past. The small talk over, we got into it.

First, he dismissed the UN report as meaningless, and it pretty much was. While it seemed important at the time, you won't see it mentioned in the history books as a marker leading to war. So, I moved on to what everyone now felt was inevitable.

"There are some in the United States and Britain," I began, "who feel that if this does in fact come to a conflict, it would be over in a week or two. What do you make of that?"

He didn't even pause. "Let them try. Let them try. They are deluding themselves in that. This nation, the people of Iraq are going to fight courageously and effectively for as long as it takes to defend their sovereignty."

"You make it sound like it will be a massive killing ground?" I responded.

"We are not killing anybody. They will be killing us, you see, and we will retaliate and that's legitimate. We are not going to the streets of New York and Washington to fight the Americans. When they come to our towns and cities, we will fight them."

I interrupted. "But how long could you hold out against—"

He interrupted back. "As long as it takes to defend our country."

Of course, Aziz was wrong about how long his forces would last against the superior forces of the United States and Britain. Within weeks, Saddam was in hiding and Aziz was in custody. But here's where he was right. Almost twenty years later, it's still hard to say it was a clear-cut victory for Washington and London. The claim they had made to justify war—that Saddam had weapons of mass destruction—was proven to be a lie. And worse, while the regime in Iraq did change, it led to years of bitter, bloody civil strife. Even now the Americans are hardly seen in a good light. Their most expensive and most fortified embassy in the world is in Baghdad, yet all these years later it still often gets attacked and surrounded with angry protestors.

When the interview ended, there were the usual pleasantries before Aziz pointed to the hall that led to the elevator and we walked along it. Part of that hallway was an atrium that looked straight down to the main floor. During the interview, he had talked about how this same building was attacked by American cruise missiles in the 1990–91 Gulf War. As we stood overlooking the atrium, I asked him whether he assumed it would be attacked again. He looked up at the ceiling and nodded his head.

"It'll come right down through there. It will be one of the first places they target."

He was right about that too. A few weeks later, just as Aziz had predicted, a missile was said to have gone straight down through the roof, raining its destruction floor by floor to the bottom. But by then, Tariq Aziz had already left the building.

POSTSCRIPT

Within days, those billboards I'd driven by had been destroyed and the statues pulled down. Saddam fled and hid in a hole in the ground north of Baghdad for a few months until he was betrayed, captured, tried, and hanged in 2006.

After he surrendered himself to the Americans, Tariq Aziz was kept in custody, tried, and eventually convicted for his role in the execution of forty-two Iraqi merchants accused of profiteering. Accusations that he had also pocketed money in Iraq's 1990s cash-for-oil schemes did not lead to charges, nor did claims of crimes against humanity. There were attempts to have him executed, but widespread international condemnation of that possibility, including from the Vatican, ensured that did not happen. Tariq Aziz was sentenced to fifteen years in prison, where he died of a heart attack in 2015.

King David's Chocolate

There's a reason that airport administrators from around the world study Ben Gurion Airport in Tel Aviv. It's because of its security measures. There is no airport with tighter security anywhere. And anyone who has ever been through Ben Gurion knows exactly what that means.

Israel ranks security above everything, and they've learned the hard way that airport and airline security is where they have to devote much of their energy. Their planes have been hijacked, their passengers attacked, and their airports the site of bloody massacres. They are determined to do everything they can not to let that happen again. And to their credit, it's been decades since they've faced any setbacks.

I've been through the Tel Aviv airport half a dozen times at least. Like others who have travelled through Israel, you learn quickly. Don't do anything stupid. Don't say anything stupid. Don't act in any way stupid. Do what you're asked when you're asked and don't argue. There are constant security checks. Some you know are happening around you, others you don't. And they're just as stringent as you leave Israel as they are when you arrive in the country.

Let me explain. In 2003, I flew to Israel for four days. I anchored *The National* from Jerusalem for three nights, travelled around the country, and, among others, interviewed Benjamin Netanyahu, who was then foreign affairs minister and was one of if not the most well-known and closely guarded Israelis of the day. So, let's be clear, I'd been checked out.

On arrival at Ben Gurion for my flight home, I showed my passport and ticket and was waved through to the area where my suitcase would eventually be tagged and sent on its way. Not so fast. First, I had to be grilled by the airport's security staff. They are a very professional mix of cool, calm, and intense. They are usually young, both men and women, and sometimes they work in teams. They looked me straight in the eye and their attention didn't break as they asked me a steady stream of questions. And they weren't just listening to my answers; they were watching my every movement, right down to whether I blinked, as I responded.

"What's your name?"

"Where are you from?"

"How long were you in Israel?"

So far so good.

"What were you doing in Israel?"

"I'm a journalist covering a story in your country."

That's the wrong answer if I expected to move through the line quickly. Israeli security love grilling visiting journalists.

"What story were you covering?"

"Where did you go?"

"Who did you meet?"

"Who did you interview?"

And if I thought dropping the Netanyahu name was going to make all this easier, I should have thought again. They became more inquisitive and they never took their eyes off me.

"Where did you meet Netanyahu?"

"How long did you talk to him?"

"Has the interview aired yet?"

"Do you have a copy of the interview with you?"

And on it went. After what felt like hours but was probably only ten minutes, they got around to a question I should have been ready for but wasn't.

"Do you have anything in your suitcase that someone gave you, or that you didn't wrap yourself?"

I paused for a moment, thinking carefully, and said, "No, I don't."

And then the Israeli security woman looked at me and said, rather firmly, "**Are you** sure about that?"

I felt like I was on that TV game show *Who Wants to Be a Millionaire?* where they always asked the contestants, "Is that your final answer?" It made me think again, through each of the days I'd been in Israel. And then I remembered.

I'd been staying at the King David Hotel in Jerusalem, one of my favourite hotels in the world. It was centrally located, had lots of workspace, even areas where we could host major interviews or panels and, best of all, they usually gave the CBC an attractive room rate. The staff was friendly, the meals were more than enjoyable, and the rooms were fresh, clean, and comfortable. And the evening staff always left a terrific little wrapped chocolate on your pillow.

Bingo. The chocolate. I'd kept the one from my last night and packed it with my things.

I looked at the security officer. "Actually, there is something that I have that was given to me already wrapped."

She looked at her fellow security member and everything about the moment changed. "What is it?"

"It's one of those little chocolates that fine hotels often leave on your pillow when they come in to turn down your bed in the evening."

They didn't seem impressed.

"Why is it in your suitcase?"

"I wanted to keep it as a memento," I said, quickly realizing that must sound incredibly stupid. But it was too late now.

"Open your suitcase."

I did as I was told.

"Show us the chocolate."

And, of course, I couldn't find it. I'd packed my suitcase neatly, but within minutes it was a jumbled mess as I tried to sort through clean clothes, dirty clothes, socks, ties—everything—on the hunt for a little chocolate. It took forever and the security team was looking ever more doubtful, but finally there it was.

"Pass it to me, please," came the order.

Which is what I did and they disappeared behind some security doors with the little hotel night gift. I'm not sure what they did with it, but I assume it was put through some kind of electronic device that X-rayed it to make sure there was nothing to be concerned about.

There wasn't.

When they returned, all they said was, "Thank you for your cooperation. You can put the chocolate back in your suitcase, and you're free to head to your check-in."

I was tempted to throw the King David's nighttime treat away, but I didn't. I packed it and brought it home to Canada. I can't remember if I ever ate it.

POSTSCRIPT

Things are even tougher now at Ben Gurion Airport. Israeli security can, and often does, demand to look at your mobile devices. They'll check recent phone numbers that you've dialed. They have even started scrolling through your social media accounts, looking at your most recent posts. They can and do go into your email accounts to see whom you've been corresponding with in the days leading up to your flight time. And they don't make any secret about the fact that they engage in profiling. Palestinians and Arabs can and should expect that their phones will be checked on an almost routine basis.

Hacks and Flacks

In the early nineties, a group of us who had known each other for almost twenty years began what became an annual January golfing trek to Florida. *Maclean's* editor Bob Lewis, former *Gazette* reporter Bill Fox, pollsters Allan Gregg and Bruce Anderson, consultants Mike Robinson, Harry Near, and Charles Fremes. And because he was a great guy, the best golfer, and someone who could be very funny, we were also joined by one of the country's greatest actors, Peter Donaldson. We called ourselves the "Hacks and Flacks" because, aside from Donaldson, we were either journalists (hacks) or political aides (flacks). We'd all met in the late seventies on Parliament Hill as young twenty- and thirty-somethings making our way up our respective career ladders. Beyond the political cut and thrust of the day, beyond the usual complaints about the media, we were friends and wanted to stay that way.

So, golf and this annual trip became the glue that kept us together as, over the years, many of us moved to new cities and new jobs. The days were long, usually two rounds of golf, and so were the nights, with friendly poker games till the wee hours. And lots of talk and gossip.

In 1998, the topic du jour was Bill Clinton and whether he could survive the fallout from his affair with White House intern Monica Lewinsky. The story had just broken in the days before our latest trip. Most of us thought he was finished and would almost certainly have to resign. But there was one noticeable dissenter to that view.

I remember the group of us sitting in the lunchtime bar at the Copperhead course, the signature course at the Innisbrook Golf Resort in Palm Harbor, Florida. Clinton coverage was on CNN, airing on the

Winner: worst dressed golfers, Innisbrook Florida.
Left to right: Charles Fremes, Peter Donaldson, me,
Bruce Anderson (crouching), Bob Lewis, Mike Robinson,
and Allan Gregg. Behind the camera is Harry Near,
who wisely kept himself out of the picture.

barroom TV, and Clinton bashing was fairly strong both there and at our table.

Sitting quietly at the end of the table was Allan Gregg, at the time the country's best-known pollster and political strategist. No one has ever accused Allan of being shy. He's told clients, including prime ministers and premiers, to their face what they were doing wrong and what they had to do to fix their situation. And now he was prepared to do the same for us.

"You guys don't get it, do you," he said. "Clinton may not have you on his side, but he does have the people. These are the 1990s, not the 1960s. Sex is not going to cost him his job. It may even increase his popularity."

He was right, of course. Clinton survived the scandal, at least in the short term, and watched his popularity increase, not decrease.

Which brings me to 2004, with Bill Clinton four years out of office and on a worldwide book tour. Presidents who used to be so hard to get an interview with while in office were easy to grab when they were flogging a book in the years after office. *My Life* was a bestseller even though it was a bit plodding, even boring at times. But his book tour wasn't. Wherever he went, there were huge crowds of adoring fans waiting hours in line for those few seconds in front of him and for the Clinton smile.

We'd agreed with Clinton's handlers to meet at the Four Seasons Hotel a few blocks from the downtown Toronto Indigo bookstore where he was meeting book buyers. We'd gotten a room on the fifteenth floor, moved the furniture around for the space we needed, and set up the lights and cameras. Then the wait began, and with Clinton one has to be prepared for the wait. He's never on time. First, he loves to talk, and second, there are always people who want to talk with him.

So, as the agreed-upon time passed, and passed, and passed again, I decided to leave the room to stretch my legs. As I stepped out into the fifteenth-floor hallway, I was surprised to see a lot of people standing in their doorways all along the passageway. I shouldn't have been. Word travels quickly when a US president is in the house and you just might have a chance to catch a glimpse. Or more, grab an autograph for the book you just bought. They were excited but orderly. Part of Clinton's Secret Service detail was keeping a close eye as well. Just in case.

Then, finally, the elevator doors opened and there he was: the silver-haired, former most powerful man in the world. And he was in classic Clinton form, circling parts of the hallway, signing books, shaking hands, and posing for photos.

By the time he reached the area where I was standing just outside our door, the buzz around him hadn't stopped. It was friendly but loud. Suddenly, the door to the room next to ours, which was closed and I assumed unoccupied, opened with gusto. A guy with serious bedhead and dressed only in his boxers peered out and half-shouted, "What the hell is all the racket about?"

Then, face-to-face with you know who, his jaw dropped.

"Holy shit, that's Bill Clinton."

It sure was, and as the Secret Service agents prepared for action, the former president prepared for charm. He put out his hand and shook Mr. Boxer's in return, which left both of them laughing and in great spirits. The agents relaxed—as much as they ever relax.

Then it was on to the interview. It was okay, but most ex-presidents just don't make the same kind of news that current presidents do. And I couldn't stop smiling about Mr. Boxer.

Later, the fellow told me he'd flown into Toronto from Boston late the night before and was hoping for a morning rest before a key afternoon meeting. He'd heard the ruckus outside, looked through the peephole and seen camera lights, and, forgetting that he wasn't dressed, opened the door to check things out. What he saw he wouldn't unsee for a while.

And neither will Clinton.

POSTSCRIPT

Allan Gregg was correct about Bill Clinton's post-Lewinsky popularity. His numbers rose and he was warmly greeted wherever he went. He raised millions of dollars for various causes, including his own foundation, and he tried, unsuccessfully as it turned out, to help Hillary Clinton win the 2016 presidential race against Donald Trump. And then the #MeToo Movement hit, and while he wasn't directly targeted, it has made life uncomfortable for the former president. In interviews he's been challenged about the Lewinsky affair and asked why he hasn't personally apologized to her. He seemed dumbfounded at the question and didn't have what was considered to be an appropriate answer. He's dropped off the radar a bit as a result. So, while Allan's 1998 assessment of Clinton was right, times have changed. But his other caution, "never count Clinton out," may still be valid.

As for "Hacks and Flacks," our routine changed as we got older. We went from two rounds of golf a day to one, 4 a.m. poker games that eventually ended at 10 p.m. And sadly, some of our membership passed. Time does move on, but the memories don't.

Acts of Kindness

You've probably never heard of the Sri Lankan city of Kalmunai. Don't feel bad, neither had I until I was standing in it.

It was January 2005, a week or so after the New Year's Eve 2004 tsunami hit countries across Southeast Asia, taking more than two hundred thousand lives. There was a massive relief effort underway from Indonesia, across Malaysia, to Thailand, India, and Sri Lanka. Dozens of countries were trying to help, including Canada, and both government and nongovernmental organizations (NGOs) were involved.

We decided that *The National* would host its broadcast in the region for a week and, with our correspondents spread out across most of the affected areas, report on rescue and relief efforts. We would anchor from Sri Lanka, so I flew into its capital city of Colombo early one morning from Toronto.

The last time I'd been in Colombo was when I was three years old and my family was sailing from our home in Britain to my father's new job in Kuala Lumpur, Malaya. I mention this only because that 1951 stop in Colombo is the background for one of my favourite childhood photos. I'm in my very colonial shorts and shirt, sitting at a patio table near one of Colombo's top hotels.

But there was no time on that day in 2005 to search out the old spot for an updated picture; instead, it was back out to the airport tarmac after clearing Sri Lankan customs. Waiting for us was a chartered Canadian-made Twin Otter for our flight to the country's east coast. The area had been battered by the five-metre-high tsunami caused by an earthquake in the depths of the Indian Ocean. Kalmunai was one of the towns hit along the very vulnerable Sri Lankan coastline, and many of its one hundred thousand residents suffered the consequences. Hundreds lost their lives in a community totally unprepared for the devastation that was thrust upon them when the waves crashed ashore. Even though it was days later when we arrived, the hospital morgue was still full, and bodies were stacked in boxes waiting outside the main walls.

I interviewed some hospital officials about the challenges they were facing, heard some gripping personal stories from survivors recovering in the hospital, and then nurses told us a story that we all knew would connect with viewers on a highly emotional level. Hours after the tsunami had hit, a three-month-old baby boy was found near the beach alone in a bucket. There was no one else around and no one came forward to claim him. Doctors called him the "miracle baby" and began telling his story in the community. By the time we arrived, eleven different families had claimed the child, but none could prove it. Authorities decided on DNA testing, but that was going to take weeks. In the meantime, they let me and my crew in the ward where the miracle child was being cared for. We already knew the video we took would go around the world, and it did.

With lots of stories in hand, we headed off to look for a place to anchor that night's broadcast. The plan was to link my stories from Kalmunai together with the work being done by some of the other CBC correspondents across Southeast Asia. As a result, I had a series of "standups" to record that would give editors in Toronto different options to string all the work together. We needed a location that would say in an instant that we were in the middle of the aftermath of the tsunami. That wasn't hard to find in Kalmunai.

We went down near the ocean, perhaps a block from the water, which was now just calmly lapping up on the sandy beaches. But all around the shoreline, things looked like a war zone, as if a tank or a bulldozer had just made its way across the landscape taking everything down in its wake. Almost everything. Trees, palm trees to be exact, seemed to somehow withstand the onslaught of water while a lot of concrete buildings did not.

We picked a spot and started knocking off the various on-camera introductions we would need. We mixed it up a bit. I did some in the normal standing position and did some in what we call a "walk and talk," moving down a pathway through the rubble while speaking. It was raining slightly, which only added to the dreary feel of the story.

After about thirty minutes, we had everything we needed, and the crew began to pack up the gear. By that time, we'd attracted a bit of a crowd, especially young kids. It's no different in Sri Lanka than in Saskatoon or Sept-Iles. Set up a camera and kids come out of nowhere to find out what's happening, even in the broken bricks and shattered glass of a scene of destruction.

The kids stood there quietly during the taping, but when it was over they moved in to play. One of them had a soccer ball and began to kick it around. It came to me and I kicked it back. Game on.

A few minutes later, one of the kids, a young girl who was maybe

"Walk and Talk" after the 2005 Tsunami in Sri Lanka.
Jon Whitten

eight or nine years old, came up to me and pointed to a small pin with a Canadian flag that I had on my gear.

"Ca-na-da," she said in broken English. "Ca-na-da . . . good."

I called our translator over and asked her why the little girl had used that phrase. Why did she think Canada was good?

I found out that morning she and her friends had been to a relief tent which was set up to give kids and the elderly vaccination shots to inoculate them against the kind of diseases that can spread after a natural disaster damages pipes, often leaving a potentially deadly mix of sewage and water. And what they remembered most was how kind the nurses were, and that the nurses were from Canada. I was puzzled. We had been told that there were no Canadians in that particular community, at least no official NGOs or regular Canadian rescue teams that had registered.

So, we asked the kids to take us and they did. When we got there,

The little girl in the story can be seen on the extreme right
with her hand on her chin.
Jon Whitten

just a few blocks away, there was a tent with a long lineup going inside. We stuck our heads in and saw three women handling the needles. And their story was something else.

They were three friends from Vancouver—nurses—who had been in their respective homes watching the stories of suffering coming in from the other side of the world. They called each other and decided they had to do something. So, they booked vacation time, withdrew money from their bank accounts, booked airline tickets to Sri Lanka, and arrived in Colombo saying they were nurses from Vancouver there to help and they would go anywhere they were asked.

And that's how they ended up in Kalmunai. They were volunteers, just three Canadians who cared and whose caring affected a little girl's view of the outside world and, in particular, Canada. For the rest of her life, she'll always remember Canada. Whenever she sees our flag or hears our country's name, she'll think of those nurses and how they came across the ocean just to help her and her friends. It's selfless actions like that, that make Canada admired by many and the envy of the world. And in one of the wonderful things about on-the-scene journalism, I got to see it all firsthand.

POSTSCRIPT

The story of the "miracle baby" did have another chapter. It took weeks, and by then we were back in Canada, but we got word that the DNA test results were in and one of the couples who had claimed that the baby was theirs proved to be telling the truth. And so the baby boy was reunited with his parents. There weren't a lot of happy endings in the tsunami, but this was one of them.

The Pope and the President

When Karol Józef Wojtyła died on April 2, 2005, it did not come as a surprise. He had been ill and suffering for quite some time, but when a pope dies, much of the world immediately goes into mourning. Karol Wojtyła was Pope John Paul II and had been for more than twenty-six years. And while membership in his Roman Catholic Church had grown, the admiration for him was even stronger, reaching beyond the religion he led. He had survived the Nazi invasion of his homeland of Poland, fought for the end of Communism in Eastern Europe, lived through an assassination attempt, and consistently taken the side of those arguing for peace in many of the world's major struggles.

For Canadians, he had a special relationship with our country. No pope had visited Canada in the past, but John Paul II came three times. First, for a lengthy coast-to-coaster that saw huge crowds all along the way, including a million worshippers for a special mass in Toronto in 1984. Because bad weather had forced the cancellation of his stop in Fort Simpson, Northwest Territories, he went out of his way to make a special stop there in 1987. And in 2002, he was back in Toronto for the Church's World Youth Day.

For all of those reasons, his funeral would attract worldwide attention and would be one of those "global village" moments. Media from across the planet would be in attendance in Rome for the final goodbye.

Like dozens of other networks around the world, we at the CBC had been briefed for some time on the funeral plans, and as a result we had many of the needed tentative preparations already. Those included picking a hotel close to St. Peter's Basilica with a clear view of where the funeral service would take place. Our resources team had found the perfect spot which would also allow us access to the hotel roof to set up our remote anchoring facilities so we could connect with our broadcasting centre in Toronto and facilitate hours of live coverage. Once the death had been officially announced, our technical team headed for Rome to begin "building" what was in effect a temporary, portable studio atop one of the city's small, affordable hotels just blocks from what would be a "world is watching" event.

The day before the funeral, I flew into Rome to anchor that night's *National* and the funeral broadcast the next day. As soon as the car driving me in from the airport got close to Vatican City, I could see the obvious—the world truly was there. On rooftops and along the hills around St. Peter's Square were news anchor positions in the final stages of setting up for coverage that would cross borders and beliefs. This was not just a religious event. The Catholic Church had more than a billion members, but John Paul II had even more admirers.

Shortly after I arrived at our hotel, the producers called for an editorial meeting. We used a workroom the hotel had provided for us to house our editing equipment and store our cameras. We discussed the plan we'd follow for the next thirty-six hours: that night's *National*, the funeral broadcast the next day, and another *National* the following night after the funeral. Every topic, from technical issues to editorial story lines, was covered.

At one point there was a knock at the door. It was a priest, who said he was from the Vatican and there to help us. "Anything you need from background, guests, access, I can arrange all of that for you," he said, offering his business card. "Just call me on the number on my card."

It was a nice gesture and we replied appropriately.

But he wasn't finished. He looked at some papers on his clipboard. "Is there a Peter Mansbridge here?" he asked.

I raised my hand to acknowledge the question. "How can I help you?" I said.

The priest explained how all international broadcast hosts were being invited to St. Peter's to pay their respects to John Paul II, who was lying in state in the area beneath the basilica's dome.

This was something that probably would not be wise to turn down. My mind flashed with the memory of the hullabaloo caused by my colleague and friend Barbara Frum twenty-five years before. The Queen was coming for a visit, and Barbara had been invited to one of the reception lines to meet her. When asked by a reporter whether she'd practice curtsying, Barbara made headlines when she was quick with a reply: "I don't curtsy, for anyone." And she didn't.

This was a bit different. I thought not only was it an invite worth accepting for the detail it might provide for later commentary but, really, how do you say no to offering last respects to someone whom almost 40 percent of your own country worships? So off a group of us went with the priest in tow.

We went through a back entrance to St. Peter's and there before us was the huge area set aside for the lying in state. John Paul II's body was very visible in the centre of the room atop a low platform area. On the other side was the public line where people had been waiting for hours for their ten seconds before their pope. We asked the priest what the proper protocol was for those of us who were now clearly in a VIP line.

"Just walk up beside the body and privately reflect for thirty or forty-five seconds and then turn around and come back," he explained.

We did just that. We walked up and stood silently. I thought about what a remarkable man Karol Wojtyła had been, far beyond the Church he would eventually lead. How he'd almost been killed by the Nazis as they overran his native Poland in 1939, how he'd championed local causes as a priest, national causes as a cardinal, and global causes as pope. How his very public support of the Solidarity movement in Poland in the early 1980s had been the first openly successful revolt against Soviet rule and helped lead to the eventual end of Communism across Eastern Europe by the early 1990s. How, after the assassination attempt that had come within centimetres of killing him in 1981, he'd sought and gained an audience with the assassin to forgive him. There was very little not to admire about this man. I thought of all those things plus his visits to Canada and the fact I'd been lucky enough to meet him face-to-face twice.

And then we turned around, walked back to the rope line, thanked the priest, and headed to the hotel.

When we reentered the workroom, people were laughing and saying, "Hey, you guys were great!"

"What?" we asked.

"You were just on television and you really should watch it."

We were puzzled and intrigued, so we grabbed the tape and pushed play. It was CNN International with two anchors in London talking about some other world event when one interrupted and said, "We have to go to Rome. A very important person has just arrived to pay his last respects to John Paul II."

All the networks were using the same feed provided by the Vatican, and there was a wide shot taken from the opposite side of the Pope's body from where we had been standing, so John Paul II's body was in the foreground. The shot slowly zoomed in to include those paying their respects, and the closer it got, the more it seemed to be focused on me in the middle of our group.

"Yes," said the other anchor. "There he is."

"The president of Poland."

POSTSCRIPT

I often tell that story when I give speeches across the country. People seem to get quite a laugh out of it and I've even been asked to tell it again during second appearances to the same group. And at times, when I'm doing a book signing, someone will ask, "Can you please sign it 'President of Poland'?"

Overlooking the Vatican moments after a special broadcast on
the papal conclave in 2013. In the background is where the puffs
of smoke emerge. Left to right: Terry Auciello, Veronique Bernardini,
Michael Gruzuk, Lara Chatterjee, me, Dave Rae, and Tom Dinsmore.
Lara Chatterjee

Beg, Borrow, or Steal

Anyone looking at me must have wondered exactly what was going on. I was on my knees in front of a plush chair in an airport lounge in Bangkok, Thailand. The chair cushions had been removed and placed over my head while I leaned in toward the cushion-less chair seat.

Prepare yourself now for the dark underbelly of on-the-fly television news production.

The year was 2005, and *The National* had just finished a week of "on-the-road" broadcasts from Sri Lanka where we had anchored special coverage of the devastating tsunami that had taken more than two hundred thousand lives in Southeast Asia. Now we were on our way to Beijing, China, where we would anchor more special shows from the famous Forbidden City, the former palace residence of Chinese emperors during the Ming dynasty. Given the time difference, we had pretaped our last Sri Lanka show so we could be in Beijing in time to do our next show.

There was just one thing left to do to finish the Sri Lanka show: a broadcast-quality version of the audio headlines that run at the top of *The National*, and those needed to be done as close to air as possible because stories could be changing. So, the plan was to record the headlines during our three-hour stopover in Bangkok.

The only place to do that was in the airport lounge. And that's why I was kneeling on the floor, my head stuck under cushions. We were trying to create as close to studio-quality sound as possible by using the cushions to baffle the noise of clinking glasses and periodic Thai Airways announcements about flight departures. We test-recorded a few versions and finally decided what we had was acceptable broadcast quality.

That's when we realized that, despite all our equipment, we did not have a way to get our recorded "voice-overs" to Toronto. We didn't have the appropriate Thailand SIM cards to use our cell phones or laptops, and there was nowhere to buy one.

The next thing I knew, producer Jon Whitten was a couple seats over talking to a travelling American businessman, who we had seen chatting on his phone.

"Seriously?" I thought. "We're going to beg some guy we don't even know to use his phone to send parts of *The National* to Toronto?"

Yup, that's what we did. He looked justifiably suspicious, but he wouldn't take any money and it all worked out. The recordings were sent to Toronto and we boarded our plane for Beijing. That's where things took another turn.

After getting through customs and immigration, checking into the hotel, changing, and having a quick bite, we headed to the Forbidden City to do our next show. When we got to the palace complex, we saw the local satellite truck we had booked waiting outside on a side street, but there was no indication that it was hooked up to anything *inside*. No wires. No satellite dish pointed skyward. Nothing. Tom Dinsmore, our resource wizard, had a look of strain on his face.

That was our first hint that this was not going to be a normal shoot. While Tom connected with the satellite person to assess the situation, we went inside the Forbidden City to find out the broadcast location the Chinese government was going to let us use. The antique complex is spectacular, every building and every room, even the one they gave us to use as a workroom.

But it was almost empty. That was hint number two. There were no chairs, just one table and nothing else. We asked where the phone was and were shown a small hole in one wall. At one time, a phone plug might have been there, but now there was just a hole in the wall with a couple of fine wires sticking out.

We were just hours away from broadcasting an edition of *The National* that the CBC had been heavily promoting. None of us were that confident we'd ever make it, but no one gave up. I'd seen technical miracles before and had confidence in Tom. We all did.

He determined—and I'll make this as simple as possible though I'm sure it was much more complicated—that if we could hook up the camera to those wires in the hole in the wall, and also run a cable from the same wires across the courtyards to that truck on the side street, we'd somehow be able to get a signal back to Toronto. We had just enough cable to do that. Just enough.

Don't ask me how they did it, but minutes before we were supposed to go on air "live" from Beijing, the connection was made. I was standing on an empty camera box in front of one of the Forbidden City's historic temples when suddenly the dead air in my earpiece began to crackle and I heard a voice boom through: "Peter, this is Toronto, we can see you fine. Can you give us a ten count to check the audio?"

The magic of television.

"We see you." Broadcasting live from the Forbidden City in 2005.
Jon Whitten

Flight of a Lifetime

There is an old black-and-white photo on one of the shelves of my home office bookcase in Stratford, Ontario. I look at it often because I think it captures the moment that began my lifelong fascination with airplanes and air travel.

It was taken in 1951 in Penang, Malaya. It shows me three years old standing with my sister, Wendy, and my mother, all three of us posing for my father on a tarmac directly in front of a Malaysian Airways DC-3. At the time, the DC-3 (also nicknamed a "Dakota" or a "Gooney Bird") was one of the largest passenger aircraft in the world. It was a huge success; first built in the mid-1930s, it starred on a number of fronts in the Second World War before achieving an unparalleled record of longevity in the highly competitive world of aviation. In fact, it's still used all over the world, including in northern Canada. But on that day, the DC-3 was making a different kind of history, at least for me. You see, I was about to board my first flight: a short hop to the Malayan capital of Kuala Lumpur. I loved the thrill of being in the air and have never looked back.

While that 1951 flight was my first, it would not compare to the many experiences that were to come. I've been around the world a few times, travelled to every continent except Antarctica (I'm working on it!), and totalled—by rough calculation, at least with Air Canada's Aeroplan—millions of miles in the air. But one flight in particular will always stay with me.

It came overseas on an assignment in 2006. During the war in Afghanistan, flying in and out of the country's capital was one thing; flying around Afghanistan was quite another. Commercial airlines still

My first flight.
Stanley Mansbridge

operated internationally in and out of Kabul, a tricky airport at the best of times because it's surrounded by mountains. But during the height of the conflict—from 2001 to 2010—coalition forces banned long, slow, deliberate approaches, fearing Taliban fighters firing or launching missiles from the hills, and instead called on flights to almost dive into a landing. It made for some harrowing touchdowns and takeoffs, but if you wanted to get from Kabul to a city in the country's south, like Kandahar, you either took a long and dangerous drive or you hitched a ride with the military (if you had the right passport).

In March of 2006, as Canada's Afghanistan role shifted from Kabul to the hotspot of Kandahar, our CBC team was hoping to get into the new Canadian base at Kandahar to host *The National* for a week. After recovering from our "dive" into Kabul, there seemed to be some confusion about how we'd get south to Kandahar. We thought we had arranged for the Canadian Armed Forces to fly us there, and when we saw a CAF Hercules aircraft on the ground in Kabul, we assumed it was for us. Not according to the crew. They didn't seem keen at all to take us. We had also spotted an RAF aircraft on the tarmac, and so we began negotiating with them. I'm not sure exactly what happened next, but it seems that when the Canadians saw us dealing with the British, they suddenly became more available. But, let's just say, this wasn't going to be like a normal commercial flight. Far from it.

We were told a couple of reasons for what followed. One was that the plane was having "issues" at normal altitudes for that flight of over twenty thousand feet, which was a relatively safe height beyond any likely enemy ground response. This meant that our trip would instead have to be a low-level flight, hugging the ground just a few hundred feet off the deck for more than an hour and a half. The other reason was somewhat similar—the crew wanted to practice low-level navigation.

Our cameraman, Dave Rae, saw an opportunity. He looked at me and said, "Let's ask to go up front and we'll record the trip. We'll get fabulous aerials."

And that's what we did. The pilots gave their okay, and the next thing we knew, Dave and I were in the cockpit getting organized for what was going to be a spectacular show. And what a place to witness the flight from. The cockpit in a C-130 Hercules is huge. For Dave and me, there was a cushioned bench to sit and strap in, but after takeoff we would be allowed to stand and move freely around the cockpit to get the shots we needed.

The other members of our crew were in the back with their baggage and the cargo. If you've ever been in a Herc, it's not exactly the most comfortable space for passengers. The few windows were very small, which can make it hard to feel settled, and there weren't any individual seats. Instead, there was a kind of lawn-chair netting stretching lengthwise on either side of the fuselage. Despite that, for normal flights it's pretty smooth, but this wasn't a normal flight. They were going to have to learn to hold on to whatever they could grab.

Starting with the takeoff. We didn't fly over the mountains; we flew through them. As we slipped through narrow passes, there were times I could have sworn the wingtips missed scraping the edges of rock by centimetres. We'd bank left, then quickly right. We'd go up a few hundred feet and then quickly down a few hundred feet. Talk about an adrenaline rush. It was a thrill a minute for ninety minutes. I didn't even want to think about how those in the back were doing. But I sure was glad I was up front where I could see what was going on.

Shortly after takeoff, Dave was up and moving around. He's a big guy and we've travelled all over the world together. Nothing seems to faze him, and this didn't either. Me on the other hand, I was trying to keep up with him, but after a while I started wondering to myself, "Where's the bag?"

Now, don't get me wrong. It was exhilarating. This wasn't covering a flood in southern Manitoba, this was the real deal. We were dancing just feet above the barren Afghan landscape in the middle of a war zone, and I had to marvel at the courage and the skill of the crew flying this machine.

We're used to seeing two pilots sitting up front, following the instruments, and guiding the aircraft from A to B. This was a lot more than that. Standing behind the pilots with one hand on the shoulder of the lead pilot was the navigator. His other hand held a map that had everything marked on it, from villages and roads to hills, mountains, and valleys. It was super detailed right down to the heights of each feature and any known danger spots where the Taliban had been seen. He had the course marked out that would take us to our destination but at the same time keep us out of trouble. And every few seconds he would bark out a direction for the pilots: "Turn ten degrees left" followed quickly by "thirty degrees right" then "up two hundred feet" and a few seconds later "down one hundred feet." This was intense stuff. At least it was for me—everyone else in the cockpit seemed to be taking it in stride.

We had been warned before takeoff that if we encountered any form of ground fire, an alarm would go off. And sure enough, about halfway along our route, cockpit lights started flashing and an alarm signaled that a sensor had detected incoming fire. Nothing hit, and nothing much happened, although everyone was very focused and the pilots took some basic evasive action. I dared not ask, but I still think maybe that was all part of a training moment, or that they wanted to give us a bit of a taste of what it could be like.

As we got closer to Kandahar and the tossing and turning kept on, I decided it really was time to find that bag. Eventually I did, and sat down convinced that any moment there was going to be an eruption from my stomach. I opened the bag and held it close. I wretched. Nothing. I tried again. Nothing. Nobody in the cockpit turned to look at me, thank God, but I'm sure they all heard. Dave was not impressed, that much I could tell. While I'm sure I was white, he looked like he was ready for a hamburger with all the dressings.

Upon landing, I'd somehow made it. The bag was empty. I folded it neatly as if there had never been an issue and placed it back where I'd found it. I tried not to think of what might be happening in the back, where my colleagues had been thrown around for the whole trip with nothing to look at except strapped-down cargo. Poor buggers. Not fair, but hey, you know what they say, "Anchoring has its privileges."

The Colonel

Sometimes I simply can't understand why the men and women of the military put up with those of us in the media. Especially in a war zone. It's not that they don't already have enough to worry about, finding themselves, as they do, in constant life-or-death situations. Yet here we are, journalists, wanting them to give us a front-row seat in the middle of dangerous operations so we can tell the story to audiences back home.

In exchange for getting access, we obey the rules the military sets for us. It's pretty basic stuff actually, like no reporting on possible future operations and no going off the base on your own. We agree to stay within the boundaries, literal and physical, that are placed on us, and in return they house us, feed us, and protect us. But, still, we get in the way and there must be times the men and women on the front lines of Canada's defences wish we would just stay home. But if they do feel that way, they rarely show it, and in my experience they've almost always been helpful.

I was in Afghanistan twice during the major combat years—once in 2003, once in 2006. During that first trip, where we broadcasted for a week out of the Canadian base, Camp Julien, in Kabul, we asked for the military to take us on a few of their patrols, both in vehicles and on foot. They agreed. Those were the early days of the war, a time when local Afghans seemed to welcome coalition forces onto their land and into their villages. After all, these were the same foreign forces that had kicked the dreaded Taliban out of power. I can remember sitting atop an armoured personnel carrier, and as we drove through small villages in the countryside outside Kabul it was not uncommon to be greeted by smiles, waves, and cheers from both children and adults.

When I returned to Afghanistan three years later, there had been a shift. The patrols were tenser, and the reactions were a lot less welcoming. As we drove through some of the villages, many of the children would either frown or they would turn their backs. Five years of conflict, five years of the heavy machinery of war rumbling by their homes, the constant harassment of the Taliban—it was all taking its toll. It was one of the first times I began to sense this was an unwinnable war.

Afghanistan had always been a dangerous mission, but by 2006, roadside bombs were common and Canadian fatalities were beginning to mount. In one terribly bizarre incident, a Canadian officer, Captain Trevor Greene, was attacked with an axe to the head, during what had been planned as a routine meeting with local leaders. That was a week before we arrived.

So, it was in that atmosphere in March of 2006 that we asked for special access. We wanted to get some aerial pictures in two key areas: one, south and west of Kandahar at a forward operating base near the Pakistan border, and the second, north and west of Kandahar over the village where Captain Greene had been attacked. The best way to achieve these goals was by helicopter. Unfortunately, Canada didn't have the

Getting ready to broadcast *The National*
live from Afghanistan.
Mark Harrison

choppers designed for those kinds of missions then; only the Americans, with their Black Hawk helicopters, did. The request went in, but I wasn't holding my breath as now we were asking for the goodwill of two countries, so getting the "sorry, no flights available" response was twice as likely. Which is why it came as a bit of a surprise when they said, "We can make that happen." We were told to be at the Kandahar airfield early the next morning.

I was excited. I'd been on a Black Hawk before with the Israelis in 2002, but I'd never been on one with American forces. The Black Hawk was the first post-Vietnam helicopter the US forces had purchased. That was in 1976. Despite constant rumours that it would be replaced, most observers now think that the Black Hawk, updated when needed, will still be around in the middle of this century. It's been a proven workhorse at all levels: as a transport aircraft; as a powerful war machine with its machine guns, rockets, and missiles; and as a highly manoeuvrable chopper that can operate at a hundred miles an hour just a few feet off the ground. It's also easy to move around the country, or the world, as it fits inside a C-130 Hercules.

Now, mind you, it still occasionally gets shot down by enemy fire—as one did in the movie *Black Hawk Down*, which chronicled a disastrous US raid on insurgents in Somalia in 1993. But that was probably the wrong thing to be thinking about as cameraman Dave Rae and I walked across the tarmac toward the spot where the fabled helicopter was waiting for us with its doors removed. The doors had been taken off for two reasons: first, so the gunners could aim their weapons of war toward any hostile forces if they appeared on the ground, and second, so Dave could get clear access for the camera shots he was hoping to record.

There was another passenger travelling with us on that day: a senior coalition officer. I think he was a colonel. All we'd been told was that he was scouting a possible operation which was planned for the days ahead in a location we'd be passing over. We were to ignore him and we did. We never spoke.

Ever since the hunt for Osama bin Laden had begun in the hours after the 9/11 attacks, there was a sense the Al Qaeda leader could be hiding out in one of the myriad caves in the rugged landscape of southern Afghanistan close to the Pakistan border. And that's exactly where we were flying within minutes of lifting off from the Kandahar base. We weren't that high, almost the same height as the mountaintops off to one side of us. I'd be lying if I didn't admit that while I was staring at the mountains, I was actually looking for caves and people who might be in them. After all, that would have been some kind of scoop: "Canadian TV crew finds bin Laden in Afghan mountaintop hideout."

I never saw anyone. Certainly no six-foot-five guy with a beard. In fact, I never saw a cave either.

The first pass on the flight was over Spin Boldak, a forward operating base on the border with Pakistan. There was great concern that the border was porous, that Taliban soldiers were going back and forth into Pakistan with little resistance. The FOB had set up patrols to try to prevent that, so far without any major success. The French had been operating the base but were about to hand those responsibilities over to the Canadians.

Then we flew on to our next stop, Gumbat, to the north and west of Spin Buldak, where the axe attack had taken place the week before. That's when the colonel on board perked up. This was clearly the area he wanted to scout. He had a pile of notes and maps with markings on them resting on his knee and attached to a clip built into his battle fatigues, and he was flipping through them as he instructed the flight crew over the Black Hawk intercom where to go. The pilots followed his directions, flying back and forth over an area that looked quite fertile and well irrigated—very different from the barren, hilly area near the border. He jotted down notes, and Dave and I respected the secrecy and confidence he clearly wanted.

Then he gave another direction to the pilots, and this time they banked suddenly. Too suddenly, I guess, because for the colonel it spelled disaster.

The notes, dozens of them, slipped out from under the clip on his fatigues. The door-less helicopter began its magic. The vacuum caused by the draft started sucking the notes toward the open space. It felt like it was all happening in slow motion. The notes flew out where the door had been. Every single one. We all tried to grab them as they passed by, but we weren't quick enough. The next thing we knew, there were all these handwritten notes and maps fluttering downward like big flakes of snow.

I looked at Dave. He looked at me. If one of us had so much as smiled, we would both have broken into a boisterous laugh. We didn't. But we also dared not look at the colonel. We had just witnessed, we supposed, the battle plan for an upcoming operation floating toward the enemy.

Needless to say, we never heard about a special operation mounted around Gumbat in the immediate days that followed.

Pearl-Coloured Toyotas

Everyone knows who Osama bin Laden was, but how many remember Mullah Omar?

Omar was the one-eyed former Mujahideen fighter who successfully fought against the Russians, helping kick them out of Afghanistan, and then led the Taliban government that took over the country. He was vicious, leading public executions in the Kabul soccer stadium; brutally pulling girls out of school, refusing them education; and blowing up centuries-old religious symbols. He also provided refuge in his country for Al Qaeda and its leader, bin Laden.

After 9/11, the United States gave Omar an ultimatum: give up bin Laden or be bombed into submission. He chose the latter and disappeared when the bombs started falling. So did bin Laden.

One person who didn't disappear was another Mullah—Mullah Naqib, also known as Mullah Naqibullah, one of Omar's key Mujahideen commanders and Taliban fighters. He decided his fighting days were over, severed his Taliban ties, and instead cut a deal with the Americans, giving them advice on how to fight his old friends in return for his freedom.

In 2006, I met Mullah Naqib at his rambling compound outside Kandahar in southern Afghanistan. He had shared the compound area with Mullah Omar, but the leader's buildings were mostly destroyed by US bombing runs in the days after 9/11. What wasn't destroyed were Omar's personal vehicles, which were known around the country: a pair of luxurious, pearl-coloured Toyota Land Cruisers–XV Limited Editions. Naqib owned them now and wanted me to see them, so he escorted me over to the garage area where both vehicles were kept parked inside. It was an odd sight—a country still so primitive in so many respects but where the gleaming twin Toyotas, sporting their leather seats and CD players, told a story of power and privilege.

Then it was time for the reason I'd come to meet with Naqib: an interview. By tradition, he wanted it outside on a large, living room–sized Afghan rug draped across the grass of his garden. We sat on the rug, face-to-face, surrounded by his supporters, and discussed the current state of the conflict between the coalition forces, including Canada, and the Al Qaeda–backed Taliban trying to take back power. He was not encouraging about how the battle was going. And even less encouraging after the formal part of the interview was completed.

As we walked in his garden, he told me that if the coalition forces couldn't defeat the Taliban within the next year, they would lose whatever support they had achieved with the Afghan people. "They just want peace," was his clear message, even if that meant being ruled again by the Taliban.

The Mullah draws a crowd.
Carmen Merrifield

He was right. Like so many foreign invaders throughout history, the coalition forces were never able to declare an outright victory in Afghanistan. Canada pulled out of its combat role and retreated home in 2014. The United States signed a peace treaty with the Taliban in 2020 and began its withdrawal.

POSTSCRIPT

Mullah Omar is said to have died of tuberculosis in 2013. Not everyone believes that.

Mullah Naqib had a heart attack and died in 2007, a year after our interview, a year in which he had told me the Taliban had to be defeated or they never would be.

I don't know where the pearl-coloured Toyotas are today.

The Northwest Passage

Between long overseas flights where connections are involved, I typically head for the airline lounge and try to find a quiet corner to relax, even catch a bit of a nap if the time allows. That's what I was doing in April of 2006. I was in the Air Canada lounge in Frankfurt; I'd just been in Tel Aviv and Jerusalem on assignment for an interview with the then Israeli prime minister Ehud Olmert about the latest attempts to find a solution to peace in the Middle East.

Those are frustrating interviews because it always seems no solution can ever be found. But you never give up hope. I remember in 1988 sitting with Barbara Frum in her dressing room at the CBC in Toronto. She was the host of *The Journal* and I was host of *The National*, and we were debating whether Nelson Mandela, in a South African prison, would ever see freedom. We were both pessimistic about the chances, because the racist policy of apartheid seemed so set in stone in South Africa. Two years later, Barbara was sitting in Mandela's front yard on the day he was released from twenty-seven years behind bars. So, you never know.

Back to Frankfurt. That day I was exhausted from my quick trip in and out of Israel and hoping to be left alone in the lounge. But that wasn't to be. I noticed a man walking in my direction. He seemed friendly enough, but he had that look you learn to spot when you're on television. The look of recognition. It's not uncommon to be recognized and not uncommon for people to want to talk. Sometimes they want to confront you about something they didn't like on the news, but usually they're very polite. After all, we're Canadian!

"Hi, you're Peter Mansbridge, right?" he asked, pulling up a chair.

"Yes, that's correct. And you?"

"My name is Marty Bergmann, and I'm a big fan of yours and *The National*."

"That's very kind of you, Marty. What do you do?"

"I'm with Fisheries and Oceans Canada in Winnipeg and I've just been at a climate conference here in Germany."

I was a little surprised. Fisheries and Oceans in Winnipeg? Didn't quite seem to make sense. "I'm puzzled. Why Winnipeg?"

He smiled a smile I would get very used to over the next five years.

"One of my jobs," he explained, "is to coordinate with the Canadian Coast Guard's icebreaker fleet for their summer Arctic voyages. We go on some of them to monitor the changing Arctic ice patterns." He leaned in, clearly wanting to make a point. "Things are happening and you, Peter, should be there."

In fact, I'd become increasingly interested in the climate story and had been looking at innovative ways for *The National* to get into the issue. We used to cover stories like this with the old "on one hand, on the other hand" approach, climate activists and climate deniers getting more or less equal time. But those days were disappearing with the overwhelming scientific and anecdotal evidence on the side of those arguing that climate change was happening and happening fast. Ironically, when Marty approached me, I was holding a recent copy of *TIME* magazine in my hand, and the cover story was on climate change and the threat it posed.

Almost as a silly dare, I responded: "Marty, if you can get me and my crew on an icebreaker going through the Northwest Passage this summer, we will broadcast 'live' for a week, telling great climate stories."

He didn't even pause. "I can do that."

Three months later, I was standing on the back deck of the CCGS *Louis S. St-Laurent*, Canada's largest and oldest icebreaker, cutting through the ice of the fabled Passage, welcoming Canadians to a part of their country almost all had never seen, and most never would.

It had been a remarkable achievement on everyone's part. Within

Breaking through the ice of the Northwest Passage in 2006.
CBC

minutes of leaving that Frankfurt lounge, I was sitting on an Air Canada flight about to leave for Toronto, emailing my executive producer,
Jon Whitten, a journalist as adventurous as me. I told him about the
idea and about Marty, gave him Marty's email address, and suggested
that he and our technical producer wizard Tom Dinsmore should get
on it. Jon leapt at the idea, so did Tom, and within days so did everyone
else at the CBC, Fisheries and Oceans, and most important the coast
guard, and a roughed-out plan was in the making. But it wasn't going
to be easy—simply getting a live signal up from our satellite dish on a
moving icebreaker in the High Arctic to a satellite above the Earth was a
challenge. Our satellite dish was huge; it was also anchored on the deck,
and there were moments when the technicians had to move it by hand
a millimetre at a time to keep contact with our home base in Toronto.

But it worked. Those five nights, which we called "Our Changing
Arctic," were fascinating. Each night our audiences grew as word spread.
Together, we all learned how the ice was disappearing at record rates,
how Inuit hunters and fishers were having to adapt, how the coastline

was changing because of the erosion caused by rising waters, and how our sovereignty was at stake—more open water meaning more shipping, some of it international. It was a summer experience unlike any other, and those who saw it have never forgotten it. I still have people come up to me and recount where they were in the summer of 2006 when they watched our Arctic voyage.

It was one of those moments where we delivered 100 percent on our mandate of being the nation's public broadcaster. We did something other networks would never have tried in those days because of the cost and the risk. But we did it and, as a result, gave Canadians, Canadians who own the CBC, a sense of their country in a way they'd never seen before, and on an issue that was about to change the country in a way they had never considered.

And it all started with me trying to hide out in a corner of a lounge in the Frankfurt airport. And a chance meeting with a Fisheries and Oceans guy from Winnipeg named Marty Bergmann.

I'd started my career in the North with that bizarre beginning in Churchill, Manitoba, but that was just a tease. Pierre Trudeau once said, "You have not seen Canada until you have seen the North." Marty gave me that chance to see the North, by icebreaker, by Twin Otter, by planes with skis landing on the ice of the Beaufort Sea. There is nothing like the North; it's spectacular, and I'm so lucky to have spent so much time enjoying it.

But it's more than just natural beauty. It's also history.

One night on that first 2006 voyage through the Passage, we played "Northwest Passage" through the ship's intercom system. The classic Stan Rogers folk song is written about Sir John Franklin, the man who died looking for the waterway that we were moving peacefully along at that moment. It runs almost five minutes. We played it once. Twice. Maybe more. It left many of us in tears.

"Ah for just one time, I would take the Northwest Passage
To find the hand of Franklin reaching for the Beaufort Sea;

Tracing one warm line through a land so wide and savage,
And make a Northwest Passage to the Sea."

We all sang along as best we could. Marty no less than anyone. We robustly toasted Stan Rogers for his tribute to Franklin and the Passage. Rogers himself had died in a plane crash in 1983, just two years after releasing the song.

Marty Bergmann became a close friend, and over the next five years we travelled the Arctic together and talked about its possibilities. He knew that if I was passionate about it, then the odds were I'd use my influence to encourage the CBC to stay passionate about it too. And that's why he approached me that day in Frankfurt. It wasn't about being a "fan." He knew if he could get me interested, he might be able to impact hundreds of thousands of others too. He was right.

In August of 2011, Marty was on his way to Resolute as head of Canada's Polar Continental Shelf Program when the plane he was in crashed. He did not survive. Canada lost a good man that day in Resolute, and the Arctic lost a loyal friend.

The one and only Marty Bergmann.
Stephanie Jenzer

True Celebrity

Sitting in a pub in Scotland is an experience. It's often noisy. There's usually a soccer—excuse me—football game on the "telly" up on the wall. And there is almost always a wonderful collection of characters in pretty much every direction you look. The Scots love their drink, love their football, and love being heard above the din. It all makes me and my golfing buddies look a bit out of place. Annually, a group of us head to Scotland, the home of golf, to whack the little white ball around the links courses we love. None of us are really that good at the game, but we do have fun. And sitting in a Scottish pub is all part of the routine.

On one particular day in early June 2008, we carried on the tradition by finding a spot we tend to frequent in a little town inland from the coastline. Soaking up the local atmosphere was perfect until the din was—somewhat—broken by the ring of my cell phone. Not a smart move. There was not a single approving eye glancing my way as I clumsily grabbed for the phone, pushing every button to try to turn the ringer off.

"Can you hold on just a minute, please?" I said into the phone, and then rushed out of the pub.

It was evening, but the northern Scottish June days often stay bright until late into the night, so it was still daylight as I stood in the parking lot.

I raised the phone back to my mouth. "Peter Mansbridge here, how can I help you?"

"Mr. Mansbridge," a woman's voice came through. "I'm calling from the Chancellery of Honours at Government House in Ottawa. Do you have a minute?"

What could this be about? I thought. "Yes, I do," I replied. "But I should warn you I'm standing in a parking lot in Scotland and I can't vouch for the reception."

"I can hear you fine. I just have to ask you one question." I assumed the caller was asking for my reference on someone but no, that's not what the call was about. "Mr. Mansbridge," she said, "the Order of Canada committee has voted to award you the Order of Canada, but before we make it official we need to make sure that if you are awarded this honour you will accept it?"

I was stunned. I asked her to repeat herself just in case I'd misheard what she had said. She did. Slowly.

I blurted out my acceptance, barely able to contain my excitement. I felt like saying I'd crawl over a mile of broken glass to get there if that's what it would take, but surely that would be unseemly for a soon-to-be Officer of the Order of Canada.

"Well, that's wonderful, and please let me be the first to congratulate you," the woman said. "Now, we do have one simple request. This will not be announced until July first, and until that time we ask you not to say anything to anyone."

"Of course, I understand."

And that was that. I was going to become an Officer of the Order of Canada, the country's highest civilian honour. I was humbled. And a bit sad. My mother would have absolutely cherished this moment, but she had passed away just a few months before, my father a few years before that. They'd been disappointed when I'd dropped out of school and then the same with the navy, but successes in journalism had made them proud. This would have been the proverbial icing on the cake.

I walked back into the pub. It was even more boisterous than when I'd left it. My buddies didn't seem to be interested in who had called or why, and I couldn't tell them anyway.

It was a strange feeling and reminded me of a story the former

governor general Ray Hnatyshyn had once told me. Ray was a friend. I'd
known him since his days as a lawyer in Saskatoon in the early 1970s,
when I was the CBC's national reporter in the province. He became an
MP, then a cabinet minister; then one day after he'd lost his seat in the
free-trade election of 1988, he was summoned to the prime minister's
summer residence at Harrington Lake. It was there that Brian Mulroney asked him to be Canada's twenty-fourth governor general. He
accepted and, after a short chat, went out to his car to drive to Ottawa.
But he hesitated before getting into the car, turned around, and headed
back to the front door where the prime minister was standing, ready to
wave goodbye.

"Prime Minister, can I ask one favour?" Ray began.

"Absolutely."

"Prime Minister, you have explained that I can't say anything about
this until it's officially announced, and I understand that." And then
came the famous Hnatyshyn sense of humour. "But if something happens to me on the drive back to Ottawa or before the announcement
is made, can you at least tell my mother that I was going to be the next
governor general?"

Ray used to love telling that story, and now years later I felt the same
way. It was almost a month before the announcement on the Order of
Canada was going to be made, and I couldn't tell anyone. Not even these
half-hammered guys in the Scottish pub!

I kept my part of the bargain and stayed silent until it was made official on July 1st of 2008. And then in the spring of 2009, my investiture
into the Order took place inside the main hall of Rideau Hall in front of
Governor General Michaëlle Jean.

I stood alongside some people I knew, former cabinet ministers like
Donald Johnston, former premiers like Frank McKenna, and two of my
sports heroes, golfer Mike Weir and hockey player Willie O'Ree. We
were among the "celebrity"—and I use that term loosely—honorees
that day. In other words, people knew who we were because our profes-

With Governor General Michaëlle Jean.
Rideau Hall

sional lives were in the public eye. But you know what? We weren't the real stars of the moment.

As I stood there listening to the emcee of the event read a few biographical lines about each person and watching the governor general place the Order around their neck, I was humbled. Some of the descriptions were so powerful in their simplicity. David Thauberger of Regina for his preservation of folk art in Saskatchewan; Shirley Westeinde of Ottawa for her volunteerism in the areas of health and education; Elinor Ratcliffe of St. John's for her philanthropy in charities and the arts in Newfoundland and Labrador; Ross Petty of Vancouver for helping improve the lives of children afflicted with rheumatic diseases; James Morrison of Halifax for his service in helping preserve Nova Scotia's multicultural heritage, especially its oral histories; and the list went on. These were people who were heroes, "celebrities" in their own communities. I sat in awe of their accomplishments.

When it was all over, I looked at the person next to me, another so-called celebrity, and said, "Listening to what so many of those people have achieved, and done for their communities, makes me wonder just how we got to be in this room with them."

The majority of those who received their Orders of Canada that day—and at most of the ceremonies—are not "celebrities." They are just ordinary people who believe in Canada and believe in the idea of "service." They're special, and so are these occasions that celebrate them.

POSTSCRIPT

While I wished my parents had been alive to see me receive this honour, I was comforted by the fact that my sister, my wife, and one of my daughters witnessed it all firsthand.

The Obama Thing

I first became aware of Barack Obama in the summer of 2004. At that time, he was in local politics, but he was about to launch onto the world stage.

The Illinois state senator had been picked as the keynote speaker for the Democratic National Convention, which would endorse John Kerry as its presidential candidate to run against George W. Bush in that year's November election. Before the convention, Obama was little known outside of his own state, and it could have stayed that way, because the commercial networks ignored his speech. But PBS and C-SPAN did not, and millions were enthralled by what they heard. Basically he knocked it out of the park with his vision of an America that could be united by a common purpose.

"There is not a liberal America and a conservative America. . . . There is not a black America, a white America, a Latino America, an Asian America—there's the United States of America."

His speech clocked out at only seventeen minutes, but it was constantly interrupted by applause and standing ovations. Thirty-three times.

A star was born.

In the end, Kerry lost the presidential election, but Obama won his, vaulting to the United States Senate as the junior senator from Illinois. Some people thought that someday, well down the road, maybe, he could be considered for a presidential run. But Obama was ambitious and convinced that the presumed Democratic candidate for 2008, Hillary Clinton, was not a shoo-in.

It was while he was a U.S. senator that I first tried to convince his office that an interview for Canadian television would be a good thing. The pitch was simple—the senator was garnering major interest as a rising figure in US politics both inside and outside the United States. We wanted to know more about his vision for the future. It didn't work. Nor did it after he secured the presidential nomination. Or during the actual race. Some of our calls didn't even get answered.

But then he won, and days after the inauguration we started trying again. My producer Leslie Stojsic pushed her contacts. Our Washington producer Samira Hussain worked hers, including going to press secretary Robert Gibbs's daily press briefings in the White House and positioning herself in such a way that Gibbs had to walk past and hear her daily pleas for an interview. And I talked to a number of mutual friends, people who knew both Obama and me separately. We tried everything, but nothing seemed to work.

Until the Monday afternoon of the long weekend in February, just a month after the inauguration. My phone rang at our Georgian Bay cottage and it was Samira. "The White House says if you are here tomorrow morning at nine a.m., you can have ten minutes with the president."

I didn't need to know anything else. I drove the two hours to Toronto, grabbed a suit, a few shirts and ties, and headed for the airport. While Leslie and Samira were consumed with the logistics of cameras and editing, I was consumed with the editorial side—I could easily do a one-hour interview, but ten minutes was going to be a much greater challenge. This was the most powerful person in the world, and only a month into the job he was faced with an economic crisis, an energy crisis, and a climate crisis—not to mention that he was leading much of the world, including Canada, in a war in Afghanistan. It was a long list. Despite all that, I actually slept soundly that night in the old Willard Hotel just a few blocks from the White House.

Shortly before eight, I began my walk toward the White House and I thought about the significance of this moment for the CBC. Canada's public broadcaster had been around since it was brought into being by the Conservative government of R. B. Bennett in the early 1930s, but this was the first time a CBC correspondent had a private, sit-down, one-on-one with the president of the United States. I was excited.

Leslie met me at the security gate on Pennsylvania Avenue, and within minutes I was ushered into the room where the interview would take place. We'd hoped for the Oval Office in the West Wing, but beggars can't be choosers. We wound up in the main backup room, known as the Map Room, where many presidential interviews are done—fireplace in the background, oil paintings from the 1700s on the wall. But it was actually hard to see any of that because the room was crowded. Aside from our six-person CBC crew, there were Secret Service people, the press secretary's staff, comms staff, household staff, and many others whom I had no idea of what they were doing.

I asked one of them, "What time will the president arrive?"

The answer was short and to the point. "9:13 and you better be ready."

I felt like saying, "Really? 9:13, not 9:14?" But I didn't. Somehow I didn't think the Mansbridge humour was going to work in this room.

I went next door, usually the White House medical office, to get a powder. And then all was ready.

At 9:13, the biggest rock star in the world at that moment walked into the room with his hand outstretched.

"Welcome to the White House, Peter, it's great to have you with us."

Gibbs was at one side of him, and principal advisor David Axelrod was just steps behind.

Alright then, I thought. Game on.

We squeezed a lot into the twelve minutes we talked. And we made a few headlines, including his honest admission—one that turned out to be quite accurate—that the war in Afghanistan wasn't necessarily winnable.

And then as quickly as it started it was over. We shook hands, and he left the same way he'd entered, with handlers moving him along. He had the presidential helicopter, Marine One, already warming up outside to take him to Andrews Air Force Base where Air Force One would fly him to his next event.

I turned to Samira, who had been sitting on the floor beside us just out of camera range. She had been there to take notes during the interview.

"So, Samira, how did it go?" I asked.

Now, keep in mind, Samira, like Leslie, was one of our best. Both were smart journalists who would go far in the business. Award winners in journalism school and destined for the same results on the job.

"I didn't hear a word he said," she replied.

"What? You were sitting right there!"

"He's so gorgeous."

Everyone in the room—and there were a lot of them still hanging about—laughed. Samira wasn't the slightest bit embarrassed. She, like most of the rest of the world in those early Obama days, was hooked.

Samira Hussain (in the white blouse) with some guys in the
foreground almost blocking her shot.
Leslie Stojsic

And then there was noise in the doorway. Obama was back with his handlers and a very tall man at his side. Obama himself is at least six foot two, so this chap must have been six five or more.

"Peter, I have someone you have to meet," he said.

I was taken aback. You have to understand what those words sound like. The president of the United States coming back to see *you* because he has determined he has someone that *you*, the one-time baggage handler from Churchill, have to meet.

Before I could get my jaw off the floor, he looked toward this giant of a fellow beside him and said, "This is Marvin Nicholson. He works with me." A pause for effect. "He's from *Victoria!*"

Yup, the president of the United States, taking time out of his day to bring a Canadian back into the room to meet, as Marvin's mother later told me, "someone he used to watch on television during his school years."

We all had a few laughs. Marvin was the president's go-to sports guy, and during the presidency when Obama was playing basketball or golf, Marvin was always with him.

"He's got no game. He's no Steve Nash," said Obama with a smile, connecting with me on another Canadian angle.

Then Marvin reached out to shake my hand and uttered words I never expected to hear in the White House. "My mother loves you!"

Aides were now tapping their watches, trying to keep the president on schedule, and so the contingent finally headed out the door, but not before the man himself said, "Come and watch the helicopter take off. It's really neat."

Neat? Clearly this was someone new to the job and nothing was routine. Yet. He'd learn.

POSTSCRIPT

Barack Obama visited Canada two days after our interview, and his rock-star status was solidified in our country. Crowds were large, the welcome was five stars, and even Stephen Harper admitted to me he was caught up in the whole Obama "thing." Over the next four years, the forty-fourth president of the United States did encounter some rocky times at home and had to fight hard for a second term, which he won. His fan base in Canada never wavered and he remains extremely popular whenever he visits.

Marvin Nicholson served in both terms of the Obama presidency, and today he and his family live in Jacksonville, Florida. Playing less basketball than he used to, but more golf, and his family says he crushes his drives 350 yards. His mom, apparently, still loves me.

Leslie Stojsic remained my main producer for two of my shows—"At Issue" on The National and my One on One series—until she relocated to Ottawa as a senior producer on the News Network broadcast Power and Politics. She moved cities again—and networks—to take the job as executive producer of Global National, based in Vancouver. We are still close and talk often, with the Obama interview a frequent cause of laughs.

Samira Hussain disputes everything I say about her in this story (It's all true!) except for one thing. She does agree she's a great journalist. I can attest to the fact because she keeps proving it. After her Washington time was up, she wanted to move up the ladder, which she deserved to. In their wisdom, the CBC felt she needed more time, so she bolted to the BBC. She's now their correspondent in New York and a damn good one. CBC's loss was BBC's gain.

The Edge of the Earth

Coming in to land on Prince Leopold Island takes your breath away. Peaking up above the waters, the island is completely flat, an oval shape almost a thousand feet above the water with a tantalizing sheer drop from all around. What struck me on this particular day in 2008 was how much it resembled a tree stump perfectly cut off by a chain saw not far off the ground—and, of course, how we were going to land on this tiny slip of ground at the junction of Prince Regent Inlet and the Barrow Strait, not far from Lancaster Sound in Nunavut.

Producer Carmen Merrifield, cameraman Peter Zin, and I were in our favourite Arctic aircraft, a Twin Otter, which is made for short landings and takeoffs. To pull off a landing, you must come in low, almost as if you were aiming directly at the daunting rock cliffs seemingly holding the island up. In fact, some of us were convinced sudden impact was only moments away as we saw the rock face looming directly in front of us. But of course that's not what happened. At the right moment, the pilot pulled the stick back, and the plane rose and landed on the flat surface above. We all breathed just a little bit easier.

We were in the Arctic as part of our continuing series looking at the ongoing effects of climate change. Prince Leopold Island is the most important breeding area for marine birds in Canada's North, and on this trip we were checking on migratory bird patterns and the natural food supplies for the different breeds to determine just how everything was changing. We met ecologist Tony Gaston, who had spent many a lonely summer in a small shack on the island studying just that. We called him "the birdman of the Arctic."

Gaston took us to a spectacular lookout at the edge to see one of the

Prince Leopold Island: a landing to remember.

breeding grounds below where thick-billed murres, northern fulmars, and black-legged kittiwakes mated and raised their young. In all, more than two hundred thousand pairs of seabirds call the island home between May and September each year. They fly thousands of kilometres, some even cross oceans, just to get to the magic, for them, of this spot. Merrifield and Zin decided to scale their way partway down the cliff to get better shots.

They looked at me.

Shaking like a leaf, I bravely declared, "Someone has to stay near the top just in case."

Nobody asked, "Just in case what?" They just shook their heads and moved on.

We got the pictures and did the interview, and then our too-short visit was over. But the excitement wasn't.

If landing on the island gave us an "edge-of-the-seat" feeling, the takeoff was even more thrilling.

The pilot checked the wind, picked the line he wanted for takeoff, and the engines roared to life as we made our way toward the cliff edge.

It was a little like taking off from an aircraft carrier where you watch the planes drop a few metres once they leave the deck, but enough to make you wonder if they're gone for good. That's what happened here. Just enough to make you wonder, but there's nothing like the feeling seconds later when you start climbing again.

Now, be honest. Don't you too want to go to Prince Leopold Island?

POSTSCRIPT

The island was discovered in 1819 by the explorer Sir William Parry and, as you may have guessed, was named after Prince Leopold, the maternal uncle of Queen Victoria.

Leopold was an interesting guy. He was a member of Napoleon's court, but he left to join the Russian army and fight against Napoleon. After that, he went to Britain and married into the royal family. When the throne of Greece came open, he was asked to fill the vacancy. He turned it down and later opted to become king of Belgium, where he remained until he died at the age of seventy-four in 1865. There is no record that he ever visited the island named after him.

Sir William Parry, who named the island, was also an interesting guy. While many other explorers get credit for trying to find the Northwest Passage, Parry may have been closer than any of them without actually succeeding. But here's why I've always liked his story. In that 1819 voyage where he discovered Prince Leopold Island, he was the first to travel with something new: canned food. That was a revolutionary advance in the way long, sometimes multiyear voyages were provisioned. There was only one problem; no one had yet invented a can opener. Hours were spent punching holes with knives to pry open the tins. Parry died at sixty-four in 1855.

King of the Sea

Ever since I was very young, I've been fascinated by the idea of underwater exploration. The story of the fated *Titanic* intrigued me from the very moment I first heard it. When the luxury liner was finally discovered in 1985, I looked at the first released pictures for hours on end. A few years later, Canadian physician and explorer Joe MacInnis sent me a signed and framed picture from his dive to the shipwreck. I'm still mesmerized by it today. When I look along what's left of the railings, I think of the last moments of those who clung to them not knowing what would happen next.

And so, when the two long-lost Franklin Expedition vessels, the *Erebus* and the *Terror*, were found more than a hundred and sixty years after they sank, I was equally excited. Seeing the photos of the wrecks, which were still in remarkable shape, stirred my imagination about those final days before they were abandoned by a crew that later starved to death trying to walk, first across the ice and then across land, to rescue.

But I've never gone beyond looking at pictures—I've never geared up and gone diving myself even to shallow wrecks. For some reason, I've never taken the lessons required to master that skill. However, I do love snorkeling, and whenever I've been lucky enough to go to tropical areas that encourage snorkeling, I've grabbed the opportunity.

Which brings me to the winter of 2009 and a little island off Antigua in the Caribbean called Jumby Bay. It's a special resort, though I'll admit, expensive, but that year the three of us—me, my wife Cynthia, and our son Will—decided to splurge and visit Jumby Bay. We had our own little house on the property, a great beach, and access to all the amenities, including exclusive snorkeling adventures. Will was only ten, and this trip was his first time snorkeling. After witnessing the colourful world of underwater sea life one morning, we had no trouble talking him into going again.

When we arrived at the beach the next day, the open-air snorkeling tour boat and its driver were ready for us, but this time there were five other people already in it: a family unit that seemed to consist of a grandfather, a father, and a son about Will's age; and two other fellows, who were sitting silently near the back. The family group asked where we were from, and when we answered Canada they responded that they were from Norway and we all exchanged pleasantries. As we headed out on the twenty-minute ride to Jumby's secret underwater spot, they explained they were on their first snorkeling adventure in this part of the world and asked what they should know about the area we were heading to.

"Two things," I said. "First, there's lots to see, many different tropical fish, but second, there are areas where it gets quite shallow, so watch you don't scrape yourself on the coral."

On arrival, Willie and I took off to areas we had found the day before. Cynthia decided to stay onshore and look for shells at the water's edge. Our newfound friends headed in a different direction.

Every once in a while, I'd look back to check on Cynthia and all seemed fine. Then, after about forty minutes, Willie asked, "What's Mom doing?"

I turned toward the shore and there was Cynthia kneeling next to the older gentleman, and from where we were, it looked like she was rubbing his stomach.

"We better get back," I said.

As we got in close, it was clear what was going on. The fellow had snorkeled into one of those dangerous shallow areas and scraped his stomach pretty good on the coral. Cynthia was making sure the injury was clean by using the only thing she had with her, hand sanitizer, which must have been painful for him. The good news was that it wasn't a serious cut, but it was nice of Cynthia to play nurse and the man was very grateful. The rest of the journey was uneventful, and by the end of it all, there were smiles and handshakes all around.

The next morning, when we started out for the beach, we saw that our Norwegian friends were heading for the departure dock, ready to leave for home. We waved goodbye and noted that the two quiet fellows who'd been in the back of the boat were now trailing a few steps behind the family, almost as if they were security.

After they had all left, a member of the Jumby Bay staff came by. "Aren't they nice people?" he said.

We agreed and asked, "By the way, who are they? We never got their names."

"What? You didn't know?" he exclaimed. "That's the king of Norway!"

We didn't believe him. We went straight to one of the rooms with a computer and logged in to Google Images. And there, resplendent in his Norwegian naval uniform, was King Harald V. Same guy.

The picture included a nice write-up about the royal family, but it definitely missed the latest headline—how the king had been caught on a Caribbean beach having his stomach stroked by a good-looking, unknown Canadian.

Wrong Table

The Bilderberg Conference is an annual meeting of politicians and former politicians—some prime ministers and presidents, some members of various European royal families—international business leaders, and leading players in the media. In total, there are about one hundred and fifty participants at each meeting. To encourage a comprehensive discussion on world issues, the three-day gathering is kept off the record and those invited agree not to discuss what's said in any detail.

But we live in a world of conspiracy theories, and those who tend to circulate and believe such schemes have a big bull's-eye on Bilderberg. They claim that those in attendance are one hundred and fifty of the most influential, if not the most important, people in the world.

So, imagine my surprise when I found myself sitting at the heavily guarded 2010 Bilderberg Conference in Sitges, Spain, a resort community just south of Barcelona. As billed, it was three days of heavy talk about big issues from world security to high tech, led at different times by heavy hitters like Bill Gates. There was agreement and disagreement, the kind of back and forth you appreciate hearing to broaden your knowledge. The conspiracy theorists—on both the left and the right—believe it's all set up to establish a new world order. If that happened that weekend in Spain, I must have missed it.

Unsurprisingly, there was a social side to Sitges as well, especially on Saturday, the eve of the final session. It was a beautiful night, and the setting was outside in the gardens of the hotel conference centre overlooking the Mediterranean Sea. There were large circular tables that sat eight or ten people each, and the seating was first come, first served. Among those I sat and enjoyed a wide-ranging discussion with were a big bank president, a social media leader, and the chair of Airbus. Only one table, and it was right beside us, was reserved for the Bilderberg elite, for lack of a better description. The queens of Spain and the Netherlands, the prime minister of Spain, and the one and only, never boring, and often controversial Dr. Henry Kissinger, who was at the time eighty-seven years old.

The meal was buffet style, with diners heading up to a well-stocked table of everything imaginable to suit any diet. Shortly after I'd sat down with my plate, I saw Dr. Kissinger rise at his table and very carefully make his way over to the buffet. He was there for a few minutes selecting what he found to fit his hunger. And then even more carefully, head down, keeping track of the plate he was balancing, he walked slowly back to the tables.

To my surprise he navigated his way to *our* table and sat down right beside *me*.

A hush formed over our group and it seemed left to me to say something. "Dr. Kissinger, welcome to our table. We appreciate the chance for a chat."

He appeared somewhat startled and looked up from his fresh vegetables and chicken. And then, this man who had sat across from Le Duc Tho of North Vietnam at the Paris Peace talks, had prayed with Richard Nixon in the nights before the president resigned, looked me straight in the eye and said, "You're not the queen of Spain."

And with that and not a word more, he got up and moved back to the table he was supposed to be at. Next to Sofia, the queen of Spain.

They must have been conspiring about something.

Jack Layton

If you ask most good journalists who cover national issues and politics in Canada what *other* journalists they follow to really get an edge on what's happening, you will likely get the same answer: Chantal Hébert. Whether it's her *Toronto Star* column or her *La Presse* column, Chantal is the one to read. The northern Ontario–born opinion writer seems to be ahead of most people when sensing trends developing in the Canadian body politic. Unsurprisingly, that's why many a provincial and federal politician tries hard to make an impression on Chantal in the hopes that their name may creep into her columns in a positive light.

It was Wendy Mesley who put me on to Chantal in the 1990s, telling me she was exactly the kind of voice I needed to persuade the bosses at the CBC that a regular political panel on *The National* would be a smart idea. The rest, as they say, is history. Eventually, that idea turned into "At Issue," the most successful branded segment *The National* has ever produced; it's still chugging along two decades after I started it. And if you ask any of its faithful viewers across the country who stands out for them on "At Issue," the answer has consistently been "Chantal!"

So, perhaps it was no surprise that as we approached the midway point in the 2011 federal election campaign, it was Chantal, Andrew Coyne, and guest panelist Althia Raj who gathered around the studio table to bring viewers up to date on the campaign trail. During her comments, Chantal mentioned she was detecting that something was happening with the NDP, that Jack Layton was hitting a chord with voters, especially in Quebec, and that the impact could affect the election result. If any of the rest of us had said that, it would have been noted but perhaps that would have been the end of it. But this was Chantal Hébert. Few people have a better ear to the ground than she does.

So I started planning, along with producer Leslie Stojsic, to get a special segment on Layton on *The National*. As we always did in the campaigns, we approached the major national party leaders for interviews. In 2011, we added a twist. We said, "You can come to us or we will come to you on the road." Stephen Harper and Michael Ignatieff went conventional, offering us straight-up one-on-one interviews, Ignatieff in the studio and Harper at a hockey rink. Only Layton said, "Hey, come with us for a few days and we'll give you access." We jumped at the chance.

It was only a couple of days, enough to follow him in Montreal, Charlottetown, and St. John's. Layton had just been through prostate cancer surgery and a hip operation, so he was walking with the aid of a cane, but he hadn't really slowed down. In fact, reporters were having a hard time keeping up with him. And the crowds. They were very enthusiastic. I've covered enough campaigns to be able to tell when something was happening. And something was happening. I knew it and he knew it.

In Charlottetown, he and I piled into the back of a van while cameraman Dave Rae positioned himself up front with his camera pointed

On the NDP campaign plane with Jack Layton in 2011.
Leslie Stojsic

back at us. Leslie was in a second vehicle behind us taking "cutaways" to help with the edit. We just rambled on in conversation as the van bumped along, and Dave tried to keep the camera steady on his shoulder. Not easy as we travelled along some of PEI's winding country roads to the next campaign stop.

At one point, I put to Layton something I'd seen a few days before joining the trip. I love watching old campaign broadcasts and had dug up the 1968 national leader's TV debate, the first one in Canada. There were Pierre Trudeau, Robert Stanfield, Réal Caouette, and Tommy Douglas taking shots at each other. Someone asked Douglas, the NDP leader, how far he thought his party could go when the votes were counted.

"Oh, we could never form the government," said Douglas, which in fact became the NDP's normal campaign response for years to come (although Ed Broadbent was so sure he might win in 1988 that some of his aides used to joke that they were "measuring the drapes at 24 Sussex").

Tommy Douglas is a revered name across the spectrum of Canadian politics and, to an NDPer, quoting him is like quoting the Bible. I decided to ask Layton about Douglas's comment, as it was becoming increasingly clear that some form of "orange wave" was hitting parts of the country with only a few weeks to go before Canadians marked their ballots. I watched Layton's face as he contemplated his answer, and it was clear he was going to choose his words very carefully.

"If I had been one of Tommy's staffers in 1968, I would have offered a different view," he said almost apologetically. And then he went on to talk about what he was witnessing on the campaign trail. And it wasn't just bloviation. I was seeing it too. He was careful to not look too overconfident, but I expected the next phrase out of his mouth was going to be quoting Yogi Berra, "It ain't over till it's over." Anything could happen.

We kept the conversation going. He talked about his cancer. About his granddaughter. "There's nothing like having cancer and having a grandchild to make you really understand the importance and meaning of life," he said.

Later that day, we had our final stop together on the docks in St. John's harbour. Another interview, and more good content for the mini-documentary we had planned.

That year, I asked all the leaders the same question: "In your political life what is the one action of yours that you regret most?"

Harper wished he'd spent more time questioning intelligence he'd received on the Iraq war.

Ignatieff wished he'd not done our interview.

Layton was the most personal.

"I wish I'd never said that Paul Martin was personally responsible for deaths because of the tainted blood scandal during his prime minister-ship. That was wrong, unfair, and inhuman."

It shouldn't be hard for a politician, even a leader, to apologize, but doing it is rare. In that moment Layton showed his vulnerability and his compassion.

The orange wave was real. Layton and the NDP won 103 seats on May 2, 2011, and for the first and only time in its history, the party formed the official opposition with Layton at the helm. It was a huge accomplishment for the NDP, but for Jack Layton there was very little time to celebrate. The cancer had returned. It was about to race through his body.

Just one hundred and twelve days after election night, the battle against it ended.

On August 22, just before five in the morning, my phone rang. I've been around long enough to know that when the phone rings in the middle of the night the odds are it's not good news. It wasn't.

"Jack just passed away. We will be announcing it publicly in a few hours. Perhaps you could make it known before then."

I got up, showered, and dressed. I drove into Toronto from our home in Stratford thinking about those last conversations we'd had during the campaign. In St. John's after that interview had ended, I'd thanked him for being so frank about his health and his hopes in the few days we'd just spent together. Standing on the dock I'd told him that while he and I had done many interviews in the years before, all my questions in those past years had been so predictable.

Before I could say anything, he smiled and looked at me. "And all my answers were so predictable too." We both laughed. It was so true. But 2011 had been different.

I parked my car and walked into the studio where Heather Hiscox was hosting her morning show and, to her surprise, I sat down, unannounced, beside her. She could tell something wasn't right and, on air, she asked me what was up.

"Jack Layton has just died."

Heather's face said it all. She was shocked and saddened, just like so many Canadians of all political stripes were, as they found out in that same moment. A person's life had been stolen from them at the pinnacle of their professional career. The country was instantly in mourning.

Two weeks later, Layton's widow, Olivia Chow, returned with me to the spot on Toronto Island where they had been married twenty-three years before and talked about what the final moments had been like.

"It was very difficult, but he had no fear. He had no fear. He was ready, so I thought, okay. So we all held him."

With Olivia Chow in the spot where she married Jack Layton.
Leslie Stojsic/Mike Heenan

The Secret of Beechey Island

There is nothing inviting about Beechey Island. Not a thing. It's uninhabited, desolate, rocky, windswept, and pretty cold even on its most summery days in August and September. Beechey is a relatively small island located in the Canadian Arctic Archipelago in Nunavut, just off Wellington Channel, not far from Lancaster Sound. Today the occasional cruise ship makes a stop near Beechey, and, trust me, it doesn't stop for the nightlife, the casinos, or the beaches. In fact, there are none of those. It stops for the history.

The island remains near the centre of one of Canada's greatest mysteries: the Franklin Expedition. To this day, no one knows exactly what happened, but for more than a hundred and fifty years, Beechey has held some clues, and that's what has led me to its rocky shores twice now, along with other journalists, researchers, scientists, and plain old tourists.

Beechey was the last place Sir John Franklin of the British Royal Navy was seen alive. It was 1846. He and the crew on HMS *Erebus* and HMS *Terror* wintered on Beechey during their fated search for the Northwest Passage, and during that stopover, three of Franklin's men died. John Torrington, William Braine, and John Hartnell were laid to rest on the island.

In the early 1980s, their bodies were exhumed by anthropologists hoping the remains would be in good enough shape to provide some answers as to what fate befell the men. They were surprised by what they saw: the bodies were pristine, as if they had been buried just hours before. The frozen Arctic tundra had saved everything. Except the answer. What they did find suggested that lead poisoning from the expedition's poorly canned food was the cause of death, but that theory has since been downplayed. Why Torrington, Braine, and Hartnell died remains a secret they took to their graves.

When I last stood at the three graves, it was a normal August day in the Arctic. Windy, cool, cloudy. But the air was pure, allowing my mind to be full of thoughts.

Mainly I was trying to imagine what it must have been like the day the crews of the *Erebus* and the *Terror* buried their mates just a few metres from the shoreline. Franklin almost certainly would have had them in their uniforms, he in his navy blue and gold braid, all of them together singing hymns, and reciting the Twenty-third Psalm, leading them "beside the still waters."

I thought about what they must have been thinking as they watched their fellow seamen lowered into the ground, their lives taken just before the crews were about to make history. Franklin and his officers were

One of the Franklin Expedition gravesites on Beechey Island.
Sheldon Beldick

convinced they were on the verge of discovering the shortcut over the top of North America to reach the riches of the Orient. When they did, they would be celebrated the world over and especially at home when they sailed back down the Thames to a hero's welcome in London.

Well, they did make history, but not the kind they had hoped for. They all perished halfway through the passage that they never discovered. The end was awful: starvation and cannibalism is all we know with certainty; the rest remains a mystery.

Except the fact that the funeral they gave their shipmates on Beechey Island was a funeral they never got themselves.

POSTSCRIPT

There is a fourth grave on Beechey Island just a short distance from the Franklin three. It's the final resting place of Thomas Morgan, and his story is a piece of history too. Morgan was a crew member for one of the ships that set sail trying to find the Franklin Expedition in the years that followed its disappearance.

In fact, Morgan was part of one of the greatest maritime searches that history has ever witnessed. There were dozens of ships from numerous countries that looked for Franklin and his men for more than five decades. It wouldn't be until much later, first in 2014 and then in 2016, that Erebus *and* Terror *were found by Canadian searchers. Those finds may, in the end, tell us exactly what happened, but as of this writing, the case remains as cold as the remote windswept island named Beechey.*

Searching for Franklin

It was September 2012, and I was seated in a chartered Twin Otter aircraft out of Cambridge Bay, Nunavut, with producer Michael Gruzuk, looking for a spot along the Northwest Passage's Victoria Strait to land. We were doing a story on an archaeological dig for the ill-fated Franklin Expedition, but first we had to meet up with a helicopter from the Canadian Coast Guard icebreaker *Sir Wilfrid Laurier*.

How do you catch up to an icebreaker in an extremely remote part of Canada's Arctic when you are in a small aircraft, you ask? It's tricky. It's intense. And it's totally exhilarating.

Luckily, the Twin Otter is one of Canada's great innovations. The De Havilland aircraft is known the world over and flown the world over because of its incredible manoeuvrability and the fact that it can land almost anywhere, on almost anything. Translation: it doesn't need an airport or a runway. And there sure weren't either of those anywhere near where we were.

But then on the horizon, a tiny slip of land came into view. Barely visible on maps or charts because for part of the year it isn't visible at all—it's submerged. But not on this day. We took a pass over the area. Along the shoreline seemed to be the pilot's choice.

"This should work," he said.

Should? I thought. (He later told me there was no evidence that anyone had ever landed before on this strip of land. Fortunately, he didn't tell me that as we headed down.)

I looked up at his grasp on the two throttles. In a Twin Otter, the throttles are in the middle of an array of instruments attached to the ceiling of the cockpit. His grip was firm. He manipulated the power up

Bare knuckle landing.
Michael Gruzuk

and down as we edged closer to the ground, reducing speed to barely above a stall. I kept myself busy taking pictures with my phone; so did Michael with a more sophisticated digital camera.

And then, just like that, we were on the ground and braking to a stop in what seemed to be less than a hundred feet. The pilot acted like it was just another day on the job. We pretended to look the same.

While it was still only September, winter that far north was preparing to set in. There was a cool breeze, and as I stood on the remote island I had a sense of what was bound to be coming in the days and weeks ahead. The pilot radioed the *Laurier* to let them know our coordinates, and within minutes we saw the icebreaker's helicopter coming toward us. We boarded and flew to the *Laurier* for a quick briefing from the captain on the rules and regulations, and then it was back on the helicopter for a ride to King William Island less than half an hour away. We were instructed on emergency procedures, shown where protective gear was in case we had to ditch the helicopter and jump into the waters below, and, in the same breath, warned that we'd be lucky to last more than thirty minutes given the near-freezing waters.

Nice.

I'd been to King William Island before, in 2006, though not the exact spot we were headed at this moment. If you know the story of the Franklin Expedition, then you know that this is the area where all one hundred and twenty-nine of Sir John Franklin's crew from the HMS *Terror* and HMS *Erebus* perished in the late 1840s. The ships, frozen in the ice of Victoria Strait, wintered there for two years, during which Franklin, their captain, died—of what we still don't know. The crew finally abandoned the ships and walked across the ice to King William Island, hoping desperately to trek the hundreds of kilometres south to mainland North America and a remote trading post. It wasn't to be. None of them made it out. Instead, they ignored suggestions from passing Inuit hunters on how to survive the remote conditions and, one by one, they died on the barren lands, most from starvation, some after staying alive only by cannibalizing their dead mates. It is a horrific story, and now I was soon to walk on the land that had cushioned their final footsteps.

The chopper approached King William Island, flying over the only other vessel working those waters, the research ship *Martin Bergmann*, a former Newfoundland fishing trawler. It was owned by the Arctic Research Foundation, which had been set up by billionaire Jim Balsillie, one of the cofounders of the BlackBerry. Marty Bergmann was a good friend of mine who got me hooked on the Arctic, and later did the same for Balsillie after I introduced the two. It was Jim's idea to name the vessel after Marty, following the plane crash that took his life in Resolute in 2011. The *Bergmann* later found HMS *Erebus* in shallow waters not far from where I was about to land. (In the interest of full disclosure, I'm a member of the advisory board of the Arctic Research Foundation.)

On the ground, we joined Doug Stenton and Bob Park who were conducting the archaeological dig, looking for artifacts of the expedition. Doug was the lead man from the Nunavut government's Department of Culture and Heritage, which claimed ownership of anything that was found. While the dig was under the direction of Parks Canada, everyone knew the area was in Nunavut, and so the territory's approval for search operations and their expertise—especially that of local Inuit—were critical to the success of the project.

We watched, filmed, and interviewed Doug as he sifted through the rocks and sand not far from the shore of Erebus Bay. We were on the northwestern side of King William Island, in the area along the waterline known as the "boat place" because it's where the Franklin crew tried to set up a camp under a longboat they had dragged across the ice to shore, a fact only discovered ten years later when, at Franklin's wife's request, the explorer Sir Francis Leopold McClintock led a search for the crew. When McClintock and his men lifted the boat, they discovered bodies huddled together under what was left of some of the ship's blankets.

The boat place is a desolate spot. As far as I could see, the land stretched away from the water to the east, mostly flat with very little except rocks highlighting the landscape. I imagined it didn't look that different when the Franklin crew sheltered from the wind and the bitter winter cold here in 1848. But while the boat, the blankets, and the

With the Nunavut archaeologists on King William Island
searching for artifacts.
Michael Gruzuk

bodies had all disintegrated over time, the land was still a treasure trove of Franklin Expedition relics. At least it was that day. Doug showed me what they had dug up before we arrived: a button, a nail, and then he carefully and respectfully held up a piece of bone, human bone. It's hard to look at things like that, especially someone's bone, and not try to picture the person it came from and the desperation of his last days. Some of the bones had cut marks on them, only intensifying, if not horrifying, my imagination.

Doug asked me if I'd like to try my hand at searching. Of course, I did. Anyone in that situation would, I'm sure. He showed me the delicate way to sift, how to pick something up that might be of significance and mark the spot with a small flag, and how to call for help if I was unsure of what to do. I looked around and found an area I thought might be promising and began.

It took me two minutes to find something. Just two minutes. A nail was first. An old square-headed one. Doug was impressed.

I continued digging, being very careful in moving things around, when I saw a small bit of something sticking up, no more than a centimetre or two, between some rocks. To me, it looked a little like the bones Doug had shown me. But as I gently moved it and pulled it toward me, I realized it was probably something else. As it finally came loose, it carried the unmistakable form of a toothbrush, an old toothbrush. Before I called Doug over to see my find, I got cold feet. I had this thought of being had, being made the butt of an archaeologist's joke. So I flipped the brush over just to make sure it wasn't a fake, that it didn't have a Shoppers Drug Mart sticker on it.

It didn't. It was the real deal.

Doug was amazed. He took a good look and gave it a preliminary dating of the 1840s. It was in pretty good shape; even some of the bristles, while worn down, were still intact and could be useful in the recovery process, which included DNA testing. The brush, like all the relics found that day, was then put under lock and key.

I had almost forgotten about the whole experience until, a few years later, a package landed in my mailbox. It was a highly polished oak box, specially designed for its contents, along with this letter from Doug:

> *I thought you might appreciate this small memento of your 2012 visit to Erebus Bay and the Franklin Expedition "boat place" site. It is a 3D printed reproduction of the toothbrush that you found; feel free to use it as proof of your status as a contributor to Nunavut's investigations of the 1845 Franklin Expedition (people still ask me if I planted it so that you could find it!).*

He didn't. I found it all by myself and, as a result, now consider myself a full-fledged member of the Franklin Expedition search team!

The replica toothbrush sits above the fireplace in my home office. I look at it often and think about what the owner of the real one must have gone through in his final days in one of our country's most unforgiving, yet unforgettable, places.

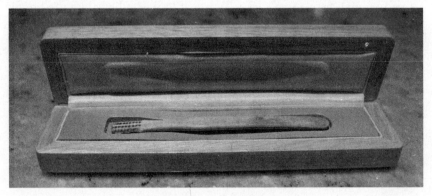

The 3D replica toothbrush.

POSTSCRIPT

In the summer of 2019, during a trip to Scotland, I found myself in Edinburgh one day with a few hours to spare. Somebody had once told me that in one of the city's older cemeteries there was a burial spot for a Franklin crew member whose bones had been brought home after being found in the late 1800s. I walked over to the beautiful tree-lined Dean Cemetery and strolled row after row looking for something that might help me find the right marker. Finally, after an hour of having no luck, I saw a groundskeeper and asked him whether he knew of any tombstones marking the final spot for a member of the crew of the famous Royal Navy Captain, Sir John Franklin. Immediately he said, "Yes, I know the spot well," and guided me to a tall Celtic cross with an inscription remembering a Lieutenant John Irving of HMS Terror. The cemetery worker left me there and I stood in silence, imagining the contrast between that barren windswept location I had witnessed where starvation and the elements had cost him his life and this beautiful, carefully manicured spot where he'd been brought home to rest.

John McCain

On November 22, 1963, John McCain was a U.S. Navy pilot flying ground-attack A-1 Skyraider aircraft off an American aircraft carrier in the Mediterranean Sea. That evening, McCain and the rest of the carrier's crew would hear the news from Dallas that their commander in chief, President John F. Kennedy, had been assassinated.

Fifty years later, to the day, I met McCain for the first and only time, and as it so happened, the Kennedy assassination was central to that encounter. Like anyone who met McCain, the moment was memorable—certainly one I will never forget—and that goes to who McCain was to his core. Before I tell you about the moment, let me tell you about the core.

During those intervening fifty years, McCain had made his mark and had become known around the world. In the U.S. Navy, he had been a reckless pilot who often "pushed the envelope"—he crashed on two early missions and collided with power lines on a third. But he kept flying and kept moving up the promotion list. By the time he was thirty, he was flying combat missions in A-4 Skyhawks in the Vietnam War. A few months later, in October of 1967, he was shot down during a bombing run over Hanoi in North Vietnam. He ejected from the cockpit but broke both his arms and one leg on the way out, and landed in a city lake where he was dragged ashore by onlookers only to be beaten by the North Vietnamese with rifle butts to his head and shoulders, suffering more injuries. They took him to a hospital where he received limited treatment, and in six weeks he lost fifty pounds and his hair turned white.

After that he was moved to the infamous "Hanoi Hilton," the

prisoner-of-war camp in the capital city. There he was frequently beaten and tortured. During one stretch, he was bound and repeatedly struck every two hours even though he was also suffering from dysentery and heat exhaustion at the time. Discovering that he was the son of a U.S. Navy admiral, his captors then offered to release him. He refused, and instead took more torture. He stayed in captivity until all the POWs were released in March of 1973. His wartime injuries combined with the torture meant he was never again able to lift his arms above his head.

After his recovery and a few more years in the U.S. Navy, McCain entered politics, serving first in the House of Representatives and then in the Senate. He kept his rebel status by having friends on both sides of the political aisle, and not being afraid to vote against his party when he felt it was the right thing to do. In 2008, he was the Republicans' choice for their presidential ticket, but he lost to Barack Obama in an election race that was closer than a lot of people thought it would be.

To me, the true test of McCain's heart came in a town-hall rally during the campaign when a Republican loyalist questioned whether to trust Obama, suggesting he was an Arab. McCain cut the speaker off, moved in, shook his head, and said, "He's a decent person and a person that you do not have to be scared of [if he becomes] president of the United States."

It was a bold move, one that some Republicans argue to this day cost him the election, but it was classic McCain. Talk straight and stay true to your heart.

Aside from his daily politics, McCain was a firm believer in international alliances, and a loyal supporter of the annual Halifax International Security Forum which was started in 2009 and attended by defence and security players and analysts from around the world. McCain was a frequent speaker and attended almost all of the forum's sessions.

And that was the reason I exchanged words with the senator on November 22, 2013.

The forum's organizers, knowing that I had just finished a fiftieth-anniversary documentary on the JFK assassination, and seeing as their major dinner would occur on the night of the 22nd, asked me to be the keynote speaker and to talk about how the world had been shaped in its attitudes toward government, security, and the media in those historic hours. Flying into Halifax that afternoon, I had the main body of my remarks prepared, but I decided I'd start my speech by recounting where some of the key players at the forum had been on that day a half-century ago.

Peter McKay, Canada's former defence minister, then attorney general, and one of the founders of the Halifax forum, was there. But he hadn't even been born when Kennedy was shot. I used that fact, and it did get a few laughs, but all it did was make many of us feel really old.

Chuck Hagel, the US secretary of defense at the time, was present too. Moments before my speech, I had gone up to him, told him what I was doing, and asked for his help. He was eager to contribute and told me he'd still been in high school in Nebraska in November of 1963 and, like everyone else, had been shocked. "Our class was very quiet when they told us."

And the McCain story I had already looked up on the Internet. He'd been on that carrier.

I started by recounting my own story about hearing the news at first in school as Hagel did, then rushing home and watching Walter Cronkite for most of the next four days (in those days the CBC often just plugged into CBS for major international breaking news). I spoke about how so many of my views about anchoring, the media, government, and even conspiracy were shaped by those first hours.

Before I moved into the major part of my speech, which would explore the angles organizers had asked for, I gave my personal opinion about the origins of the assassination. I'd just returned from my second trip to the School Book Depository building in Dallas and had walked the floors and the stairs where Lee Harvey Oswald had been, driven through his old neighbourhood, stood on the corner where he'd shot officer J. D. Tippit, passed by the movie theatre he'd been arrested in, and drove by the Dallas police station where he'd been questioned and in whose basement he'd been shot dead. I talked about the dozens of books, articles, documentaries, movies, and theories that I'd read and seen. How I'd spent my earlier years believing at various times that the assassination had been ordered and organized by either the Mob, or Cuba, or the Soviet Union, or right-wing US-based Kennedy haters. But I told the audience that after many years of studying the issue, my own personal belief was that Oswald had done it all by himself. There was no second gunman standing behind an old wooden fence beyond the grassy knoll. Just Oswald, a former U.S. Marine sharpshooter with albeit an old, cheap rifle, but also with a shot that, when you stand in the Book Depository building looking down to the street, wasn't that hard. And then I moved on.

Twenty minutes or so later, when I had finished my remarks, the audience gave me a generous round of applause, and one member even stood up. As I walked down from the podium, I was stunned to realize that the person standing was none other than Senator John McCain.

As the applause continued and I passed his table toward mine, he moved forward and wrapped his arm around me and half-whispered in my ear, "That was a great speech, son."

I felt pretty special. Before I could react to the compliment, he added, "But how do you explain Oswald being in the Soviet embassy in Mexico City just weeks before Dallas?"

I stopped cold. I knew the Mexico City story. It had been around for decades, explained away by the theory that it was just kooky Oswald trying to get a visa to travel to Minsk, where he used to live and where he'd met his wife. Clearly, McCain didn't believe that.

I looked at him, this senior senator from Arizona, who had come close to being the forty-fourth president of the United States just a few years before, and who had been a kind of personal hero of mine ever since his POW experience.

"Not you too?" I said. "*You're* a conspiracy theorist too?"

And then came the McCain closer. "You're damn right I am, and I'll

Two bald guys in Halifax.

always be one till someone gives me a real explanation as to what the hell Oswald was doing with the Soviets in that embassy. No one ever has."

And as far as I know, no one ever did.

POSTSCRIPT

Senator John McCain, war hero and former presidential nominee, died on August 25, 2018, just a few days shy of his eighty-second birthday.

Political friends and foes alike praised McCain in both formal and informal eulogies, including former presidents of both parties, many of whom had knocked heads with the "rebel" over the years. There was one notable exception—Donald Trump, who had claimed more than once that he had no time for McCain because the enemy had captured him. "I like guys who don't get captured," said Trump. This from a man who had used a questionable claim of bone spurs to avoid serving his country in the same war that had left John McCain beaten, tortured, and almost dead.

Johnny Hihgney

Who was Johnny Hihgney? And what was he thinking when he etched his name on this underground wall? Those were my thoughts as I half crawled along a long-ago abandoned First World War tunnel thirty feet below the earth's surface.

The year was 2014 and I was in northern France, not far from the city of Arras on the very land where the Battle of Vimy Ridge had been fought in 1917. CBC London producer Stephanie Jenzer had convinced a group of former British miners who were responsible for exploring this particular war tunnel to take us along, so for the first time, television cameras could chronicle what had happened there almost a century ago.

Vimy was and still is a significant moment in the Canadian story. Some argue Vimy was the real birth of a nation, even though it was fifty years after Confederation. Others say it was a significant military battle, worth remembering, but beyond that it's an overstatement to call it much more.

Almost four thousand Canadians drew their last breath at Vimy Ridge, in a fight so brutal and bloody that bodies are still found in the earth all these years later. In the years before 1917, both the British and the French had tried to take Vimy from the Germans, but they were pushed back. The Canadians, though, were not, and the strategic ridge overlooking a vast stretch of northern France fell into Allied hands. The Canadians accomplished this feat under Canadian command, not British, something that hadn't happened before during the war, and thus the legend about the "birth of a nation" began. But the war did not end at that moment; in fact, battles around Vimy continued and, in some cases, the Germans recaptured some of the ground they had lost.

Preparing a script at Vimy Ridge.
Stephanie Jenzer

Vimy remains sacred ground to all who fought there. Two thousand Canadians lie buried within sight of the spectacular Vimy Memorial. More than forty thousand Germans have their final resting place just a few kilometres down the road.

In part of my family's convoluted history, I have a connection to Vimy. My grandfather, Harry, fought in the battle as an enlisted man in the Canadian army. He was badly wounded in the leg after being shot by a German infantryman and had to be evacuated by hospital ship back to England, where he wound up in a care area in Folkestone near Dover. He fell in love with his nurse, they got married, and not long after, my father was born. So, whenever I've been to Vimy, I've often considered the fact that if it wasn't for that German sniper, I might never have come along.

More than a million visitors come to Vimy every year, many of them Canadians of all ages. School tours are popular as a part of a living history experience. It's so much more than a magnificent memorial. There are trenches re-created in the exact spot where both sides faced each other, sometimes just metres apart. There are short stretches of reinforced tunnels that you can walk through. And throughout the area, there are fields still zoned off by barbed wire because there are unexploded ordnances from the time of battle.

But Stephanie wanted to find something for a documentary we were doing that had not been converted to 2014 standards, and that's when, during research in England, she learned of the former British miners and their work in a tunnel that had been discovered only a few years before.

During the First World War, tunneling had become a tactic both sides were trying to master. It was a way of avoiding the bloodbath of no-man's-land, the area between the trenches that the opposing armies would try to cross at times. Going "under" gave the men a strategic advantage—they could literally pop up at the last minute instead of being exposed all the way. The Canadians were considered some of the best tunnelers of the war, and miners from different parts of Canada were called on for their expertise.

In June 2014, the Brits met Stephanie, myself, and our London-based cameraman Pascal Leblond in the visitors parking lot not far from the memorial. We then followed them by car in the opposite direction, deep into a nearby forest, down what looked like an abandoned country grass road. At a certain point, we had to leave the cars and walk into what was a makeshift half-cabin half-tent. We had some tea—or it looked like tea—and received our safety briefing which included reminders that the tunnel we were about to descend into was pretty much in the same shape as it had been when the last soldiers climbed out ninety-six years before. A few months earlier, there had been a cave-in at one part of the tunnel, and a miner had been seriously injured. We got the message: it's dangerous, be careful.

With a hard hat on and a rope tied to my waist, I climbed a rickety aluminum ladder thirty feet (ten metres) from the forest to the tunnel floor. It was dark and damp, but things became visible because of our hard-hat headlights and Pascal's camera light. Within the first few steps, it was clear that the soldiers had left in a hurry. There were old rifles on the ground, and even a discarded grenade had been left behind. I couldn't tell if the pin was still in it and I wasn't about to fiddle around to find out.

Hunched over, sometimes on our knees, we moved along the tunnel. It was a far cry from the neatly groomed "tourist tunnel" near the memorial; instead, it had been roughly cut out of the earth with jagged outcrops here and there, so there was a good reason for the hard hat.

When we reached an area where the walls of the tunnel were almost white, like chalk, we were told that the whole area around Vimy was really an extension of the same ridge that is seen above ground on the other side of the English Channel—what the world knows as the White Cliffs of Dover.

The white was the perfect background for what we saw next.

Names. Lots of them.

And regiments. And hometowns.

As if they had been written yesterday, but in fact they had been drawn on the walls a century ago. The Canadian soldiers of 1917, waiting below ground, sometimes for hours, sometimes for days, not knowing what would await them when the whistle sounded to attack, had scribbled their stories on the walls.

And who knows, for some it might have been the last thing they ever wrote. In fact, almost certainly, for some it was.

There were names like:

L. McDonald, Woodford, Ontario
Pte. W.E. Richardson, 4th C.M.R.
J.A. Hope, 2nd C.M.R.
H. Bambrough, Canada
J. Lamb, 4 D.L.I.

The etchings went on and on as we moved along the passageways strewn with old ration cans, shells, and other relics of war. Then we reached a stretch where the soldiers got more imaginative. Aside from their names and regiments, they added some basic artwork depicting where they came from.

A fellow from Nova Scotia drew a fish.

A chap from Victoria went beyond drawing and carved a face in the soft chalk wall. Was it his face? His buddy's? A face in his dreams? We'll never know, but it stands there in silent tribute.

From Kingston, Ontario, another soldier drew a moose. And that was John Hihgney, from the 4th C.M.R., whom I've been wondering about ever since.

I later asked a friend at the Canadian Forces for help, and he went into the archives armed with Hihgney's service number, which was also written on the wall. Within half an hour, he found out everything I needed to know.

John Hihgney, or rather John Hingey, as his military record confirmed, survived the war. He moved back to Kingston to be with his wife of more than twenty years, Janet from Scotland. They had five children, four sons and a daughter. One of the sons, Frederick, had joined

Century-old writings in the tunnel.
Stephanie Jenzer

the army at the same time as his father. They even served in the same regiment. He survived the war too.

A Vimy story with a happy ending.

But back to the tunnel. I spent about two hours underground. When I climbed out, it was early evening. A beautiful early evening in June with the sun beginning its descent over the French countryside.

There I was on the other side of the world, but in my mind I'd just been in Canada. And I'd never felt more Canadian than I did at that moment.

POSTSCRIPT

Private John Hingey may have been fooled by the lack of lighting in the tunnel. He had etched his name as "Hihgney" on the wall, but all his military records, his census data, and his wedding certificate say it was "Hingey." Whatever the case, he had a distinguished war record and lived a good life. He died in 1947, at the age of seventy-three, in his hometown of Kingston.

I mentioned that my family history is convoluted. I should explain. My great-grandparents were in a travelling theatre company and moved from Britain to Canada in the late 1800s and toured southern Ontario. Their son Harry, my grandfather, was born in Canada and joined the Canadian army in 1914. After my father was born in Folkestone, England, and the war ended, the family came to Canada and lived in an apartment above a store on the Danforth in Toronto. But my British-born grandmother never felt at home in Canada, and they returned to England in the 1920s. And that's why in the late 1930s, my father joined the Royal Air Force to fight for England in the Second World War. The Mansbridge family didn't move back to Canada until 1954. Confused? Me too.

Chancellor Mansbridge

Paul Martin looked at me with a hint of a smile but didn't blink an eye. "I didn't hear a thing," was all the twenty-first prime minister of Canada said in reply to my question.

And what was my question? First, a bit of background.

It all began in 2008, when former Mount Allison University chancellor Purdy Crawford and then president Robert Campbell asked me whether I'd be willing to take up the chancellor position. I'd given a few lectures at Mount A in the past, and had been awarded an honorary doctorate there as well, but chancellor? Needless to say, I was shocked. I would have been stupid to pass up such a wonderful opportunity, so I said yes, and after serving two four-year terms I have no regrets.

Part of my duties as the university's chancellor involved awarding honorary doctorates on Convocation Day, something I always looked forward to. Over the years I'd given doctorates to business leader Heather Reisman, environmentalist Sheila Watt-Cloutier, Governor General David Johnston, and many others. Once the brief honorary degree ceremony was over, the honorees would sit beside me as I performed my main Convocation Day function: offering my congratulations and having a short word with each of the four hundred or so students graduating that year.

But strange things tended to happen during this part of the day's proceedings. While some graduates were occasionally overcome by the moment of realizing that all that hard work, all those exhausting hours of study, had finally reached a rewarding conclusion, others wanted to make a different kind of statement during their few seconds onstage. Some would pull a camera out from under their graduation robes, wrap their arms around me, and ask for a selfie. Some would suddenly ask me to give a shout-out, like a real shout-out, to their mom in the audience. And still others would be even more innovative. Like the day one young woman stood before me and reached out to shake my hand, and as she did I could feel there was something in her palm as she grasped mine.

"What's that?"

"It's for you," she said.

As I relaxed my grip, I looked at what was now in my palm. It was a thumb drive, a USB stick. "Okay, so what's on this?" I asked cautiously, almost afraid to know.

She leaned in close and whispered, "My résumé!"

This young woman was going to go places! She wanted help in finding a job and was tapping whoever she could. I was impressed. It was a pretty ingenious way of enlisting aid, and I promised that when I was back in Toronto, I'd see what I could do. As it turned out, before I could do anything, she found a job. After seeing how she improvised on her graduation day, that didn't surprise me.

All this brings me to Convocation Day in 2014. That year I had the honour of presenting Paul Martin with an honorary law degree. Afterwards, we sat side by side on the main stage in Convocation Hall in Sackville, New Brunswick, and watched as the graduating students came up to receive their diplomas. As each student walked across the stage, some would stop to congratulate the former PM. It was nice and showed the respect many had for the man who had once guided the country's economy, becoming what most would agree is its most successful finance minister, and then spent two difficult years leading a minority government as prime minister.

On this day, someone very special was graduating: my brother Paul's eldest son and my nephew, Christopher Mansbridge. So, it was a nice family moment when Christopher walked onto the stage to receive his degree; we embraced and the audience applauded.

A few hours later, in the afternoon convocation session, the second wave of graduates was receiving their diplomas. A young woman arrived, we shook hands, and before I could say anything she launched into her question: "Chancellor, do you have a moment?"

I assumed this was going to be another selfie request or something along those lines. "Of course," I said.

"Is it true that Christopher Mansbridge is related to you?"

"He sure is, he's my nephew. Is he a friend of yours?"

"Oh, yes," came the reply. "We slept together in second year."

I froze. She smiled. I nervously laughed. And then off she went with her new degree toward a new life.

And that's when I turned to Paul Martin, the man who once occupied 24 Sussex Drive, and, still a bit dumbfounded, asked, "Did you hear that?"

The former prime minister had been at my shoulder for the whole encounter, but he clearly wanted no part of this: "I didn't hear a thing!"

Did I say he had a half-smile on his face? He did.

I never told Christopher what happened because even all these years later I still don't know whether her story was just part of the convocation

I always enjoyed Convocation Day as chancellor.
Mount Allison University

hijinks I'd seen in so many other ways over the years or whether it was real. I tend to assume the former because her expression at that moment was pretty mischievous. And besides, I don't plan on asking Christopher if it was true, but maybe I'll send him a copy of this book.

Finally, a word about having the honour of being the chancellor of a prestigious university like Mount Allison. While it's primarily a ceremonial position, being chancellor does give you a front-row seat during a critical moment in the lives of those who have reached the pinnacle of educational success.

When I'd address the packed hall on Convocation Day, I could always feel the importance of what was happening. To the families and friends who'd come to witness the moment, mothers and fathers, often in tears, so proud of the accomplishment of their child, but also knowing this was likely to be the beginning of a new era for their family. To the professors and teaching assistants who had always been there to help, to advise, to mentor. And finally to the graduates, who knew that as they walked out of the hall that day it would be the last time they would tread that path. Instead of heading to their dorms, they'd be heading into a new world, one in which they would be joining the leaders of tomorrow.

That was always heady stuff for me, and I'd get somewhat quietly emotional too. I never had had that walk myself, having never been to university or college. And while I have always envied those who did, I also have enormous respect for what they did to achieve their goal.

So, thank you, Mount A, for all those times you let me share the moment too.

POSTSCRIPT

In late 2020 Mount Allison awarded me a new honour: chancellor emeritus. Again I was humbled, and very happy to keep the connection.

The Real Stephen Harper

I have never been close to any of the prime ministers I've covered. I have had, for the most part, good relations with all of them, some better than others, but never by much.

Some were impossible to get close to. Pierre Trudeau was known as aloof and that was a pretty accurate description, especially in my case, because I was very green when I arrived on Parliament Hill in 1976, a prairie stubble jumper in my twenties. I ended up doing more than a few major interviews with Trudeau over the next eight years but still, I never sensed that he knew or cared who I was, and nor for that matter, did he need to. In the spring of 1984, after he'd taken that legendary walk in a snowstorm and decided to retire, I'm sure that when someone plunked a picture of Trudeau and me from one of those interviews in front of him for signature, he had to ask who that other person in the photo was. When I look at the way he wrote my name, you can see he stopped halfway through, and I imagine him looking at his aide and asking, "How does he spell that?"

While they were polar opposites, Stephen Harper was a little bit like Trudeau in that it was hard to say I ever really knew him.

I'd covered Harper in his first days as an MP on Parliament Hill. He left in the mid-1990s, clearly unhappy with the leadership of Preston Manning at the Reform Party. But he didn't want to leave the political scene, so he became an analyst, and a good one at that. It was the late '90s before we initiated the "At Issue" days on CBC Television, but I was road-testing the idea with an occasional political panel on *The National*. Harper often became the voice on the right and the voice of the West. He had great political instincts and wasn't shy about making his views

Who caught the bigger fish?
CBC

clear, even when those views criticized the conservative side he was on. He also showed an occasional sense of humour. Okay, very occasional.

As Canada moved into the new millennium, Harper was one of those Conservatives who knew that the only way they could ever retain power was to form an alliance between the two right-wing parties: Reform, by then known as the Canadian Alliance, and the old Progressive Conservatives. When merger was finally achieved in 2003, Harper became its first leader. He held the Liberals to a minority in 2004 and then won the first of three elections in 2006.

Conservatives, many of them anyway, don't like the CBC, convinced it is inhabited by Liberals, if not Communists. Many Liberals, mind you, think the corporation is full of Conservatives. Funny what happens when a party comes to power and realizes that the public broadcaster is there to serve the public, not them. In other words, it really is a *public* broadcaster, not a *state* broadcaster. Harper never went as far as some of his party, but he wasn't a fan of CBC News or, for that matter, most media. I'll give him this, though—he rarely said no when I asked for an interview. We might haggle over dates and interview length with his office, but in the end something almost always got worked out.

Interviewing Harper was often like interviewing an academic, especially when the questions involved the economy. After all, he had spent time as a professor of economics at the University of Calgary. That often made it hard to have a good conversation. I needed to look for a moment to break the monotony, but I'm sure most viewers wore glazed-over looks trying to follow the arguments.

In one of our one-on-ones during his prime ministership, he was delivering what we call "message track," the party line rehearsed in preparation. He was doing that and I was trying to break him out of it. I had noticed that lately in some of his public statements he occasionally prefaced an answer with the phrase: "Let me be honest here." And on that day he used it again.

"Let me be honest here, Peter . . ."

So, I interrupted. "Surely, Prime Minister, you're always honest, no?"

He looked momentarily stunned. He sheepishly smiled. And said something like, "Of course, it was just a phrase." And then moved on.

When the interview ended, he turned to me and said, "You really got me there on the honest thing. I have to stop using that phrase."

I don't think he ever did use it with me again.

As tough as it was to get to know Stephen Harper, I felt fate did allow us that moment.

The morning of October 22, 2014, dawned peacefully enough in Ottawa. It wouldn't turn out that way.

I was in Toronto having a breakfast meeting with a source at the historic York Club on Bloor Street West. I'd left my phone on, which was unusual for me in such a setting, but when it suddenly started ringing, I grabbed it.

"There's been a shooting on Parliament Hill, you better get in." It was Michael Gruzuk, a senior producer with CBC.

Fifteen minutes later, I was on the air, shuffling through the developments, trying to sort out fact from rumour, and that's where I stayed for the next few hours.

What we learned was that a lone gunman, armed with a 30-30 Winchester hunting rifle, shot and killed a soldier standing on guard at the National War Memorial, then ran across the street and into the Parliament Buildings, shooting up the Hall of Honour, including the doors to the various party meeting rooms—full in each case because it was a Wednesday morning, the regular caucus meeting day. And then in a final shootout, the gunman was shot dead outside the Parliamentary Library. There were lots of rumours about other gunmen and more shootings, including in a nearby shopping centre, resulting in a locked-down downtown core. But in the end, the story was as first outlined above. A lone gunman. A dead soldier. And that was awful enough.

Our coverage had gone around the world on various international cable-news operations with solid and responsible journalism from the likes of Rosemary Barton, Julie Van Dusen, and Evan Solomon. When I handed the story over to my colleagues at CBC News Network, I headed into a quick story meeting on how we would cover things for *The National* that night. We also decided that I should anchor from Ottawa the next day, and so early the next morning I headed to the airport.

In Ottawa, I went to our bureau first and then straight to the House of Commons to watch Question Period. It was emotional and honest. No showboating on this day. All MPs had had the scare of their lives, persistent gunfire outside their caucus rooms spraying the doors as the gunman ran down the main hall. The leaders crossed the floor of the Commons and hugged each other in a display of unity that was raw. Some had tears in their eyes. I sat in the press gallery overlooking the floor, witnessing it all. At one point, I saw Stephen Harper look up at the gallery and see me there, but his face was expressionless.

About half an hour after QP, I got a phone call from one of the prime minister's senior staff.

"The PM would like to see you at five p.m. It will be off the record."

Those are offers you don't refuse, especially on a day like that one.

With the building still locked down and no visitors allowed, I went to a prearranged spot on the back side of the Centre Block behind the Peace Tower, where I was met by security and one of the PM's people and began a walk I'd never been on before. It wasn't a secret path but it was a route I didn't know, and I'd been in and out of the building for almost sixty years. A series of narrow hallways, marble stairs, and solid wooden doors took about five minutes to travel, and then the doors opened to a room where Stephen Harper was sitting. He motioned me to a couch beside him.

He started the conversation by congratulating the CBC for its live coverage the day before, suggesting it was the most reliable and responsible information he and his caucus colleagues received while the scene had been unfolding. (I've often thought that may have been the only time I ever heard him saying nice things about the CBC!)

Now, there was a story already floating around Parliament Hill that when the shooting got close, the PM hid in a caucus room closet. No one denied it, but no one would talk about it either. So I asked him.

His reply was short and to the point. "I can't talk about anything that occurred immediately during the incident until the investigation is complete." But then he went the extra mile, adding along these lines, this: "Peter, when I first became PM in 2006, the RCMP put me on a rigorous training session for situations just like this. How to protect myself, how to seek cover, how to lead from a very difficult position."

I took that to mean the closet story was true and that it was exactly the kind of thing he'd been taught by the RCMP.

As we spoke, it was clear that he wasn't very happy about how the building had been defended. He couldn't understand how a lone gunman could make his way from a car in front of Parliament, up a staircase, through the entrance, and down a long hallway, with guards all around who couldn't stop him. Part of the reason was that some of those guards were almost like tour guides. Unarmed and therefore unable. It was clear from the prime minister's expression that things were going to change. And eventually they did; within months, the guards were moved under the control of the RCMP.

Our conversation went on for about half an hour. He filled in some blanks, but not many. He was careful about what he said.

Before I left I went personal for a few moments. "Were you scared?"

He wouldn't answer directly but he did say, "The noise of that gunfire was deafening. You couldn't help but think of what might happen at any moment."

Then I tried one more ask. "Who did you call first when it was all over?"

He paused, but not for long. "My mother. I knew she would have been watching and I knew she would have been very worried."

For the first time in almost twenty years of interviewing him, I sensed the real Stephen Harper.

POSTSCRIPT

A new, armed security detail now guards Parliament Hill.

Stephen Harper has never talked about the closet.

Tens of thousands of people came to the National War Memorial a few weeks later on Remembrance Day, the largest crowd the capital had seen for the occasion in years. They were there for two reasons: we always gather on November 11th, and also to remember Corporal Nathan Cirillo, who had been shot in the back and killed as he stood on guard at that same memorial just three weeks before. He had been carrying a Colt C7 rifle, but because his duty was ceremonial, by custom, it was not loaded.

Peter Moosebridge

There's something about me and airports. I got my first job with the CBC because of an airport experience, I ended up going through the Northwest Passage because of an airport encounter, and of course, like many other travelers, I've spent hours and hours sitting in airports around the world contemplating the life around me.

I remember sitting in the Baghdad airport just weeks before the US invasion of Iraq in 2003, an invasion everyone knew was coming. It was about two in the morning and I was waiting for a much-delayed Royal Jordanian airline flight to Amman. The flight had originally been booked for 10 p.m., and I passed the time by staring at the terminal building's ceiling. I must have been quite bored because I found the ceiling fascinating. While on one hand, the whole building seemed relatively modern in design, it was also not built to last. The roof seemed to be constructed of a rather flimsy sheet metal and would certainly not withstand incoming cruise missiles, which was to be the case in the days ahead. Airports are often high on a first target list, and I sat there imagining how easily one of those missiles, fired from a US warship in the Red Sea or the Mediterranean Sea or the Persian Gulf would glide through that exterior like butter.

But I digress. This is not a story about war, but a story about a cartoon character. Seriously.

In the spring of 2015, I was on my way to Vancouver to give a speech and I was passing through security at Pearson International Airport in Toronto. Even for experienced fliers, the security perp walk is always a challenge. Different rules don't just apply in different countries—they also apply in different airports. Some want all shoes off; some want only some shoes off. Some want laptops and phones out of the carry-on; others don't. And so on. The secret here is to be calm and just go with the flow. And whatever you do, don't talk for fear something you say may be misinterpreted.

So I was quietly minding my business, shoes off, phone and laptop in the tray, and waiting for my stuff to come through the X-ray machine, when I heard someone behind me say, "Hey, aren't you Peter Mansbridge?"

I'll admit that does happen fairly often and it's always flattering, and even in an airport security line I try my best to act appreciative of the recognition. But this one came with a job offer.

After exchanging pleasantries, my new acquaintance said, "I was just in a meeting and we were talking about you."

"Really?" I said.

He nodded. "My name is Greg Mason and I'm a vice president with Disney and we want you in our next animated feature."

Sure, I thought. Some random guy wants to make me the next Mickey Mouse. This was definitely a joke. Was *Candid Camera* still a TV show? Were they lurking somewhere in the background?

But Greg didn't stop there. With the security line starting to back up, we stepped off to the side to let others through.

"We're in production for our next blockbuster animated children's feature," he told me. "*Frozen* set new records for us, but this one, *Zootopia*, will be even bigger. And we want you in it—well, your voice anyway."

I was still suspicious and told him the CBC had rules against its journalists starring in movies, so it was a nonstarter. He wouldn't give up, thrusting a business card in my hands and saying he would be in touch.

Quite frankly, I never thought I'd hear from him again, but I was wrong. A few days later, he was in touch with a detailed offer to be the voice of a character that they had designed especially for me. It was a moose news anchor in the city of Zootopia, by the screen name of Peter Moosebridge. They'd pay real money, cover all expenses, and fly me and my family to Los Angeles for the studio recording work.

"How long is the part?" I asked.

"Well, it's actually more of a cameo, probably about ten or fifteen seconds," Greg said.

"And you are going to go to all that trouble for ten seconds?"

"Hey, this is the real deal. This is Hollywood."

I explained how I wouldn't and couldn't accept money—it could go to a charity instead. I also said the hurdle with the CBC's policy about its journalists still existed and I would have to check that. My inquiry went all the way up to the president of the CBC, Hubert Lacroix. And he, buffeted at the time by various issues at the CBC, ruled against my involvement. There was an irony in his decision. He made it while with his family on vacation at—wait for it—Disney World.

So that was that. Or was it? I decided to appeal. By then, I knew I was soon going to announce my retirement, and this was something to do for my grandkids—Honor, Hope, and Ryder—as much as it was for me. Plus, Disney and the CBC had been partners since the 1950s, with no controversial issues surrounding that alliance. I'd done, at the CBC's request, other appearances on other CBC kids shows, why not this? It would be seen by hundreds of millions of people around the world, why would we pass up the opportunity?

To his credit, Lacroix reconsidered, changed his mind, and as a result, I was ready for my close-up. The Hollywood recording session was set for August.

But, not so fast. Now it was Stephen Harper's time to get in the way.

The prime minister decided August was the time for an early election call. There would be an eleven-week campaign leading up to October 19. And that meant, because of my duties at *The National*, I couldn't leave the country for some boondoggle in California.

I called Greg and told him that while I was upset, Disney should look for someone else. But he wasn't giving up that easy. If I wouldn't fly to Disney, Disney would fly to me.

And so, in mid-August, Disney arranged an elaborate setup with a high-tech video connection from the studios in Hollywood to a recording studio in Toronto. It was booked for four hours. Limos, food, and lots of people to help with whatever I needed, which of course was next to nothing. The whole process took about forty-five minutes.

I did a number of "takes" to give them options on inflection and pacing. Everyone seemed happy. I signed my contracts, waived my fee, and had it sent instead to a Canadian-based charity.

A few weeks later, Greg called and said there was a problem. To meet the rules of Disney's agreement with the Screen Actors Guild, I had to receive *some* money. We agreed one dollar seemed appropriate. And that's what I got. A Disney cheque for one dollar made out to me. It's framed and hanging in my office. Of course, it's worth more than a loonie because it's US currency—I don't come cheap.

Zootopia was released in 2016, and I finally got to see it at its Toronto premiere. It really is a good movie, and not just for children. While it tells an entertaining story, it also touches, and not so subtly, on the need and the value of a country accepting its diversity. A lesson, in some ways, that was before its time.

You have to be patient, though, waiting for Peter Moosebridge. He's teased in a few visuals but it's near the final scenes before anchor Moosebridge delivers his big lines. Both of them. All ten seconds or so.

Without trying to explain the movie, let's just say that these were critical lines to the unfolding plot. At least I thought so.

First, Scene 29: "Meanwhile, a peace rally organized by pop star Gazelle was marred by protest."

Then, Scene 38: "Her predecessor, Leodore Lionheart, denies any knowledge of her plot, claiming he was just trying to protect the city."

I waited for the theatre to explode in applause. It didn't happen. But people loved the movie, the first sign for Disney that it was going to be the success they predicted.

But the moment that really got me was in the credits. They moved slowly, but eventually they rolled to the key line. Key for me anyway.

PETER MOOSEBRIDGE   PETER MANSBRIDGE

That sure looked good. An airport encounter had struck again.

They didn't get the eyes quite right.
© *Disney Enterprises Inc. Used with permission.*

POSTSCRIPT

Zootopia *was a huge success. It set national and worldwide box office records and won a Golden Globe and an Oscar. I like to claim that my ten seconds was really what put it over the top. And who's to argue?*

The grandkids loved it. To them Zootopia is my career achievement—much more important than all the other "stuff."

By the way, I'm still waiting for a call about a sequel.

–II–

What Is "It"?

I KNOW WHAT YOU MIGHT BE THINKING. I TOLD YOU AN interesting story about Howard Stringer and CBS (pages and pages ago), but I didn't answer the key question.

Why did he want me? There were more than three hundred million people in the United States at the time and he had to come to Canada to find an anchor? It doesn't make sense, does it? I've asked that same question about some other parts of my life too.

Why did those producers from the National Film Board decide I was the one they wanted to work on their 1958 film? Why did Gaston Charpentier decide I was the guy he wanted at his radio station in Churchill? Why did producers for Disney Productions name a character after me and want my voice to match their animation? It's not like anyone asked for a résumé. No one asked for anything beyond meeting me in the flesh and hearing my voice.

Back in the fall of 1988, in my final meeting with Stringer, I did ask *him* the question. "Howard, why me?"

And he had the classic TV business answer. "Because you have 'it.'"

Now, no one, not even Howard Stringer, can really define "it," but you sure hear that argument used to justify a lot of decisions in the TV business.

"It" may not be definable in words, but it's something anyone can notice. When you're watching television, whether it's news or not, do you find yourself favouring certain people over others? And I'm talking about first appearances here, before you have any real chance to judge a person's actual ability. Your feelings after that initial contact are often based on the "it" factor. Does that person make you feel comfortable and does their eye contact with the camera, and therefore with you, make you feel they are credible? Do you think they are someone you could be friends with? Do you think, knowing nothing about them, that they probably care about what you care about?

As you can see, "it" is a very personal thing; different people look for different qualities. But in the end, it's remarkable how many agree that certain people have "it." And people like Howard Stringer and Gaston Charpentier and the NFB fellow and even the Disney people look for "it" almost before anything else.

If you think that sounds like an imperfect science, you're right. It is. Making instant judgments based on the "it" factor is a heck of a gamble, and worse, making judgments based on *not* seeing "it" in others can leave some truly talented people on the sidelines of a much-coveted job.

So, back to the CBS example. Stringer makes his initial judgment based on what he saw on a tape of someone he's never met, in fact, never even heard of before. He has a one-hour meeting to confirm his initial assumptions. And then, days later, he makes a multi-million-dollar offer to fill one of his network's prime pieces of news real estate. Now, Howard Stringer was no flash in the pan. His office was stacked with Emmys and prestigious journalism awards. He had a glorious international reputation. He would go on to higher executive positions at CBS and then leave the company, eventually becoming the chairman of SONY worldwide. He was the real deal, and in November of 1987 he was telling me, the baggage-handler kid from Churchill, that I could attain the heights

On Parliament Hill in the winter of 1978 doing publicity
photos for what turned out to be the 1979 election
campaign. Left to right: Knowlton Nash, David Halton,
Mike Duffy, Don McNeill, me, Brian Stewart,
John Blackstone, Ken Colby, and Mark Phillips.
CBC

of TV journalism in the United States. Maybe he was right, but perhaps
he was wrong. The fact is, in my case, we will never know.

In the many years since, I've been in Howard's position more than
a few times. I've watched new people arrive hoping to break into the
big leagues of Canadian TV news. They seemed to have all the basics:
presence, appearance, a good voice, and a résumé that puffed up what,
at that time, was a relatively short career. More than once, we took a
gamble only to realize disappointment. It's one thing to fake your way
through local news, quite another to pull it off at a more senior level.

One of the most serious journalists I ever worked with was the *Globe
and Mail*'s Jeffrey Simpson. He was so serious, some felt he was just a
couple of zones above the rest of us, maybe even one above his own
limit. I liked Jeffrey and felt, when I included him on our political pan-

els, he gave us a heft and class we didn't have without him. But Jeffrey often found television shallow—just not deep enough—and he may have had a point there. He had a sense of humour about it, though. One Christmas in the late 1980s, with a not-so-concealed smile, he gave me a little marble plaque for my desk with these words printed on it: "Bullshit baffles brains."

I didn't take it personally, but I also didn't disagree. I'd witnessed the truth of those words many times, even been deserving of it on occasion. I guess that's why I still have the plaque, and secretly award it to deserving anchors every once in a while.

Welcome to the world of network television news. It is a strange world. Careers are often made or broken overnight. And sadly, so are standards.

Journalism is based on trust. Or so it should be. And trust is often gained through the pathway of truth. The two "T's."

Trust has taken a beating over the past few years. People's faith in institutions has waned, and professions once seen as rock-solid aren't so

Covering Joe Clark in the 1979 election campaign. I'm in the bottom left.
University of Toronto Archives

invincible anymore. From politicians to journalists and the many voca-
tions in between, these professions at times now rank at the same end of
the trust spectrum as what we once called used-car salesmen. (Wisely,
the men and women who sell older cars now describe their products as
"previously owned" vehicles, which seems to have added a new layer
of prestige and class to their work and allowed them to up their profile
slightly and their "trust factor" too.)

But it will need more than a name change to help journalists. The
profession must reestablish its position of trust in the ever-expanding,
ever-powerful information age. We live in an era where there is more
information available, literally at our fingertips, than at any other time
in the history of the planet. But how trustworthy is that information?
Sadly, in far too many cases, not very.

It's due, in part, to the fact that the news landscape is extremely
different than it was in the half-century since I started. Back in those
dinosaur days, there were two major networks in Canada, the CBC
and CTV. One national newspaper, the *Globe and Mail*. Three major
networks in the States. No 500-channel universe, no Internet, no cable
news, no streaming services, no Facebook, no Twitter, no Instagram, no
TikTok, no whatever new social media platform was invented yesterday.
It was a very different world, a world much easier to trust.

The media is, of course, not a monolith. Different news organizations have different values, guidelines, policies. And some have none at
all. Yet somehow, to many, they are all seen as equals. And so, when one
has a problem, often it means they all have a problem.

When Facebook circulates proven falsehoods and conspiracy theories, consumers who care (and not all do) demand fixes and corrections.
But Facebook, which claims it's not a news organization—even though,
in my view, it clearly is—takes no responsibility and no accountability.
Ditto for Twitter and the others. Far more people go to social media for
their news and information, and as a result, they are drinking from a
polluted news well.

But you can't blame it all on social media. Traditional media gets sloppy too. Even the best of the best. And when the best of the best gets things wrong, even when it's one story out of thousands, the damage is devastating.

Take the *New York Times*. In 2018, it ran a brilliant podcast series and an accompanying print series about ISIS which relied heavily on a Canadian who claimed to be a former ISIS member and whose sordid stories of torture, rape, and murder left listeners and readers gutted. The journalism won numerous awards, including a Peabody. There was only one problem. It didn't stand up to scrutiny and further fact-checking. Awards were withdrawn, apologies were made, careers were held in limbo. For the *Times*, which was enjoying one of the best runs in its storied history, the whole episode was more than embarrassing, it was a disaster.

None of us is perfect. Mistakes do happen. Fortunately, unlike the "Caliphate" story, most mistakes are small. But mistakes they still are. They damage, even destroy, your credibility. Your trustworthiness. And they must be addressed. Even the little ones. That's why newspapers have page-two correction boxes and why television networks—at least ones that care about their credibility—find ways to fix their mistakes too.

During my thirty years anchoring *The National*, I had my share of fixes to do, and while the natural impulse was to bury the corrections near the end of the newscast, some argued the opposite. "This won't hurt us. It will only enhance our work by proving that we care about getting things right." That was the attitude people like senior editor Mark Bulgutch would take. Even today, with my podcast *The Bridge*, I follow that same guidance. It doesn't hurt to admit when you're wrong. It helps.

One night in the mid-1980s, we lifted a clip out of the House of Commons television feed because a spotter quite correctly pointed to a sequence saying, "That sure doesn't happen often." Prime Minister Brian Mulroney had just given a speech on an issue that had caused divisions between the parties, but there on the feed was opposition leader John Turner walking over to acknowledge Mulroney and shake

Sitting between two real icons, Barbara Frum and David Halton.
CBC

his hand. We ran the clip and I commented about how even partisan debate has its limits.

However, things aren't always as they seem. It wasn't Turner. It was Mulroney's silver-haired fisheries minister, Tom Siddon. The shot was of Siddon's back, and from that angle it sure looked like Turner. But it wasn't. None of the principals were upset. In fact, most thought it was funny. But they all wanted an apology delivered and we wanted to give one. The next night, the fix was made in our broadcast.

Being transparent about our work is critical to improving the dilemma that many journalists find themselves in. With our audiences second-guessing the value of our work, we can't ignore or dismiss their concerns.

In 2018 and 2019, I gave a few lectures about journalism at the University of Saskatchewan and the University of Toronto. I wanted those in attendance—students, alumni, and members of the general public—

to give me one word, or at most a short phrase, they would use to describe what they think is wrong with journalism today. Hands shot up in the rooms where I was lecturing. People weren't shy. They were armed and ready, and it wasn't pretty: biased, disconnected, corrupt, wrong, depressing, boring, one-sided, irrelevant, phony, unfair, a lack of transparency, activist, sensationalized, and yes, even fake.

How did I feel hearing that parade of condemnation? After five decades of devoting my life to journalism, of defending it, of privileging it, and having it so ingrained in who I was, the words cut deep. But I couldn't rightly defend against them. It was the middle of the Trump era and it had become the wild wild West of bashing the media by calling it the enemy of the people, a claim that had significant support. But on the other hand, those defending the media were openly calling the president of the United States a blatant, sexist, misogynistic, racist liar. And that was on just a normal day. It was, and still is, an ugly time.

When I asked my audience how to fix the media, the answers often came down to earning trust through the most basic of qualities—being more connected to the lives of ordinary people and less so to the power elite—and being more transparent about how journalists make the decisions we do.

All this takes me back to that elusive question: What is "it"? Well, I think it has to do with trust. (Though *trust* me, I wasn't always trusted!) But when I think about the times when I felt I had "it," I think about these moments and the trust viewers placed in me:

Standing on the hills of Rome surrounding the Vatican waiting for a puff of white smoke.

Standing on the Great Wall of China in the last days of Mao in 1976.

Sitting with Barbara Frum watching the Queen and Pierre Trudeau sign the 1982 repatriation of the Constitution.

Standing near the Brandenburg Gate in Berlin in 1989 watching the Wall come down.

Standing on the beaches of Normandy, numerous times, where so much Canadian blood was spilled.

Standing in the tunnels below Vimy Ridge where young Canadians gathered before they went into a cruel and brutal battle.

Facing the balcony of Buckingham Palace where Charles and Diana, Andrew and Sarah, Will and Kate embraced to celebrate marriage. (Well, one out of three ain't bad.)

And strangely enough, that's how so many people relate to me even today, years after I left the anchor chair.

I often have people ask me, "What was it like to . . . Be at a royal wedding? Be at Nelson Mandela's funeral? Be at a papal conclave? Sit across from Barack Obama in the White House? Meet Diana? Be in Afghanistan? And how did you remain so calm on 9/11?"

What they're asking boils down to this: What is it like to be an ordinary human being in the middle of extraordinary circumstances while at the same time being the vehicle for an entire country to witness those events? Fires, funerals, weddings, bombings, wars, birthdays, election nights, leadership convention victories and defeats. When I hear questions like that, I realize that it was through my eyes, my words, my heart that many Canadians were viewing these events, learning through my lens—not a bias but a lens. I spent a career trying to keep Canadians guessing about my biases. Some felt they noticed a bias through a twitch of an eyebrow; others saw the opposite. Now, I'm not a robot. I feel things. But I wasn't being paid to express my feelings, and I didn't. The pressure and the responsibility were tremendous. As was the privilege of being trusted to show and tell and help Canadians experience the world and what matters to them. It sounds so obvious, but when I was sitting in that anchor chair, I didn't often think of it that way, but I certainly felt people's trust, curiosity, and confidence, and I promise, at no time did I ever fake any of that.

It was only after I retired from day-to-day news coverage that I realized people had spent years getting to know me in a very personal way. I've had new Canadians, dozens and dozens of them now, come up to me to say they arrived in Canada unable to speak English, but they learned English by listening to me each night. Can you imagine

Seconds before air for the last time on *The National*
set in Toronto, June 28, 2017.
CBC

what that feels like to hear someone say that about your work? It's over-whelming. They're not crying. I am.

And for others, I was guiding them through a rapidly changing world. I'm not sure I ever fully appreciated that connection. But today I get glimpses of it—in airports, in grocery stores, in hotels, on the street. People will come up to me, more so now than even when I was on the job, to say hello, mention a big event they watched, and sometimes sim-ply to say thank you.

Let's be clear, it was my job. I got paid. But that job exposed me to public service in a way that went far beyond what I ever did on my own. It was a different kind of "it," but it was an "it" nonetheless. And it was an "it" based on trust and truth.

When I think of how I got to those moments I mentioned, the an-swer is by standing on the shoulders of and being propped up by the smart men and women I worked with in my career even when, some-times, they could have left me floundering. I haven't always behaved well. I haven't always deserved the opportunities I've had. But others either covered for me or found ways to smooth over any issues caused by my actions. I'm not talking about gross offences, just silly things that I've seen others stumble over while I seemingly got a pass and was able to move onto "greater glory," if you will. That too, I'll admit, is a benefit of having "it," of having trust.

All the excitement, all the privilege, all the glory that came with the job could at times go to my head, even when it really wasn't about me. But there was a safety valve just in case I got carried away with how important I felt. You see, for all the credit I would receive for a job well done, even when much of the credit rightly deserved to go elsewhere, like to those behind the scenes, I often stood there alone when the crap started flying in our direction. Often, I became the target. I understood. It was part of the job.

And it still is, I realized, during those university visits. Lack of transparency, loss of trust, the blurring of the lines between traditional news and opinion—these are real issues and have led to a questioning of journalistic methodology that has become more wide-ranging with time: The partisan nature of the media—is it by design, necessity, or human nature? As the world becomes more polarizing, as the rules are broken by the rule makers, as facts themselves become seen as partisan, how do you tell a story objectively? Facts were facts, until there were "alternate facts." Truth was truth, until there was "my truth, and your truth." It all becomes even more difficult to untangle when the loudest voices are too often misconstrued as the most important voices.

Is balance always about representing both sides? So, do you have to have a climate denier on a climate panel? Okay then, do you need an anti-vaxxer on a vaccine panel? Fine, then how about a racist on a racism panel? See, it's complicated. What is bias? What is balance? How do you tell both sides of a story when both sides are not equal, and who decides they're not equal?

These are not new arguments, but the times are new, and it makes searching for the answers all the more challenging. And the stakes are as high as ever, perhaps even higher. It's not a stretch to say the future of journalism, in a world that's redefining the practice, is very much at risk.

As the old fart in the room, my tendency is to argue for a return to the basics: focus on facts not bullshit, admit mistakes, understand responsibility, serve the people not the elite. But that just may not cut it anymore. Too much has changed. The tools, the pace, the expectations, they're all different. In the end, if this wonderful profession is going to remain a pillar of democracy, then it may have to be the consumer who finally demands more and demands better. And demands now before it's too late.

Whether it's the journalist or the consumer, affecting change will take courage, but that's okay. Because courage is contagious.

Paris

It was Friday the 13th, not that those kinds of things bother me, but at the same time I'm not surprised when something bad happens. And it did on that November day in 2015.

I had the day off, so I left Toronto and headed to our home in Stratford for the weekend. By the time I arrived in the late afternoon, news started to trickle in from Paris. There had been an explosion at a football stadium, the Stade de France, where President François Hollande had been in attendance. The first reports said that there were two bombers, one of whom blew himself up in the process. But the night was just beginning. Within minutes of the explosion, a few kilometres away in the heart of Paris, gunmen with high-powered assault rifles strafed a restaurant, then a nearby bar, and then a nightclub. The attacks seemed coordinated, and the casualties, including scores of dead, were mounting.

I looked at Cynthia and said that I had to get back to Toronto. She understood, the way journalists' partners tend to understand.

On the two-hour drive, I talked with the office and we started putting together what we hoped we could accomplish for that night's *National*. It was a story that was changing by the minute; rumours—as they always are at times like that—were chased down, dismissed, or built upon. Our London bureau was racing to get to Paris any way they could. Reporters, producers, editors, all heading to the French capital.

The broadcast that night was very strong and responsible, given the ever-changing details and the crash edits being performed in CBC suites in London, Paris, and Toronto.

When we were off the air, we immediately went into an editorial meeting about what to do next. The decision was no surprise: get to

Paris and mount programming that would capture the horror of what had happened, but also move the story forward by trying to understand the motivation of the killers and how they'd held one of the world's great cities hostage. By then, the death toll was staggering—one hundred and thirty—and another four hundred and thirteen were injured.

We flew out the next day and on arrival in Paris went straight to one of the hotels where we had booked rooms. It was situated not far from a small plaza and park called Place de la Republique, a stone's throw from one of the restaurant-bars that had been shot up on Friday night. We walked toward the restaurant, but it had been zoned off by Paris police holding back the crowds of onlookers. However, next door was a patisserie that was still open even though some of the gunfire had ricocheted through its windows. Behind the pastry counter, there was a clock on the wall. It was early afternoon, but the clock read 9:40. One of the bullets had hit it, stopping the mechanism, freezing the hands in the moment of the shooting. The owner told us he would never have it fixed.

The plaza was full of people, at least ten thousand by my guess. Everywhere, there were Parisians in tears, hugging, and bringing flowers for makeshift memorials. In times like these we conduct what we call "streeters"—we go up to people and just ask what they are feeling and how they are explaining what happened to themselves and their friends. It was emotional for many, and they weren't shy about showing the range of those emotions from fear to sorrow to anger. We spent an hour or so trying to make our way through the crowd, but it was hard because the small plaza was really packed. At one point, what sounded like gunshots could be heard and panic took over. People were running in all directions. Journalists were trying to stay safe but also cover the story at the same time. Within minutes, it was clear it was a false alarm—a car backfiring seemed to be behind the moment. People returned, relieved but solemn.

We were on a tight schedule to assemble enough material for our part of that night's special broadcast, and next on our agenda was an interview with a terrorism expert who had thoughts on what we were witnessing. We grabbed a Paris taxi near the plaza and headed to a restaurant patio about twenty minutes away where producer Stephanie Jenzer had prearranged to do the interview. With that done, it was back to the hotel to begin an edit. Stephanie had paid for the taxi on the way to the interview, so I said I'd pay for this one.

When we got to the hotel, I reached into my pocket for my small wallet that contained my credit cards, some cash, and my hotel card.

Nothing.

I checked all my pockets.

Nothing.

Stephanie paid the driver. I was beside myself because I'm not one to lose things. I'm very careful. Standing on the sidewalk outside the hotel, we called the terrorism expert we'd just interviewed in case he had seen it. He checked the patio where we'd had a coffee.

Nothing.

Then I thought about the time we'd spent in Place de la Republique— an hour or so crammed into an area with thousands of people bumping into each other. Could I have somehow dropped it from my pocket? Could it have been a pickpocket? I'd once had my pocket picked in Dublin in 1986 while covering an anti-divorce rally in one of the city's squares. I decided that must be what had happened in Paris too.

I knew what this meant. A night on the phone cancelling all my cards with VISA and American Express and trying to get replacements, not the way I wanted to spend my time with the biggest story in the world unfolding in front of me.

We walked into the hotel and toward the front desk. It was one of those hotels where you have to give your key to the attendant when you leave for the day.

"The name is Mansbridge," I said, adding my room number.

"Oui, monsieur, we have something for you," he replied. And then he passed me something wrapped with a piece of paper and an elastic band. It was roughly the same size as my small wallet. Could it be?

It was. My wallet. With everything intact.

The desk clerk said a man had been by a few minutes before, said he'd found the wallet lying on the ground at Place de la Republique, saw the hotel card inside, and brought it to the address on the card.

I looked at the piece of paper. It simply said, "Jean," with a Parisian phone number.

I called the number that evening and thanked Jean profusely. I told him I was going to send him something, but he actually seemed insulted. He said he would accept nothing.

"It was the right thing to do," he told me.

All these years later, I still carry Jean's piece of paper in my wallet, the same wallet. I take it out every few months to remind me that the world we live in is not always as we see it. That weekend in Paris was full of horror, the kind where you realize that our world can be a very, very nasty place, but even in the midst of all the ugliness, it can still be a place of goodwill.

Ringo

Ringo is a germaphobe. I discovered that the instant I met him in a bookstore in Los Angeles where he was promoting a new book of pictures he'd saved from over the years.

As the CBC crew and I arrived, his executive assistant said, "These are the Canadians, and this is Peter."

And then the most famous drummer in the world said, "Hello, Peter from Canada."

I reached out my hand. Ringo offered his elbow.

"Bumps, my boy, that's the safest way," said the one-time Richard Starkey made famous as Ringo of the Fab Four. (This was 2015; he was ahead of his time.)

I was thrilled to meet him and was hoping above hope that I wouldn't be disappointed. I wasn't. He was as you'd expect: funny, charming, and ready to talk. The only surprise was he's short. Very short. Barely over five feet. We had less than an hour together, but he was happy to chat about old Beatles stories, and even though I'm sure he'd told them a million times already, he made it sound like the first time with everyone. I'll admit it was a big deal for me, having grown up in those same years. I even told him how, after their first Sunday night appearance on *The Ed Sullivan Show*, some of the boys in my Ottawa high school who had been sporting Elvis-style greasy haircuts on Friday turned up on Monday looking like they'd just arrived from Liverpool. Moptops. That's how fast everything changed.

Anyway, we had a great interview, and I played fanboy at the end, asking for a picture. We both did the peace sign into my producer Lara Chatterjee's lens.

"You probably only wanted to ask about Paul," he teased her, somehow knowing, probably from years of experience, that even though she'd been born decades after their most popular years, she was one of those young women who swooned for Paul.

And then, sadly, it was time to move on. But I must have made an impression because Ringo suddenly reached out his hand to shake.

"Bumps, my boy," I said, and bumps we did.

Yeah Yeah Yeah.
Lara Chatterjee

The Burden of Service

I don't think I've ever seen anyone who looked more like he was carrying the weight of the world on his shoulders as the man who was walking toward me just at that moment.

I was on the top floor of the stadium hosting the Opening Ceremony of the Salt Lake City Olympics in 2002. It was literally minutes before the ceremony, which would be broadcasted to billions around the world, was to begin. And ahead of me was the director of the Federal Bureau of Investigation, Robert Mueller, flanked by four men with earpieces visible to anyone nearby.

This was to be the most heavily attended, most watched, and most hyped event to be held in the United States since the horror of 9/11 less than five months previous. Security was incredibly tight; we had been told to be at checkpoints at least six hours before the ceremony was to start, while lineups for the public started four hours before the event. We already had security clearance and were carrying Olympic media badges and cards with authorized photo IDs. Every bag, every pocket, every phone was inspected. Nothing was being taken for granted.

Mueller was a legend in Washington. He was a decorated Vietnam War hero, who had received a Bronze Star for rescuing a wounded marine under fire in 1968 and a Purple Heart after being shot in another firefight in 1969. In all, he was awarded more than half a dozen medals for bravery in Vietnam. Upon his return to America, he achieved his law degree and ended up in government, serving four presidents from both Bushes to Clinton and Obama. When he was nominated for the job as head of the FBI, he was approved by a unanimous vote of the U.S.

Senate. He took office in August of 2001, just weeks before the nation was attacked that September.

No wonder he looked like he was carrying an enormous burden on that February 8th evening in 2002.

Moments before, I had been in our location inside the stadium standing alongside Brian Williams of CBC Sports waiting for the hours to tick by till we'd be on air. Not far from us, Tom Brokaw and Bob Costas of the NBC team were doing the same. And broadcasters from around the world were lined up in their spots as well. With about thirty minutes to airtime, I told Brian I was going to go for a final walk to stretch my legs, so I headed up the stairs to the walkway that surrounded the top of the stadium. That portion was closed off to the public; it served the media and, more important, the VIPs and heads of government from many of the attending countries.

It wasn't long after I reached the top of the stairs and began my walk that I recognized Director Mueller coming the other way. He seemed totally focused on the job before him. As the distance between us closed, I saw him glance at me staring at him. It was for only a fraction of a second, but in that time he appeared to give me the slightest of nods. And then he and his bodyguards were gone.

You may wonder why I even tell this story. Perhaps because I've never forgotten that moment. As I watched Mueller through his special counsel investigation of Donald Trump after the 2016 US election, I often thought of that brief passing—and of the qualities he had spent a lifetime exhibiting as a public servant. In the jungles of Vietnam carrying a wounded buddy away from further danger, in a country devastated by terrorism trying to protect its citizens, and in the hallways of Congress battling the partisan attacks of some elected officials who had no right to question his honour.

Mueller had been guilty only of serving his country and bearing the weight of that responsibility all his life. And that's what I saw on his face that evening in Salt Lake City.

High Flight

My passion for aircraft and flying, combined with the profile of my job, twice allowed me to go up in Canada's most advanced fighter jet: the CF-18.

Once was out of the CF-18 base in Cold Lake, Alberta, in 2017, when I had a chance to capture what for me is an iconic picture. It was a short flight, and while up in the air, I interviewed Lieutenant-Colonel David Moar, who was one of our combat pilots in Iraq, and to my extreme delight had a few seconds of my own at the controls. Now, I'm sure the colonel was ghosting my every move, but when I was at the controls, a second CF-18 cut through the air behind us, which gave me, thanks to

Up, up, and away on a CF-18 with Lieutenant-Colonel Dave Moar.
Lara Chatterjee/Dave Rae

an installed GoPro camera, a great shot where I look like I'm in a dog-fight. My Tom Cruise, *Top Gun* moment.

However, I'd been in a CF-18 before for a longer, quite engaging experience for a very different reason altogether. It was 2002 and I was working on a one-hour documentary that would mark the first anniversary of 9/11 and focus on the untold stories of what had happened in Canada on that day. Part of the video we needed was an intercept of a passenger plane by a CF-18 to illustrate what Canada's new air defences looked like. We begged and we begged the Defence Department, and finally we got the okay.

Early one morning, we arrived at CFB Trenton, which was home for a squadron of CF-18s that had been prepped and readied for quick action if it was needed in the weeks and months immediately following 9/11. For our documentary, the idea was that a CF-18 would be scrambled to go up and intercept an incoming, unidentified aircraft flying into Canadian airspace. Playing the role of the mystery plane was an old Canadian Forces Viscount aircraft normally based in Ottawa. The simulation was that the Viscount would be coming in from US airspace without clearance and not responding to Canadian air traffic control.

We took off and went straight up and out over Lake Ontario. Within seconds, we were at altitude and the Viscount was visible in the distance. Seconds more and we were literally at its wingtip. I don't know whether I could tell the colour of the other pilot's eyes, but it sure did seem that close. We waggled our wings and did all the other things pilots need to do to communicate visually, and then the exercise was over. It was exhilarating for sure.

But it was also a very clear reminder. If it hadn't been an exercise, and if the other plane hadn't responded to the commands we were giving, the closer we got to Toronto the more likely the CF-18 pilot would have to use its missiles to end the threat. The military had put on a show for us to simulate what could happen in what was a very tense few months following 9/11—the skill and bravery of these pilots have always impressed me to no end.

Trending

I wrote my first tweet in front of Buckingham Palace on the day Will and Kate got married. Seriously. I barely knew what Twitter was at that point, but there I was tapping away on my phone.

I really enjoyed the royal wedding and had fun during the 2011 broadcast. It's not often we get to cover enjoyable events, so when we do, I've always felt it's okay to have a good time doing it. And I did, so much so that during a break, one of the crew told me that I was "trending" on Twitter, something else I didn't quite understand. When it was explained that it meant people were talking about some of the things I was saying on air, they asked me why I never "tweeted."

The CBC had signed many of us on to Twitter a few years before and encouraged us to use the social media platform to promote our programming. I figured we had a multi-million-dollar communications department to do that, so I'd focus instead on the news and let others worry about public relations. But others became addicted to Twitter, sometimes creating controversy when they let their opinions filter into their tweets in a way they never did with their on-air reporting. It was and still is a problem.

In any event, I decided that day, let's explore this platform for a bit. Ten years later and I've got three hundred and thirty-five thousand followers, and sometimes get carried away myself in what I tweet.

In the summer of 2020, I was so charged up watching my favourite hockey team, the Toronto Maple Leafs, rebound in the final four minutes of a playoff game against the Columbus Blue Jackets that I stretched my Twitter vocabulary a bit. The Leafs were down 3–0 when they went for broke, pulled their goalie for an extra forward, and stormed the Blue

Jackets' net. They went on to score three times to tie the game in regulation and then win it in overtime.

On that tying goal, with just seconds left in the game, I grabbed my phone and tweeted: "Holy shit."

That tweet tells you something. No other tweet I've ever sent was "liked" by as many people. But that's Twitter. Often, the more outrageous the tweet, the more popular, especially when it's from an unlikely source.

I run hot and cold on Twitter. I admire the chance for people to smartly argue their positions and engage in a debate that can be informative for all who follow it. I'm dismayed, though, at the times—too often, actually—where Twitter and other forms of social media turn into a sewer of hate, sexism, and racism. I don't tweet often and often when I do, it's a retweet of someone else's article or commentary that I find worthy of consideration even when I don't agree with it.

But I did write one tweet of which I am quite proud. I was in Washington on Friday, January 20, 2017, for the inauguration of Donald Trump. I'd also been at Barack Obama's first inauguration in 2009.

With Canadian ambassador David McNaughton the night before
the Trump inauguration in Washington.
Lara Chatterjee

There was no comparison between the two events. Obama flooded the area with a huge crowd. Trump had a good crowd, but it did not in any way compare.

But on Saturday, the day after the event, Trump sent his staff out to claim it had been the largest crowd ever assembled for an inauguration. I knew he had told untruths throughout the campaign that put him in the White House, and that wasn't dissimilar to many who had preceded him. But I thought the lying would stop when he took office. I was wrong. Very wrong.

On Sunday I flew out of Washington on a 6 a.m. flight from Reagan Airport. Passing overhead near the White House, I tweeted: "Flying out of DC this hour feeling disturbed. When POTUS or his people flat out lie, a fundamental pillar of democracy is threatened."

POSTSCRIPT

It was the first of more than twenty thousand lies or untruths the forty-fifth president of the United States told during his time in office, according to the Washington Post, *who made it part of their journalism to keep track. As it turned out, the lies did more than just threaten democracy, they destroyed it at the edges. It may take generations to restore what the country was founded upon.*

Gord Downie

The storm clouds were coming. I could see it in the sky and I could feel it in my bones. This could be nasty. Lightning almost certain.

And to top it off, I was exactly where I shouldn't be for weather conditions like that. A golf course—the Ladies' Golf Club of Toronto to be specific, an immaculately groomed, Stanley Thompson–designed course built in 1924. As its name suggests, the course is for women, the members are women, but men can apply for "guest card" status, as I did back in the early 1990s. I was lucky to be accepted and loved the opportunity.

On that particular summer day in 1990, I was playing with my longtime friend and fellow "guest cardholder" Allan Gregg, who had brought along two pals of his from the music industry, two guys he was helping make their way through the hoops of a tough business. Their names were Paul Langlois and Gord Downie. Yes, that Paul and that Gord from the Tragically Hip. I was keen to meet them because not only did I like their music, but my two daughters, Jennifer and Pamela, both in their late teens, were huge fans and never missed a Hip concert when the band passed through their hometown of Winnipeg.

As it started to rain and the clouds got even darker, we discussed whether we should get back to the clubhouse, but foolishly we opted for the "it's going to blow over" choice.

Wrong.

It didn't. In fact, within moments the lightning started and we ran for cover. Allan and Paul went one way, Gord and I went another, where we made another bad choice. We headed for shelter under a huge tree. We were lucky. Lightning did not strike us or the tree, but it could have, which left my daughters imagining the headline "Downie and Mans-bridge trapped in a lightning storm on Toronto golf course" when I later told them the story. It almost sounded like they wished that would have happened just to give them talking points.

After that, Gord and I stayed in touch. Over the years, I helped him out fundraising for a water conservation project he was involved with, and then one day he asked me to introduce the band at a sold-out concert they were doing at what was then the Air Canada Centre in Toronto. One of my dreams in life had always been to play with a rock band and stand in front of thousands of screaming fans. The fact I can't sing or play any musical instrument (I did play the tuba in high school—poorly) meant that would never happen. But this would be a close second.

Walking out onto the stage with the lights flashing and the crowd pumped for their rock heroes was quite something. The sound was deaf-ening. It was a rush. A real rush.

Then I said, "Ladies and gentlemen, the Tragically Hip," and the noise metre must have doubled in strength. I stayed onstage for an extra moment just to drink it all in. I'd had my rock star moment and every second was worth it.

In the spring of 2016, the Hip shook the music world. They an-nounced that Gord Downie had terminal brain cancer. He was receiv-ing treatments, but there was no cure. The news shocked not just the band's fan base, but the country. I sent Gord a message of support and told him that I wouldn't bother him unless he ever decided he wanted to talk, and if he did he knew where to find me.

But Gord had decided he would use what time he had left to write and perform. He and the Hip went on one last hugely successful tour across the country, and he wrote the passionate ode to Indigenous rights with *Secret Path*, an album which told the story of a runaway from a res-idential school. This was something entirely different for him, and his illness had inspired him to work harder at making it happen.

And while the summer of 2016 tour sold out everywhere it went, and while the final show in the band's hometown of Kingston, Ontario, was attended by the prime minister and watched by eleven million people on television, and while his voice seemed as pure as ever, it was a constant struggle. The cancer was tugging at his memory, and songs Gord had sung for thirty years had to be written out in long-form and put up on a teleprompter just in case he needed them.

After the last concert in late August, he was exhausted. But he wanted the opportunity to talk. We agreed to an interview in October in one of his rehearsal studios in downtown Toronto.

I don't usually get too nervous before an interview, but I was that day. Gord wasn't just a friend, he was an icon. His fans loved him and his country loved him. For many Canadians, he was almost the country's poet laureate—crafting music that talked of our landscape, our values, our people. And yet while his music would last forever, we were losing him.

His cancer had made him emotional around people, all people. Those he knew and those he didn't. Hugging and kissing were things he now did all the time. When producer Lara Chatterjee, who'd been a Hip

Gord will always be missed, but we'll always have his music.
Lara Chatterjee/Jean-Francois Bisson

fan almost since she was born, met him that morning for the first time, he embraced her and kissed her.

We sat down to get ready for the interview. The room was cramped, full of instruments and stacks of papers and books, but we had managed to squeeze in two small chairs. This was someone's home turned into a studio and there was nothing sterile about it.

I told him that we could stop anytime he wanted to take a break, and he said that was good because he would need to take one every five or ten minutes. As it turned out, we talked for more than an hour, and he never took a break.

Just before we started, I saw him print out something on his left palm. And then I realized what it was.

PETER.

I felt that in my whole being. He was afraid his memory would fail him. That he'd forget my name. This after we'd known each other twenty-five years. In fact, his palm was filled with writing, little "notes to self" about other names and places and dates. Just in case.

I looked over at Lara. She was crying. She wasn't alone.

He was amazing in the interview. He didn't hold back. He answered questions about his struggle against cancer, about his concerns for Indigenous Peoples, about his hopes for one more album.

Near the end, I asked him whether he was prepared for what was coming.

"What scares you?" I said.

"What scares me? I don't want to die because my son's just ten. My youngest son, Clemence. That really scares me, yes. Obviously. I sure want to do this right on the way out, so that he's not worried. Not too worried."

I was close to tears now. "You're fighting what's in front of you, though, right?"

"Yes, for sure. I can get more time. More time."

As I thanked him, he leaned forward, asked if it was okay to kiss. "Of course," I responded and kiss we did.

Lara Chatterjee

He then moved behind the piano and started to rehearse the title song for his soon-to-be-released album, *Secret Path*. It tells the true story of twelve-year-old Chanie Wenjack, who ran away from a northern Ontario residential school and tried to walk hundreds of kilometres in freezing weather to get back to his reserve. He never made it.

We sat there, watching Gord as he played.

You could not hear another sound in the room.

Only a dying man singing.

POSTSCRIPT

Gordon Edgar Downie, Canadian rock singer, songwriter, musician, activist, and member of the Order of Canada, died on October 17, 2017.

Each year, at least once, I take a marker pen and print out on my palm: G O R D.

The Trudeaus

My political reporting career has been bookended by the Trudeaus. First Trudeau the elder, then Trudeau the younger. Two very different politicians: one who often acted aloof and above the rest of us, the other who seems to love being with the people. One considered an intellectual, the other thought to have more street smarts.

I never had much of a relationship with Pierre Trudeau even though I interviewed him more than a few times. I never had the impression he knew who I was before the interview started, during it, or after it. I was just something he had to put up with for a few minutes, and then he could bat me away like some bothersome fly. Having said that, I'm still proud to have and show off to my kids and grandkids a signed picture of the two of us with David Halton in his office on Parliament Hill. In the

Don't spill the water.
CBC

moment of the camera click, one could argue he even seemed to know who he was sitting with, although I doubt it.

Justin Trudeau was and is a different experience. For starters, I was there almost at the beginning. I remember watching him as a baby on the front lawns of Parliament Hill during an early Canada Day party. Then watching him visit the Hill with his father in the early 1980s. His eulogy for his father in 2000. His decision to run for office in 2008, then for leader in 2013.

I got the first interview the day after his election as leader, the same day as the Boston Marathon bombing. The bombing had just happened, many of the details weren't known, but the blood from the victims still wasn't dry on the Boston streets. I asked the new Liberal leader what he would be saying in that moment if he were prime minister.

He didn't hesitate. He said we all had to understand the roots of such terror.

It was the wrong time to try to understand the bombers. It was the right time to show compassion for the victims. His office knew it had been a mistake. An unforced error, something which would later plague his prime ministership at times. They almost begged me not to run that clip. I said no, that was something we do not do. That clip was used over and over by the opposition parties in an attempt, unsuccessfully as it turned out, to hammer Trudeau as soft on terror. Instead, in October of 2015, Trudeau took his party from third to first place with a crushing majority victory over Stephen Harper.

On November 4, 2015, Trudeau was sworn in as Canada's new prime minister. My producer, Lara Chatterjee, had negotiated exclusive and unprecedented access to his first hours in the office, which she would then crash-edit into a long-form documentary for that night's *National*. It would be a tough assignment because of the short turn-around time; it would have its rough edges, but it would be something unlike anything Canadians had ever seen before. It was history, and the raw footage should be in the Public Archives of Canada.

We spent hours following Trudeau, asking questions when the

The kickoff interview for the 2015 election.
Lara Chatterjee

moment was right and watching history unfold. Things started with Trudeau taking two of his children, Ella-Grace and Xavier, into the prime minister's office—the same office his father had taken him to for the first time all those years before. (And the same office I'd interviewed his father in all those years before!)

Then it was up the Peace Tower to raise the flag. And I mean up the Peace Tower. Clutching Xavier, Trudeau scaled a very narrow iron staircase up the final steps until they were both on top of the Hill, their heads popping up in the raw November air. Moments later, the flag fluttered over the home of Canada's democracy.

Then we all headed back to the prime minister's office for a strategy session between Trudeau and his top aides. It was real. It was not staged. This was his last chance to prep for a scrum at Rideau Hall after the swearing-in of his new government. Among the questions expected to come up was the fact that half the new ministers were women.

Trudeau asked his staff, "If a reporter asks why, what's the right answer?"

There was a pause, and then Gerry Butts, Trudeau's longtime friend and now his principal secretary, said simply, "Because it's 2015."

Butts's suggestion became the line of the day when Trudeau, seemingly off the top of his head, used it verbatim a few hours later.

Meeting over, it was time for the ten-minute drive to Rideau Hall by the RCMP-guarded prime ministerial limo. Trudeau changed into a suit in his office while I waited by the limo outside. We would use the ride, with GoPro cameras fixed inside the vehicle, for some final, "before the big moment" remarks from the soon-to-be twenty-third prime minister of Canada.

But two other things are what I remember most from that short jaunt.

As we sat together in the back seat, I suddenly realized we were wearing similar suits and the *same* tie. The *exact* same tie. A grey-blue Hugo Boss. We looked like teammates, just what the conspiracy theorists who are convinced there's some kind of deal between the Liberals and the CBC want to believe. (If you believe that, then ask the various Liberals who have had to resign over the years because of CBC journalism exposing their wrongdoing just how true *they* think it is.) But it was too late now on the tie. Let's just say it was a good day for Hugo Boss.

Then we arrived. I was going to have to get out fast or some viewers watching on television might be misled into believing *I* was going to be sworn into the cabinet. I wished the prime minister luck, grabbed the door handle, and started lifting it up and down.

Nothing.

I tried again.

Nothing.

The prime minister just sat there, not making a move.

"Oh," I said. "I guess I have to wait until they open it . . ."

Without turning to look at me, he said quietly, hands folded in his lap, "Yep."

It was the prime minister to be, calmly explaining to the guy who thought he was a political veteran that the doors to the prime ministerial limo don't unlock until the RCMP is convinced the outside area is secure.

POSTSCRIPT

The beginning of the Justin Trudeau prime ministerial years signaled the emergence of a generational change in the realm of politics and media that I had joined in the late 1960s. That showed me that it was time to begin the process of moving aside from The National. I'd been in the anchor chair for almost thirty years and in the CBC for almost fifty. By July of 2017, I made it official. Time to move into new areas, like documentaries and podcasts.

A River Runs Through It

In my final years at the CBC, it was not unusual for young journalists to come by my office to talk about their careers and seek advice. Sometimes they would be upset that they had been passed over for a promotion they applied for, and I would try to keep them interested and involved.

"Do you know how many times I was passed over when I tried to get ahead?" I'd say.

Most, of course, having heard the story of my beginnings, thought I'd somehow gone straight from baggage handling in the Churchill airport to anchoring *The National*. It had not been that way. Not by a long shot.

I'd been a local reporter in Churchill and then Winnipeg for five years, and when I applied to become a network reporter, I was turned down three times. It was depressing, but I never considered myself a failure. I just felt I'd hit a roadblock and had to try harder. And I did, for years.

I had to learn perseverance, I would tell the young hopefuls in my office, and part of that process was learning from an experience I had on the job.

During my travels in northern Manitoba and northwestern Ontario, I met many Indigenous leaders who were dealing with issues far worse than the challenges of making headway in the CBC. One summer, I was interviewing a First Nations elder about an issue his band members were having on their reserve, and afterwards the conversation swung toward a version of the meaning of life. To him, it was all about nature and I was a willing listener.

"Life is like a river," he said. "We tend to think it runs straight, in one direction. But it doesn't." He talked about how rivers or creeks bump

Somewhere in northern Ontario, circa 1973.
Steve Solilo

into logs or stones or riverbanks. Sometimes the water stalls or even bounces back. "But eventually it always finds its way."

The message was clear and simple. Setbacks happen. They should be expected. But they can be overcome.

I've never forgotten that story, though I have forgotten where I was and who told it to me. But that elder should know that I—and many others—have taken comfort in those words many times.

Life. A river runs through it.

–III–

Canada

DURING THE MID-1980S, NOT LONG AFTER I STARTED AN-choring *The National* on the weekends, the CBC came to me and asked me to start accepting outside speaking engagements. I'd been shy about accepting the few invites I used to get then, unsure of just what I'd talk about at luncheons or dinners, but the CBC felt this was a great opportunity to meet our audiences while at the same time promoting CBC programming. They even supplied draft speeches that hyped everything from *Mr. Dressup* to *Street Legal*. So, to be the good corporate soldier, I said yes.

Initially, it was only a few speeches a year, usually to Rotary Clubs and Lions Clubs and the odd small-town chamber of commerce. It didn't take long before I got comfortable, enjoyed the events, and realized the value in them. Meeting and hearing from people who weren't part of the Toronto-centric crowd that formed our office bubble was a major plus. When I lived and worked on the prairies, I used to worry that our perspective at CBC National News was too narrow, too focused on downtown Toronto chatter, partly because that's where so many of the senior CBC brains lived, worked, and raised their kids. I worried about that—until I became one of them. Guilty as charged. Speeches allowed me to branch out, going places and meeting people from different walks of life and hearing their concerns in a social setting that, at least occasionally, broke down the barriers of the studio. Speeches helped me burst the bubble.

Meeting Canadians at Vimy Ridge.
Mark Harrison

I also got pretty good at it. I started getting a lot of invites to bigger venues and bigger crowds. Speech agents and speaking fees followed and again the CBC encouraged me to keep doing them as long as they didn't interfere with my work. In fact, they even used the argument that I was making money speaking and factored that into the equation when my contract was up for negotiation. I quickly put aside the CBC-written promotional speeches and replaced them with speeches *I wrote* about journalism and my own experience: the achievements and the challenges.

I didn't then, and still don't now, charge for charitable events or for talks with journalism students—though these lectures, done properly, take a lot of preparation. However, I do charge elsewhere because of the time and effort that I put into some of the events in different parts of the country. I've used a good portion of the money I've earned to set up scholarships for journalism students, grants for promising young people who have joined Junior Achievement Canada to learn about entrepreneurship, and also a foundation to support worthy charitable causes like the hospital in my hometown of Stratford. Over the years, I've spoken to teachers, doctors, environmental groups, lawyers, Indigenous leaders, nurses, oil executives, farmers, truckers, judges, social workers, bankers, engineers, educational assistants, municipal workers, CEOs, small-business owners, tech professionals, and many, many others. You name a group, I've probably spoken to them. All with similar messages about journalism and about Canada. I don't pretend to know anything about their business, but I can explain mine, and I try to narrow some of the wide gaps that exist between journalists and the people they cover.

Some critics, including some of my own colleagues, took exception to a speech I once gave to oil executives and complained that I was obviously in their pocket. I was literally a last-minute fill-in for a US journalist who was booked to speak but had to cancel. They were holding their event across the street from the CBC in downtown Toronto, so I agreed to head over and ad-lib some comments, most of which were imploring the companies to be more transparent about the issue of pipeline safety. It wasn't a "secret talk," as some later suggested. It was open to anyone who walked into the convention hall. But it was too late. Times were changing and the CBC, who ironically had pushed me into public speaking and never expressed problems with speaking fees, was now faced with both some internal and external criticism; they changed their policy, and the speech-fee days were suddenly over. I chose not to argue.

A few years later, after I retired from *The National*, I hung my speaking shingle back up, and business is busy once again, although the pandemic has taught those of us who ply this trade that virtual speeches can work pretty well too—the bonus is that you can stay in your sweatpants! But nothing beats face-to-face and being in the same room with your audience. That's where real discussions take place and real value can be had for both those in the audience and those at the podium.

I tell stories, like some of the ones you've read in this book, always with the hope they express something, not just about me but about the profession of journalism, the country we call home, and who we as Canadians are. The best conversations are when I learn something too, when I meet someone who is fascinating and who lets me into their world.

On stage for CBC fall launch, 2017.
CBC

Most good sessions end with a question-and-answer period. Delegates to the conventions I'm invited to seem genuinely interested and curious about my profession. Not surprisingly, there are certain questions that come up a lot: Who was your favourite interview? What was your worst moment on TV? What was it like on 9/11? Do you get nervous?

But I think my favourite one is this: What is a Canadian?

It's the question that gives us all so much trouble because it's laced with so many sub-questions: Who are we? What do we stand for? What do we believe? The question delves into Indigenous representation, how we handle immigration, and how national identity can be co-opted by dark forces as to "who qualifies to be a Canadian?"

I've been asking myself that main question for as long as I can remember. Through various constitutional talks, conferences, and crises, two Quebec referenda, the patriation debate, Meech Lake, Charlottetown, the Trudeau years, the Mulroney years, the Chrétien and Harper years . . . through them all, the key question almost always came down to "What is a Canadian?" We would organize town halls, eminent persons' panels, debates, poll nights, major interviews—you name it, we tried everything looking for the answer. I'm not sure we ever found the definitive answer beyond "We're not American!" but the question haunts me still.

I find the easiest way to answer the question is by telling stories of moments I've witnessed from around the world, making the argument that sometimes you learn more about Canada when you're not in Canada, from those who watch us. I tell what I call my trilogy.

I recount the story of the little girl in Sri Lanka after the 2004 tsunami who pointed to a Canadian flag on my field jacket and said in broken English: "Ca-na-da good."

The crowds in the tens of thousands who still line the streets of the Dutch city of Apeldoorn on major anniversaries thanking Canada for liberating their communities from the Nazis in the spring of 1945. As their mayor once told me, "We will never forget Canada because we learned the very hard way that you don't appreciate freedom until you've suffered from occupation. And because of that you never forget who was there to liberate you."

A woman named Roya Rahmani, who spent the years immediately following her graduation from McGill University in Montreal in Afghanistan helping Afghan women understand their rights under a new constitution. Roya was a new Canadian, emigrating with her family *from* Afghanistan just a few years before to flee the Taliban. She went back because she wanted to tell the citizens of her former country what real freedom was like. She was using us as an example of what is possible. Could there be a greater, more flattering description of what Canada is?

So, what's the answer in the trilogy? In its simplest form, it boils down to one word. A Canadian *cares*.

The little girl in Sri Lanka felt Canada was good because she and her friends had just received vaccinations from three volunteer nurses from Canada who had *cared* enough to spend their own money and time to fly to Sri Lanka to help.

The people of Apeldoorn were on the street to welcome some old Canadian veterans, many in their late nineties, who were back one more time. The Dutch still pass the story of the Canadians, young kids at the time who had *cared* enough to volunteer to fight an evil empire, down from generation to generation.

And Roya Rahmani, who turned down a postgraduation, guaranteed job in the Canadian tech sector because she *cared* enough to help out in a war zone.

You and I could tell a dozen trilogies of Canadians who care. That's who we are. And we can be pretty proud of that.

But Canada is also a country that still allows injustice within its own borders and, knowing it's wrong, doesn't push back enough. Every time there's a change of government in our country, the shameful history of how Canada has treated First Nations peoples comes up and the new government will say this time things will be different.

Take something as simple and as uncomplicated as water. And I use this example because it *is* simple. Surely, clean drinking water is a necessity that everyone understands. We see it in the television spots that play again and again on daytime TV—poor children in third-world countries unable to find clean water, asking for the generosity of Canadians to help them. And yet that necessity isn't being met in our own country. And that's shameful. Clean drinking water is a basic human right for every community in Canada. Every community. Not just non-Indigenous communities. Every community.

But that's not what's happened. It's 2021, and the most favourable statistics show there are still more than fifty communities where there is a boil-water advisory. You can't drink the water unless it's boiled first. And, of course, every one of those communities is on a First Nations Reserve. In Canada. In 2021. In the country that stands as a beacon in the world for its stance on human rights, and yet it fails on its own standard.

We proved in 2020 and continue to do the same in 2021 that no amount of money is too much to protect our citizens from a health threat. We have spent billions—hundreds of billions—of dollars in the fight against the coronavirus. Very few have stood in opposition to the expenditures, and no one has any idea of how the debt will ever be paid off. In fact, it probably never will be paid off. It will most likely end up being *written* off. A fraction of that number, whatever it is, could solve Canada's water problem. But it doesn't happen. Why?

You know why. Canadians—and our history proves this—have decided, to our shame, that there really are two classes of Canadians. Those who were here first, and those who came later. And while some have tried to change that, most of us, including me, haven't done enough. We've stood by and let it happen. Accepted it. Watched while non-Indigenous communities like Walkerton, Ontario, when suddenly faced with a contaminated water supply in May of 2000, became national priority number one. It was bad: people died; people got sick. The country and the province were all in on fixing the problem, and those responsible went to jail. Racism? Maybe. Probably. Definitely. After all how many Indigenous People have died over the years, and have got sick because their water was bad? We may never know. But it's still happening.

It's not just water that separates us. Health care, education, and the justice system all are examples of the divide that shows systemic racism is not just part of our history, it's part of our present. And unless there is drastic systemic change, it will be part of our future, and that is not only undeniable, it's unacceptable.

Gord Downie died pleading with us to change; Senator Murray Sinclair showed us how we could change in his report for the Truth and Reconciliation Commisssion in 2015. After listening to thousands of witnesses in hearings across the country, Sinclair warned of the horrendous likelihood that unmarked graves would someday be discovered near former residential schools. For the most part, the country yawned. That may sound unfair, but it's true. Nothing changed. By mid-2021, Sinclair's predictions came true when more than a thousand unmarked graves were discovered across the country—and thousands more are expected to be.

Prime minister after prime minister promised their government would affect change. Stephen Harper stood in Parliament and apologized for our history's past ills; Justin Trudeau admitted the problem was systemic and just this year committed billions of dollars in new promises to fix things.

But here we are. 2021. Dozens of communities without drinkable water, Indigenous kids not given the privileges non-Indigenous kids get

On the Neskantaga First Nation cleaning fresh fish in 2018.

in both education and health care, and our prisons disproportionately filled with inmates of Indigenous descent—all seeming to prove that the scales of justice, equality, and fairness are thumbed down against them, while some of the most brutal aspects of our history are still denied or doubted. It's unacceptable.

I could end my story there, but I won't. I'm a believer in hope, not in despair. I believe that we can keep striving for an even better Canada, and I believe someday, perhaps long after my time, we will find it. So, let me end on this.

As I mentioned earlier in this book, I spent part of the early summer of 1979 on board a local police vessel bouncing in the waters of the South China Sea not far from Hong Kong. I was filming a documentary for one of the popular CBC news programs of the day, *Newsmagazine,* and we were in the sea looking for the latest arrivals of what the world had dubbed the "boat people," hundreds of thousands of ethnic Chinese who were fleeing Vietnam and the persecution they were suffering at the hands of the new, postwar Vietnamese government. To leave the country, they had to pay exorbitant fees for a spot on overcrowded, often unsafe boats just to get them and their families somewhere, anywhere, that was a better place. Some of those voyages ended in horror—passengers robbed by pirates, women raped, husbands and sometimes even children thrown overboard. But even knowing that could happen, the exodus continued.

We intercepted some of the boats and later visited the people in the refugee camp in Hong Kong, and I asked those who had given every penny they owned for the escape why they had taken the risk. The answers were remarkably similar. "For our children. Not for us. To give them a chance for hope." Those were some of the phrases I remember coming back at me through translation.

At one moment, as I was standing in the Hong Kong refugee camp, one woman thrust her months-old son into my arms. She had heard that we, my crew and I, were from Canada and she wanted us, me in particular, to take her child to Canada where there would be "hope." I couldn't, of course, and as a result I have never felt more helpless. How desperate could a mother be to place her little boy in the hands of a complete stranger and hope that somehow, some way, that stranger could accompany her child to a far-off promised land? His mother was weeping as I handed her son back, and I'm not ashamed to admit that my eyes were blurry too.

Filming with the "boat people" in Hong Kong refugee camp in 1979.
University of Toronto Archives

The thing about this job is that sometimes things come full circle.

In the early 2000s, one of the organizations I helped with my time and donations was Junior Achievement Canada, where I sponsored two major, annual scholarships for bright young Canadians who aspired to one day have careers in entrepreneurship. On the night of the big celebratory gala at the Canadian Business Hall of Fame, which I emceed, I handed out the two scholarships.

In 2008, one of the winners was a young woman from Milton, Ontario, by the name of Priscilla Tang. She was incredibly impressive, scoring 95-plus marks in high school while starting her own business at the same time. As I called out her name, she came onstage for the acceptance, a short speech, and the obligatory ceremonial photos, and the audience clapped. Before she went back to her table, she asked, "Would you mind if my parents came up at the end of the evening and we took a picture?"

"Of course, I'd be honoured," I said.

And sure enough, as the evening drew to a close, I saw Priscilla and her parents heading toward the stage. As the photographer positioned us, Priscilla's mother turned to me and said softly, "I was a boat person. I came to Canada in 1979."

Hearing those words, I was silently overcome. In that moment, I remembered the stories, the faces, and the determination of those people I'd met, a determination that they were doing this, risking their lives, for their children, to give them hope. Priscilla's mother would have been only a child in 1979, fourteen she said, but I saw in her eyes that night in Toronto what I'd seen in the eyes of those refugees in Hong Kong all those years ago. I saw hope and the realization that it could be achieved. Priscilla was living proof of that.

Canada delivered hope for thousands of boat people and their families, just like it has for many others, those who have grown up here and also those who have come from elsewhere to our shores, my family included.

But our job is not done. I believe Canada can do the same, should do the same, and will do the same, for all, especially those who were here long before the rest of us.

Traffic Agent Required

By the time I was getting ready to step down from *The National*, I assumed that everyone I had worked with knew the story of how I got hired back in 1968. The Transair ticket agent with the "great voice." But I was wrong.

One night in 2017, I was out for dinner in Washington, where Paul Hunter was our correspondent, when the two of us began talking about how I had started at the CBC. He was stunned to hear the Transair tale and wanted to know more, in particular how I'd ended up at Transair in the first place.

I told him that when I was nineteen, fresh out of the navy and right

With Paul Hunter moments after my final *National*
in Ottawa, June 30, 2017.

out of work and therefore money, I was desperate for a job. I was sitting in the Winnipeg bus depot early one morning waiting for the next bus to Portage La Prairie where I was going to see my girlfriend, when I picked up a discarded edition of the *Winnipeg Tribune* on one of the nearby chairs and started flipping through the want ads. Among all the general job listings, a small ad leapt out at me. It had a headline that said something like "Traffic Agent Required." That caught my attention, and instead of going to Portage I went to the address mentioned at the airport. I aced the interview, got the job, and the rest is history.

We both laughed, then went on with our dinner and discussed how we both saw the latest Trump story unfolding.

I didn't think about any of that again until Paul turned up in the Toronto newsroom a few days before my final broadcast. He was carrying a bag.

I opened it up and pulled out a T-shirt with a copy of that 1968 ad printed on it. In his spare time, Paul had spent a few weeks online searching the old *Tribune* archives for it and miraculously found it. He even had a copy of the ad turned into a fridge magnet. I was floored.

Looking at it now, as you can see from the copy in this book, one thing becomes very clear. They must have been hard up for a new agent because, aside from being single, I didn't have one of the other requirements.

Just lucky, I guess. Whatever the case, it was an ad that changed my life.

TRAFFIC AGENT
required

Applicants must be single 20-28 years of age, minimum Grade XII education and preferably some experience in meeting and dealing with the public.
Duties will include answering enquiries over the telephone and counter, reservations, and passenger check-in.

- 40 hour week.
- Salary commensurate with qualifications and experience.
- Generous employee benefits, including free and reduced rate Air travel privileges.

Letters of application stating age, qualifications, experience, salary desired and telephone number should be directed to the:

Personnel Manager.

TRANSAIR LIMITED
Winnipeg International Airport.
St. James 21, Manitoba.

Acknowledgments

Any book of remembrances by its very nature has to rely on memory, and this book is no exception. As a result, many of the conversations and quotes included in the anecdotes you will find on these pages are based on what I can recall from particular moments, and you can be sure that they are not exact. But I'm convinced that they accurately reflect my memories of conversations that occurred, in some cases, decades ago. Some quotes, though, are direct and have been taken from transcripts or videos of actual interviews.

Many of these stories I've kept notes on over the years and they have been a valuable resource for me. But so too have been the numerous human resources, people whom I have recounted stories to during my career or, better still, have been part of the stories. The same goes for many of the photographs that are here—some are mine but most came from colleagues like Brian Stewart, Fred Parker, Leslie Stojsic, Jon Whitten, Stephanie Jenzer, Sheldon Beldick, Carmen Merrifield, Lara Chatterjee, Paul Hunter, Michael Gruzuk, and Mark Harrison. Lara produced the final years of my work at *The National* on CBC, and in some ways, she helped produce this book too by suggesting, vetting, and polishing anecdotes and by being responsible for collecting and cataloguing the photos. Thank you also to the archives at the University of Toronto for making available many of the photos that are found here. And a special thanks to my son-in-law Jordan Hinchey for his work restoring some of the older 1950s and 1960s photographs.

A special mention to my children—Jennifer, Pamela, and Will—who reminded me of some of the stories I've told them over the years that have made their way into the book. Especially Will, who remembered things I'd forgotten and fought for them to be included. He's also the custodian of some others I felt were just too risqué for me to share!

And to my wife Cynthia, my thanks for allowing me the space and the time to write, and the ability to often listen to me read back a story to her and for her to say, "You must change *that* word" and for me to quickly realize she was right.

The 2020 instant #1 bestseller *Extraordinary Canadians* that I coauthored with my longtime friend and colleague Mark Bulgutch ensured I would take his advice on this book as well. While he didn't write anything here, he was instrumental to me as a fact-checker of sorts, as he witnessed many of these moments with me.

Simon & Schuster Canada publisher Kevin Hanson has become a friend as well as a boss, and I'm grateful for both.

And, finally, to my editor for the past few years, Sarah St. Pierre, who has the amazing ability to flatter you with compliments while at the same time getting you to rewrite, and then just when you thought you were done, rewrite again. So kind yet so firm.